LOVING PSYCHOANALYSIS

LOVING PSYCHOANALYSIS
Looking at Culture with Freud and Lacan

Ruth Golan

First published in 2006 by
H. Karnac (Books) Ltd.
6 Pembroke Buildings, London NW10 6RE

Copyright © 2006 by Ruth Golan

The rights of Ruth Golan to be identified as the author of this work have been asserted in accordance with §§ 77 and 78 of the Copyright Design and Patents Act 1988.

Hebrew edition published by Resling, Tel-Aviv, 2002.

Translated by Jonathon Martin

All rights reserved. No part of this publication may be reproduced, stored in a retrieval system, or transmitted, in any form or by any means, electronic, mechanical, photocopying, recording, or otherwise, without the prior written permission of the publisher.

British Library Cataloguing in Publication Data

A C.I.P. for this book is available from the British Library

ISBN: 1-85575-379-0

Edited, designed, and produced by Communication Crafts

Printed in Great Britain

www.karnacbooks.com

Dedicated to the Friend I'll Never See

CONTENTS

ABOUT THE AUTHOR   ix

PREFACE   xi

1   Introduction: psychoanalysis and language—getting to know Lacan   1

I
LOVE, PHANTASY

2   What can we know of love?   21

3   Phantasy—from Freud to Lacan and from Lacan to the artist   35

II
JOUISSANCE, WOMAN

4   Paul Celan and the question of feminine *jouissance*   49

5   One eats—the other eats "no"   73

viii   CONTENTS

| 6 | "A woman's voice is *erva*":
the feminine voice and silence—
between the Talmudic sages and psychoanalysis
with Admiel Kosman | 78 |

III
TESTIMONY

| 7 | The secret bearers—from silence to testimony, from the Real to *phantasme* | 101 |

IV
ART, LETTER

8	The letter as place and the place of the letter	127
9	The Act in psychoanalysis and art	133
10	The return of Orpheus— a psychoanalytic view on realism in contemporary art	150

V
DEATH, ENTROPY

11	True grace—the blood is the soul	167
12	There is no such form—*Arbeit macht frei*	179
13	Myth and Act on the crater's edge	191

VI
EVOLUTION

14	Is interpretation possible?	201
15	About narrow-mindedness and the Real	206
16	*Eppur si muove!*—nevertheless, it does move	215

| REFERENCES | 227 |
| INDEX | 233 |

ABOUT THE AUTHOR

RUTH GOLAN is a clinical psychologist, a Lacanian psychoanalyst, and a poet.

She lives, works, and teaches in Tel-Aviv and is a member of GIEP (the Israeli Group of the New Lacanian School, headed by J.-A. Miller). She teaches and writes on the way psychoanalysis and culture mutually influence one another. She is also a member of IEF—a foundation for the study of the evolution of consciousness, headed by Andrew Cohen.

Loving Psychoanalysis and four anthologies of her poetry have been published in Israel. She co-edited a translation into Hebrew of an anthology of Freud's papers on love and sexuality.

Ruth Golan is interested in all that is human.

The following poem, entitled "The Path of Man", is from her most recently published anthology, *Flood*.

> From the low to the high
> The winding to the direct
> Hidden into manifest
> Gross into subtle
> Matter into spirit

From the living to the dead, to the eternal

From confinement to the unlimited
Hesitance to resolution
Dimness into brightness
Masculinity into femininity
Inexorability to resilience

From void into fullness, into emptiness

From the approximate to the precise
The many into the one
Fitfulness to constancy
Fragility into steadfastness
Rigidity into flowing

From the partial to the whole
Reservation into confidence
Adulteration into integrity
The recurring to the novel
Pollution into purity

From ignorance, to knowledge, to not knowing

From the sexual to the erotic
From something, into nothing
Darkness into illumination
From dust, to the heavens
From serpent into bird

From the personal to the all-embracing
Limitation to infinity
Deficiency into abundance
Desire into contentment
Slavery into freedom

From God to the devil, back to God

[translated by J. Martin]

PREFACE

> Why do you look at me through the white curtain? I did not call for you, I did not ask you to look through the white curtain at me. Why does it conceal your face from me? Why can't I see your face behind the white curtain? Don't look at me through the white curtain! I did not call for you. I did not ask you. Through closed lids I can see you looking at me, you who look at me through the white curtain. I shall pull the white curtain aside and see your face, and you will not see mine. Why can I not pull the white curtain aside? Why does it hide your face from me?
>
> Wassily Kandinsky, "Sounds" (1982, p. 336)

The interrelating essays and lectures contained in *Loving Psychoanalysis* have been written over the course of the past few years in an attempt to codify and transmit what I have learnt through the study and praxis of psychoanalysis.

The differing perceptions of psychoanalysis that they reflect form a complex mosaic of beginnings and finales. They examine psychoanalysis from various cultural aspects, the overriding theme being the sense of discontent that they express. I have attempted to weave the various viewpoints into a web of perceptions, that it may catch fragments of significance and reveal thereby the "holes" through which everything beyond meaning runs.

In addition, I hope to raise questions that those intrigued by life and their own make-up can ponder on. For those who are ready to ask and take the winding path of psychoanalysis, this book is a means to pass on the fruits of my own understanding—a kind of guidebook. It also ought to provide the key to *la passe*—that process devised by Jacques Lacan to negotiate the crossover from the stance of analyst and analysand, the juncture at which the analysand begins to refer to his or her own analysis in an attempt to contribute something new to psychoanalytic knowledge.

Although *la passe* referred originally to psychoanalysis and the reader is not about to find direct references to my own analysis, whoever does trouble to read between the lines should perceive not a few realizations and quandaries (including mine) arising from what has occurred in the clinic.

* * *

It must be emphasized time and time again that psychoanalysis was born neither of philosophy nor university—it developed in the clinic.

Freud was taught by hysterical women speaking of their pains and anxieties and exhibiting their physical symptoms, enabling him to formulate his theories in regard to the existence of the unconscious. These women demonstrated the difference between biological instinct and drive, between anatomy and the human body—which is constructed according to the degree of libidinal investment, and its erotization.

Lacan began the construction of his theory—his return to Freud—through meetings with psychotics when he was working as a psychiatrist in a psychiatric hospital. In 1932 he wrote his thesis on a psychotic woman whom he called *Aimée* [loved].

Psychoanalysis is neither a theory nor a philosophy of life; rather, it is a form of ethics (the manner in which the subject relates to the world) that is unlike any other set of ethics. Whether or not psychoanalysis in itself constitutes a science is arguable, but there is no argument regarding the fact that it owes its existence to science. It could be termed "the science of the particular" because of the way it deals with the particular truth of the subject. Lacan termed it "the conjectural science of the subject", whereas the theoreticians aspiring to universality would rather have the subject beheaded.

While nobody seems to be interested in the desire of the theoretician or even of the artist, knowledge of psychoanalysis cannot be detached from the desire of the psychoanalyst.

In his XIth seminar, *The Four Fundamental Concepts of Psycho-Analysis*, Lacan referred to this thus:

> Analysis is not a matter of discovering in a particular case the differential feature of the theory, and in doing so believe that one is explaining why your daughter is silent—for the point at issue is to *get her to speak*. . . . It might be said, therefore, that in the last resort, it amounts to overcoming the barrier of silence. . . . The symptom is first of all the silence in the supposed speaking subject. If he speaks, he is cured of his silence, obviously. But this does not tell us anything about why he began to speak. [Lacan, 1973, p. 11]

* * *

It is important to bear in mind that the principal factor in psychoanalysis is not language, but, rather what is missing from what is said, what is left out. Psychoanalysis is not just another aspect of a civilization, for it relates to the discontent that is embodied in a civilization.

In certain cases, cultural and artistic expressions can serve as examples to explain psychoanalytic concepts, but balance is lacking in the relationship between psychoanalysis and art. Psychoanalysis can be studied through art but not the other way around—certainly not in a direct and simplistic manner. According to Lacan, rather than reflecting psychological creations, works of art give birth to them.

When Lacan is perceived as a philosopher, structuralist or post-structuralist, psychoanalysis is discussed in terms of two spheres—the imaginary and the symbolic—while the vital and important sphere of the Real is ignored, similarly to the way in which American psychoanalysts chose to ignore the death drive.

Psychoanalysis is the ethics of the Real. The Real cannot be set apart from psychoanalysis as the theoreticians and philosophers would like it to be.

Psychoanalytic research is not scientific, philosophical, or even psychological research.

When the term "self" is studied, it is not just an examination of philosophy, despite the philosophical connotations. Research of this nature takes the researching subject into consideration. Such is the practice and such is the ethic. This type of research intends not only to gather information or knowledge, but also to discover something about the truth or the reason, in a way that will bring about transformation. This applies equally to both praxis and study.

* * *

Lacan did not refer to the clinical concept merely in relation to the treatment of patients. He saw it as a means of leading us to reconsider our own practice—that is, our treatment and transition from the position of patient to that of analyst, as well as the position we take regarding transference in our own patients.

It seems to me that it is easier for us to forget what Lacan had intended while we make do with the intellectually stimulating aspect of psychoanalysis. Indeed, it would be tempting to maintain the sheltered intellectual position—the position of the gazer who is not gazed upon—rather than trying to understand the implications of our own psychoanalytic practice: those implications in regard to the position we take as analysts but also in regard to our lives. Such a line of thinking would be likely to make us wake up, but we could also find it disturbing.

* * *

Thinking or suffering individuals who turn to analysis because "something isn't working in my life" or "something's wrong", or due to frustration, confusion, and dissatisfaction, want to know the reasons and even to make changes in their lives. They have two questions: "Who am I?" and "Why do I suffer so?"

Through investigating the question "Who am I?" psychoanalysis hopes the individual will find other answers to the question "How can I live in a way in which I will suffer less?"

Delving into psychoanalytic knowledge out of mere curiosity is not the same as embarking on investigation motivated by a sense that our fate depends on new breakthroughs being achieved in the field. Usually when questions begin to be asked, real answers are to be found, but genuine answers tend to be hard to bear because they require one to change one's position. Thus most of us prefer the answers to be safely wrapped in intellectualism—"this is really interesting . . . I'd like to learn more"—in a way abounding in *jouissance* (see chapter four herein).

* * *

Thus the motive for investigation is important. I believe that people who draw near to psychoanalysis are principally interested (even if they are not consciously aware of it) in truth that relates to them personally. I refer to it as "living" knowledge or "erotic" knowledge, as opposed to intellectual knowledge. It reflects a craving that stems from dissatisfaction with what already is and a desire for deeper subjective experience.

That same motivation lies behind the creation of symptoms, just as motivation lies behind any creation. If we awaken to the knowledge that psychoanalytic investigation reveals to us, we will become aware of the extent to which we are occupied with preserving what already exists—pathological *jouissance* that works against ourselves and against life.

* * *

Fellini's film *Rome* depicts the revealing of subterranean catacombs. As the researchers illuminated the cavernous darkness, they beheld exquisite murals. After the murals had been duly restored and recorded for posterity, the public were invited to view them. As time went on, researchers realized that exposing the murals to light was actually causing them to fade away. Now, are murals really being destroyed? Can they even be said to exist unless there is someone's gaze to illuminate them? Like the unconscious, the murals seem to be present somewhere between appearance and disappearance—which is the source of their significance.

Since completing my formal studies I have been trying to illuminate those murals with fleeting shafts of light from various angles, in order to facilitate ongoing alternate discovery and disappearance. That is how I attempt to work my way through Lacan's dialogue and—with Lacan's aid—through Freud's dialogue. In the course of this journey I am aided by guides (guides in the full sense of the word) such as Jacques-Alain Miller, Collette Soler, Salvoj Žižek, and many others.

* * *

My most important teachers have been, and still are, the patients. I am primarily grateful to them, but not only to them. Psychoanalysis is something of a cooperative society. All analysts need a professional community—a board of trustees to accompany them on the complex and challenging path they have chosen. The trustees form a chain in order to transmit a line of those who either influence or are influenced

My companions on the path have granted me companionship, knowledge, support, love, and constant brainstorming, all of which together grant the courage to dare, to investigate, and to write.

Of the extensive list, I am particularly grateful to Rivka Warshawsky, Gabriel Dahan, and the people from The Freudian Place in Jaffa: Liora Goder, Mona Zupnik, Avi Rybnicki, and Shlomo Lieber. Also Susanna Huller, who guided me in the initial deciphering of Lacanian theory, and teachers and friends at GIEP (The Israeli Group of the European School of Psychoanalysis).

This book first saw light in and was inspired by The Freudian Place in Jaffa. The Place was, between the years 1991 and 1996, a centre of activity that provided an environment conducive to querying and bringing about the consequences that are inherent in psychoanalytic discoveries. The Place was intended to be involved in the dissemination of psychoanalytic knowledge, to facilitate research into the connection between psychoanalysis and other fields of knowledge, and to introduce psychoanalytic dialogue and ethics to Israeli culture.

I am grateful to Avi Rybnicki and Benny Gleitmann for their care in reviewing and their edifying comments. To Jonathon Martin for his studious translation and Helen Eisen for her meticulous editing. My thanks are also due to the following artists who in their generosity have allowed me to use their works: Michal Heiman, Moshe Gershuni, Michal Na'aman, Michal Rovner, and Tsibi Geva.

LOVING PSYCHOANALYSIS

CHAPTER ONE

Introduction: psychoanalysis and language— getting to know Lacan

The poetess Tirza Atar, daughter of the poet Natan Alterman, who met her death by falling (or jumping) out of a window, wrote thus:

Words are never mistaken.
They themselves say: "Error, pardon".
Only they are shouted out: I am mute
Only they are sobbed: I do not weep!

[Atar, 1979, p. 150; translated for this edition]

In this introduction to psychoanalysis, I intend to focus on the contrast, as expressed in the poem, between false words and what is really being said.

The title "getting to know Lacan" raises questions such as getting to know whom? And what is actually meant by "getting to know"?

Lacan claimed that he was a Freudian. He spoke of the return to Freud. A return to what had been suppressed from the initial, radical significance that Freud's psychoanalytic revelations contained.

When Freud was first invited to the United States together with Jung, he told Jung on the deck of the ship—"They do not realize that it is the plague that we are bringing them."

From Lacan's point of view, Freud's work, in its entirety, had been adulterated and tamed by the generation that followed him, in order to make it easier to digest and for society to accept.

In other words, the following generation took the sting out of Freud's great and revolutionary discoveries, whereupon the training of analysts became institutionalized and authoritarian. Lacan thought that reductive and harsh interpretation led to a decrease in the significance of Freud's ideas, and he intended to instil new spirit into psychoanalysis.

In view of this we should not be speaking about knowing Lacan but, rather, about recognizing him, or recognizing Freud through Lacan—all by means of illustrating specific concepts and contemplating their implications.

* * *

Lacan's theories cannot be read in the same way as the theories of others. Studying him is a great endeavour that requires a teacher—as well as ample will and stubbornness. In the process of study, it is essential to examine many of the sources that provided the basis for Lacan's reading of Freud—Socrates, Hegel, Heidegger, Sartre, linguistics, the philosophy of science, structuralism, and so forth. But most important of all, perhaps, is that the study of psychoanalysis requires that the desire for knowledge be retained. Therefore, in order to know Lacan, one has first to be able to recognize desire and the limitations of knowledge.

So what are the limitations of knowledge? Can I explain what I know of Lacan? If I did, the reader would more than likely get to know me rather than Lacan. Here, therefore, we are dealing with levels of knowledge in the context of degrees of consciousness of the I—together with the unconscious level of the subject, which appears at the conscious level as an unexpected and surprising factor.

The I and the subject

One of the principal distinctions made in psychoanalysis is that between the ego, which comprises our identity, and the subject, which is alien to us. In a similar way to the unconscious, the subject appears and disappears unexpectedly, and we only become aware of it in retrospect. According to Lacan, the I is the reflection of ourselves as both we and others perceive it—in the context of the system of identifications that we create with people, opinions, and beliefs. The subject is alienated from the I. It is an effect of the unconscious. Psychoanalysis attempts to go beyond the alienation by facilitating the appearance of the subject. Lacan contends that in the context of psychoanalysis, when we speak we are unaware of what we are saying, because when we speak, the unconscious participates, occasionally even leading us to state the opposite of what we had consciously meant to say.

To be precise, this is a discourse on language, the sole tool of psychoanalysis, which Anna O.—one of Freud's first patients—referred to as "the talking cure".

* * *

Psychoanalysis is ethically different from other medical or research models in the way it relates to language. When someone goes to a clinic of whatever type, saying, for example, "I'm drunk", the psychiatrist or researcher will probably ask questions such as "Since when? How many glasses do you drink a day?" and so forth—thereby relating to linguistic statement as authentic fact.

Psychoanalysts, on the other hand, would ask, "Who told you that?" or "Speak more about it". For Lacan, language was the paradigm of the psyche's make-up. The unconscious is structured as language, and symptoms are also embedded within language. Unlike the linguist Ferdinand de Saussure, he views the linguistic unit not as a sign, but as the signifier, which is a component of differential (defined by the difference between it and another signifier). Speech is the basis of the discourse that produces social links.

Psychoanalysts (particularly if they are Lacanian) relate to the subject's statement, to the actual formulation of his suffering. In every treatment there is a therapist and a patient, but there is also a third element—language.

In psychoanalysis there is speech, through which the symptom is supposed to change, following which logic it may be concluded that there is a connection between speech and symptom. There is homogeneity of the unconscious and of speech. In the wake of de Saussure, Lacan distinguishes between language and *parole* and demonstrates how, through the use of language—the sole tool of the psychoanalyst—it is possible to effect change on things that are not expressed in the speech of the subject.

* * *

Getting to know Lacan, therefore, is a detective process in the sense that what has to be detected is whatever it is that we do not know—the question has to be discovered, so to speak. In getting to know Lacan we distinguish between the symbolic dimension and the imaginary dimension—a distinction that he had already made in the 1950s. Acquaintanceship with Lacan means entering the imaginary dimension found within the boundaries of the I—the portion of the I that is constructed out of identification and phantasy.

* * *

Psychoanalysis does not, therefore, function according to a set of norms, but it does relate seriously to language. Using language, on the one hand it attempts to lead people to perception of the general structure that conditions all their reactions and decisions in life; on the other hand, it tries to lead them to perceive what makes them unique, their own particularity. Psychoanalysis relates to sense or signification. It tries to reorganize the sense of life, and speech provides the means to do so. What is said cannot be verified using material or authentic evidence. It can only be verified through comparing other things that are said by the subject and then checking for coherence and consistency. Reality, which is scanned using language, is language itself. Here I should point out that the truth referred to here is the truth of signification, rather than of the Thing itself. When speaking in a clinical context (where there is also, it to be hoped, listening), it is an attempt to use speech to bring about change in the structure of the subject.

The object

The fact that something is being discussed means that it begins to exist at the level of speech while disappearing from the level of reality, of the Thing itself. Therefore, should we encounter the same object in reality, it will never be the same as that which we spoke of or read about. In this sense, language eliminates the object, or, as Lacan (following Heidegger) put it: "The word is the death of the thing." We are talking about that which has no existence *because* we are talking about it. We use various means to represent it and various adjectives to describe it. In the sense of the object being erased by the word, the symbolic dimension is connected with lack and the object is represented by its absence. Freud called this method of approach "castration".

A social link

One needs to distinguish between the etymological signification of words and the signification underlying a person's intention. If a patient says "I'm depressed", the analyst would respond "What do you mean by that?" "Depressed" is one of the most commonly used words by people coming for treatment. When people complain of depression, what do they actually mean? They need to say more about it.

As well as conscious intention, there is always unconscious intention. The therapist relates to the patient's speech as if it were a foreign language. Beneath the indication of depression he puts an X—for "obscure". Therapists that already know all about depression from studying, as well as from plenty of experience with patients suffering from depression, actually become therapists who do not listen, since words for them have become objects that have taken on a fixed meaning.

For example, in psychiatry one of the criteria for diagnosing psychosis is what is called "linguistic disorder". What does this mean, and what are the implications for the individual? If we discover that someone has some linguistic disorder, we will know either that they are schizophrenic or that they have some other type of personality disorder—in accordance with theory and statistics. However, if we do not *listen* to people, we will know nothing of their truth. What if that truth just happens to be masked within their disorder?

If we relate to their disorder as a symptom or merely as a phenomenon for analysis, we will be attempting to listen to the message that they are trying to impart to us, a message of subjective truth. This message should be sought through analysis. Once again, we are discussing subjective truth here, rather than what is commonly accepted as reality.

* * *

Lacan defined therapy as a kind of social link. Such linking would not be possible without language. The psychiatrist and the psychologist relate to words as being superficial, a superficial stratum behind which there are Things—as if language were merely a manifestation of phenomena. From the psychiatric point of view, the word is equal in value to medication. The patient is asked "Where does it hurt?", and just as magnetic-resonance imaging can be used to scan the brain, language can be used too—albeit being a less accurate tool.

According to this definition, words have diagnostic and therapeutic value. Universal norms are determined by a group of respectable citizens. These norms define what makes a healthy person and who is sick. There is a norm for healthiness, and words can bring one into line with that norm, to existing order. In this approach anyone can be compared statistically to the norm and to normative language.

In contrast, analytic exegesis dwells on the level of "what the patient wants to say", and such signification is closer to day-to-day interpretations.

Should a man call home and say "I have a lot of work at the office", his wife is liable to interpret this as: he doesn't love me any more. Should he later bring her flowers, she is liable to think: he has someone else. Significance is always determined in retrospect, as in the sentence: "When I was little, my father used to hit me—said the patient." The significance of what is said is determined by what is said afterwards. The effect of significance is always retrospective: from the last signifier to the previous one—from S_2 to S_1. We refer to this as "the chain of signifiers".

Each signifier indicates something for another signifier. What does "I want to kill myself" mean? Perhaps, I want you to do your best to stop me from killing myself—thereby showing me that you love me?

The value or significance of each signifier is derived in contrast to, or by distinguishing it from, other signifiers.

* * *

As creatures of speech, facts for us (including biological facts) do not actually exist in their own right, except in relation to their significance. Biological facts exist only in relation to the degree of significance they have in the history of the subject. What is unique to each and every subject is its significance. The significance of a sentence such as "My father used to hit me" can vary depending on age. At one age it could be explained by contending that he was angry with me, whereas in regard to another age it could have been a part of my receiving a proper upbringing. At yet a later age—perhaps he had something against me. Even when the word "love" is used, one cannot know its meaning in relation to the subject concerned. One person might interpret it in the context of sexual relations while another might interpret it as alluding to abstinence from sex.

Symbolic order

Symbolic order is the linguistic structure into which we are born, a kind of net enveloping our lives. Every newborn baby arrives bearing a gift—that of the plan of its destiny. To a great extent, symbolic order determines both our nature and our destiny: what is said about us even before we are born, the name that we are called by, our significance to the primary carers in our lives, and what they want from us. The question "What does he or she want from me?" constructs us as subjects. We seek the response of others, their recognition. The answer that we create in response to this question constitutes our *phantasme*. There is language in the world into which we are born. It exists for us from the very moment when our crying calls "someone else" to fulfil our needs. From the moment that the shout becomes a call, which then becomes a demand, the primary carers—usually our mother—represents to us the original Other.

* * *

The "Other" is a Lacanian term alluding to that place wherein lies the entire treasury of signifiers, the place that gives certainty to truth. Therefore, if the mother—the archetypal Other (the mother is only a representative of the Other, since she herself, like everyone else, is a subject)—herself identifies with that same Other, the results are liable to be tragic. There was a case in the Northern Israeli city of Carmiel of a mother who drowned her two little daughters. Our response tends to be to ask, how could a mother do such a thing to her own children? One respected psychiatrist was quoted in a newspaper saying that the deed was due to chemicals in her brain.

In contrast, Lacan asks how it could be that mothers don't gobble up their children. A third factor is responsible for that—the symbolic order, which is built on lack represented by the "Name of the Father", according to Lacan.

The father, who comes between mother and child, represents culture and law. He enables the child to enter the Oedipus complex and to detach him/herself from the mother as an object, in order to build his or her own separate subjectivity.

* * *

Language could be described as being a somewhat murky field, because it can give rise to so many meanings. The murkiness clears at a certain point—specifically when the listener decides to grant significance to what is said, or to halt at the point where meaning disappears. At the point where another interprets, the subject's message becomes precise. Interpretation can also alter previous significance. Freud discovered the fact that if one interprets actions such as examples taken from the psychopathology of everyday life, one accepts the facts of the language, by means of which one can reach the realm of the unconscious.

Truth is not something that is known by the subject; rather, it is something that is created between two subjects. The subject responds with surprise upon hearing what he or she is saying, and these things depend on the attentiveness of the analyst in listening. Interpretation is what gives the symptom meaning.

I should emphasize that when Freud speaks of the unconscious, he is not referring to something that wants to express itself. The unconscious is not an expression; however, it does manifest through the failure of expression, of speech, memory, and action. Such failures had no significance at all until the attention of the interpreter was directed to them—that is, before Freud. Inadvertent slips of the tongue and quill and every other kind of failure, dream, and symptom imaginable were occurring for countless ages—but all were of little significance. Significance only exists in speech, through the mediation of the interpreter.

* * *

How can we know the value of the significance that the interpreter detects in a patient's words? The sole criterion for verification is whether, following interpretation, there is change in the appearance of the symptom. Truth, therefore, is not necessarily connected with accuracy. The truth of the subject is only one form of truth, produced in speech, as the experience of the subject changes.

What we refer to as the subject is not the person. It does not constitute a person's reality in its entirety. We become aware of the subject by implication, through an event of language.

In referring to intercommunication between two people, we do not really mean two people but, rather, two couples—two Is and two subjects in the realm of the unconscious.

In referring to communication or relations with another person, we need to know whether the reference is to the imaginary axis or the symbolic axis. Does the other person constitute an imaginary object—an ideal of the self or Other (in a symbolic dimension)? Communication usually occurs on the plane of imaginary identification. When communications function, uniqueness is diminished until it is lost, producing a common denominator founded on identifications, with the Other functioning as an object for the I.

Both Lacan and Freud mention that subject-to-subject relations are possible but that such occurrences are rare. They do not enlarge on the matter (in contrast to Martin Buber, for example, who contrasted the connection between I–Thou and Me–You).

* * *

The unconscious is a structure of memory, created by a certain number of linguistic elements called "signifiers". People are born into existing languages that are comprised of series of signifiers, which are interconnected by association. A signifier can be a word, syllable, or nonverbal sign. It is a series of concrete linguistic elements, linked up to form some kind of structure.

The significance of a signifier is never bound to the indicating word but, rather, to a series of words. A signifier always denotes something for another signifier. Wherever a signifier appears, various things are signified that can connect with it. These essential signifiers determine the nature of the subjective.

In analysis the subject is, in a certain sense, merely an effect of language, an amalgamation of signifiers. These signifiers do not depict reality; rather, they construct it. Such premises are indispensable to the point of view that speech and interpretation in psychoanalysis can change the subject—how can speech be used to influence something unconnected with speech? How can symptoms be alleviated through speech if they themselves are not held to be a form of speech? Freud called symptoms "hieroglyphs"— codes that have to be deciphered.

Desire

When people come for analysis, they formulate their suffering. Their approaching an analyst is in itself a formulation of their suffering. They state it, and they seek something. According to Lacan, everything said in psychoanalysis is a demand. The person being analysed is demanding something, but underlying the demand lurks something that cannot be formulated into words—and all that the patient is really demanding is merely a substitute for that something. In the Lacanian approach, underlying the demand is desire, just as it is the signified that underlies the signifier.

For example, a child being put to bed at night suddenly returns to wakefulness, wanting something else—water, story, lullaby, toilet, or whatever. What desire really lies behind all these requests? All the child's requests might be fulfilled, but that underlying desire will always remain unrequited. It is something that cannot be expressed in words, although it does exist and does persist. In fact, the object of desire is a lost, primal object, linked—according to Freud—to infantile sexuality. Freud enumerated two such objects—the breast and excrement. To these Lacan added the voice and the gaze.

* * *

The journey of desire begins with such lost objects. We seek them throughout our lives, finding all kinds of strange substitutes for them, from which any satisfaction gained can only be incomplete and temporary. In the end we say of all such substitutes "It's not it", and we go on seeking incorrigibly for "it".

In analysis there is avoidance of satisfying the demand, since doing so would in effect be blocking the path of desire.

* * *

It could be said that we do not use language; rather, language utilizes us. This is what is meant by the term "unconscious". Language cannot express all that there is to say—as we have said, language blots out the Thing.

We could use endless descriptions to describe, for example, a table, but it would not be possible for us to impart the object itself. The Thing becomes language as an empty object for which language does not have a word. In other words, a certain lack develops in the transition from signifier to signifier. The entire theory of desire is constructed on this lack, which is a lacking in one's very being. The neurotic construct centres on this lack.

The lack relates to man's encounter with sexuality—a traumatic one, in the sense that there are not really words that can describe it. Lacan refers to the encounter with sexuality as "the missed encounter". In his attempt to compensate for what is lacking, the neurotic exploits all kinds of objects but with scant success. Men try to compensate for that which is lacking by using women, but a new car or some other idealized object might also do—each according to his own *phantasme*. It is actually psychotics who use language as a set of signs, as regular codes. For them, there is no such thing as lack, the Thing is not hidden—it becomes the word itself, meaning that language takes on the value of the object: instead of a dialectic chain, there is certainty.

* * *

In an article entitled "The Unconscious", Freud (1915e) described the case of a woman who had quarrelled with her lover. To relate this she used an expression to do with squinting eyes. Here Freud differentiated between the hysterical and psychotic structures, contending that while a psychotic would say that her eyes squint, a hysterical woman would actually create the symptom and start squinting. In the same context, relating to language in a different way will enhance diagnosis. In both cases there is a retreat from the unbearable reality of being hurt, but the types of response differ. In the structure of the psychotic, symbolic order is given real value—which is to say, the word is the Thing. Rather than complaining that others have hurt her, the psychotic woman complains that her eyes have actually been made to squint, whereas a hysterical symptom enables the hysteric not to feel the injury on the one hand, while on the other hand it allows her to maintain symbolic order.

Language without meaning—indications of jouissance

In his later teachings Lacan emphasized the material element of language—its Real, jouissant aspect. Instead of, or in addition to the subject, he referred to the speaking being [*parlêttre*]—linking language with *jouissance*. He invented the term *lalangue*, denominating meaningless tonal language, such as that of a baby's.

Such language is linked to *jouissance*—the primal language upon which or from which symbolic language is constructed. Lacan also referred to the aspect of *jouissance* in discourse, characterizing it by means of another play on words—*jouis-sense*—denoting the sense of *jouissance* or the *jouissance* underlying the meaning.

Accordingly Lacan emphasized the Real core of the symptom, a core enveloped in symbolic significance that cannot be interpreted, deriving pleasure from suffering or *jouissance*.

* * *

During that later period Lacan resumed his development of the term "sign". The definition of the term "signifier" was changed, and signifiers were held to be signs for other signifiers—in effect, the things that indicate being, presence rather than absence.

Signs should be perceived as codes rather than as language containing a message. They usually have only one meaning; the sign represents something for somebody. In contrast, signifiers derive their significance from other signifiers. A sign requires one signifier, whereas signifiers require at least two. One signifier always constitutes the subject for another signifier, which is the way symbolic order is constructed. In the case of paranoid psychosis, for example, the paranoid would hear signs whereas the neurotic hears signifiers. The sign derives its significance from the Thing itself, in which sense it is similar to codes in primitive cultures in which everything symbolizes something. Signs are always immutable; they bestow names: a black cat is a sign of bad luck, a thunderstorm is a sign of the wrath of God, and so on. As a psychotic once told me: "Your gazing at me is a sign that you want to kill me."

Analysis and language

Let us go back to the subject of psychoanalysis and language. For the subject who turns to analysis, the analyst occupies the place of Other. This is the place where one turns to, to which one directs one's speech, the place of otherness. It is the patient's unconscious that places the analyst in that position.

In consulting with the analyst as one who is supposed to know of his suffering and his symptoms, the patient allots him that role. This is the significance of transference. The analyst has to speak from that place, the place from which he or she is the guarantor or master of truth—at least for the duration of the session. The analyst conveys the subject's own words back to the patient—words that the patient has uttered many times without exploring their significance, words that have been engraved within him or her. This is the speech of the Other, or, alternatively, the superego.

The analysand consults with the analyst as the one who will demand of him to speak of that of which he does not know, rather than about that of which he does know, thereby believing that talking might help him become aware of something.

The analyst has to leave the patient in that place of "I do not know". This "do not know" could be the meaning of the unconscious. He could say to the patient, "When you say you don't know—you do know." In his paper "Negation", Freud used the example of a patient relating the contents of a dream, saying "it's not my mother!"—therefore it clearly is his mother, precisely because of the negation (Freud, 1925h).

Negation confirms the fact of repression, which is to say that it confirms the fact of a signifier being registered in the symbolic dimension, where the knowledge that lies in the unconscious emerges. The patient assumes that the analyst has this knowledge and it is desirable that the analyst acquiesces to occupying the position of being the Other, as long as he does not identify with it. Such a kind of identification would be characteristic of the "ego psychology" approach, of the psychiatrist or the sort who "really knows" what's best for others.

* * *

The Other is a creation of the unconscious and has no existence in its own right. There is actually no guarantee of truth but the patient is likely only to discover that while undergoing analysis, when the analyst casts himself from the position assigned to him as being the one who knows. From this aspect the analyst is not located beyond the unconscious but, rather, within it.

From the moment that the process of transference commences, the patient in analysis dreams his dreams for the analyst, or, as Freud said, the symptoms join the conversation. In analysis the diagnosis is made under transference, which is to say that observed behaviour cannot be translated into statistics as in the medical procedure. Not all doctors can conduct analysis. Today, science recognizes the importance of the observer in determining the results of observations, a fact well demonstrated in the process of transference.

* * *

The fact of transference came as an unpleasant surprise for Freud. He discovered it precisely when the patient manifested resistance. Speech therefore acts as a sort of wall. It is not a means of expressing what we are thinking, it is not a means of expression. It acts, rather, as a defence against the unconscious.

When resistance arises it indicates something, when there is actually a halt in the discourse (e.g. silence, fixated thought, or some impediment to speech), a sort of aperture forms, through which the unconscious can peep out and disappear. Lacan referred to this as having to speak to the beauty at the window behind the curtain. The unconscious is also referred to as "the stranger", or, as Freud called it, "the uncanny". From this aspect, the meaning is not an explanation but, rather, a deciphering that has the effect of surprise since it leads to this feeling of foreignness—the otherness that exists within you.

The analyst's position is not that of understanding but, rather, suspended confirmation, since he really does not know the significance of what the patient is speaking of. The analyst's position is to stimulate speech and then to guarantee the work of analysis. How can the patient know whether he is understood? When he is being listened to and heard? Only if the analyst, as listener, discovers truth that is not his own, since basing his interpretation of the patient's words on his own truth would constitute projection, rather than interpretation.

The sole demand that the analyst makes of the patient is for free association (saying, "All that rubbish that you think you are saying is valuable and will be of use"), but the paradox is that associations are never actually free. Free speech facilitates the appearance of the subjective structure. Things that are uttered apparently by chance are actually predetermined by the structure. The motives are revealed.

An eye for an eye

I would like to use one of Lacan's examples of interpretation—one that emphasizes the symbolic dimension. Lacan told of a patient who had a symptom related to the use of an arm. The first interpretation, given by another analyst, explained the symptom according to motive, relating to the original prohibition of masturbation. However, prohibition of masturbation is of a general nature—not particular. Other interpretations connected to Freud's theories could be found, such as self-punishment.

The same patient later came to Lacan, who paid particular attention in listening to the patient's symbolic context. Lacan noticed that he lived in an Islamic context and that he found the law of the Koran particularly deterring. The analyst's attention in listening to the symbolic dimension produced the dimension of the Other, that same Other that is the place of discourse of the culture. The question that the analyst always has to ask himself is in regard to the position of the subject in relation to the surrounding symbolic order. Lacan discovered something else about his patient: as a child he had overheard that his father, who was a government clerk, was a thief and that his hand should be cut off, as written in the Koran. Three places can be located at this point: father/thief, son, and a verse that exists in the Other, in this case the Koran—"whosoever steals shall have his hand cut off". The symptom is the realization of the law of the Koran—the hand's function is cut off. Here we are talking about two objective events—the verse and what the patient heard as a child.

The interpretation stems from the connection of those two objective facts—it is of no importance at all whether the father actually stole. Lacan is only telling us about the signifier from which the interpretation stemmed. From this point, the way opens to many possible interpretations. Perhaps the significance of the paralysis could be: I myself am a thief, perhaps—I have to pay my father's debt. The subject did not want to know about the Koranic law into which he had been born. He did not want to know about it consciously, but the unconscious and the symptom do remember the law. In analysis one can perceive a process of symbolic integration of the patient's history with the parts of it that have been suppressed—history, not in the sense of actual facts but, rather, in the sense of linguistic facts, organized according to the significance that the subject places on them.

* * *

As said above, the objective of the analyst is to listen to the subject and to open before him the question of desire, the path of passion. For this purpose, the analyst has his own desire, a different desire from that of his desire as a subject. It is the desire *not* to identify with the Other, *not* to want to be the ideal, mentor or model, the desire to respect the patient's individuality. The opening up of the path of desire—that attention to what the patient is saying—not only reveals significance but also creates it. We are not talking here about the revival of past memories but, rather, about construction of the past—the acquisition of significance, through looking back on the subject's own particular history. Such construction facilitates the revealing of the *phantasme* that is created in response to what the Other said or demanded, which made the subject fixated. In other words, the purpose of analysis is to temporarily put aside all the substitute objects that man is driven to pursue and to unveil something new—the existence of the lost primal object.

* * *

When the analyst assumes that position of the Other, love is generated—the love out of transference. It may thus be said that in transference the analyst not only constitutes a symbolic signifier, he also constitutes a desire-inducing object. In light of this, the analyst must be prepared to be rejected. When, for his patient's benefit, he becomes the Other, he must be prepared to be cast aside and abandoned at the end of the process, like so much detritus. The end of the process involves the analyst being rejected as the master signifier, the master of truth or of significance. Within the framework of such a state of affairs, the subject can change from being an effect of the speech of the Other to being an effect of his own speech.

PART I

LOVE, PHANTASY

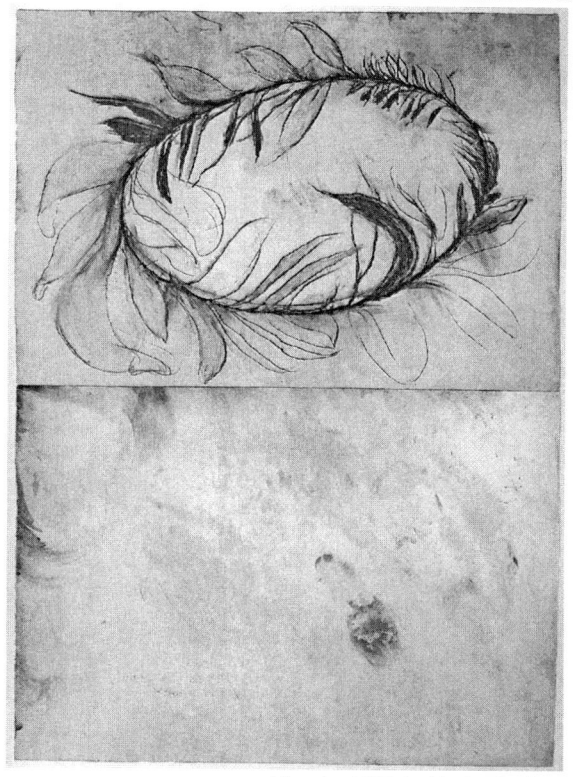

Wreaths, 1990, by Moshe Gershuni

CHAPTER TWO

What can we know of love?

Can one enter the realm of love without getting hurt? The title "What Can We Know of Love?" was inspired by the section "From Love to Libido", in Lacan's XIth seminar, *The Four Fundamental Concepts of Psycho-Analysis* (Lacan, 1973). Having decided on the title, I then realized that I had got myself into some sort of a trap. This title could be the inspiration for a Haiku, a Beatles song, or perhaps a weighty doctoral dissertation. But for this chapter, I attempt to approach the theory of love in various ways, to profile it, and to examine its connection with knowledge—starting with that wondrous stanza from The Song of Songs:

> ... Love is strong as death; jealousy is cruel as the grave; the coals thereof are coals of fire, which hath a most vehement flame. Many waters cannot quench love, neither can the floods drown it: if a man would give all the substance of his house for love, it would utterly be contemned.
>
> [Song of Songs, 13: 6–7]

In his XIth seminar, Lacan poured cold water on the romanticism of the Song of Songs. The conundrum he used in commenting on

Freud's way of relating to love—"The drives necessitate us in the sexual order—they come from the heart. To our great surprise, he [Freud] tells us that love, on the other hand, comes from the belly, from the world of yum-yum" (Lacan, 1973, p. 189)—constitutes a point of reference in this essay. Can the two statements be reconciled? On the one hand, the connection between love and death, the divine fire—worth all the wealth in the world. And on the other, merely something associated with a most basic physical need—perhaps the most straightforward need of all.

Lacan added: "On one side, Freud puts the partial drives and on the other love. He says—*they're not the same*" (Lacan, 1973, p. 189). Despite the fact that both partial drives and love are connected with libido, Lacan states that libido is neither streaming nor liquid matter, not energy but an *organ*—an organ in two senses: (1) a component of the organism and (2) a musical instrument.

Lacan followed the writings of St Augustine, who said that love is a form of appetite—hunger. In her book *Love and St. Augustine*, Hanna Arendt added that craving and appetite are linked to a specific object. Such an object is necessary to ignite the spark and to serve as the object of the hunger. Appetite is determined by the object being sought after by a particular individual, just as motion is determined by the objective that it moves towards (Arendt, 1996).

As St Augustine wrote, love is a form of movement and all movements are made towards something. The movement of love, according to this approach, stands in contrast to the movement of desire: from a certain object rather than towards it. In this case, the object is the reason for movement, rather than the objective.

But why should we have to make do with Augustine when such things can be found in the Song of Songs: "I charge ye, O daughters of Jerusalem, by the roes, and by the hinds of the field, that ye stir not up, nor awake my love, till he please" (Song of Songs, 2:7).

The Hebrew word for "please", *tehfatz*, has a double meaning: the desire and the object that are signified in one word—*hefetz*. Love should not be awakened until the object appears.

In that context arises a doubting question—has psychoanalysis anything to say at all about love? Such a question seems strange considering the fact that our patients hardly complain about anything other than their love life—and they complain far more frequently (nowadays at least) than they do about their sex life. This question, and the hesitancy around any subject connected with love, were also the lot of Freud and Lacan. Perhaps this was well justified considering their far more outstanding contributions in the area of understanding sexuality. While the fields of love and sexuality have many points of contact, they do not overlap and are sometimes even contradictory.

* * *

In 1910, when Freud set out the essential conditions for love in his essay "A Special Type of Choice of Object Made by Men" (1910h), he apologized for invading the territory usually occupied by poets. He contended that science must step cautiously through the field of love—if only because the touch of science is far coarser than that of poetry, and it produces less pleasure. However, according to Freud, on psychoanalysis rests the responsibility of dealing with love, because poets display but little interest in the source of mental states (Freud, 1910h). We may understand from this how Freud, in the same year when he was busy formulating the first theory of love, wrote to Jung thus: "I do not think that our flag of psychoanalysis should be raised on the territory of normal love" (in Bergmann, 1987, pp. 156–157).

In his VIIIth seminar, *Le Transfert* (1991b), Lacan too said that it is not possible to make significant or logical statements regarding love. In the XXth seminar, *Encore* (1975a), which deals mainly with love, he contended that one descends to the level of stupidity as soon as one starts talking about it. Following all these words of caution, we cannot but discuss it or at least take note of some landmarks.

* * *

Freud provided us with three theories about love or three stages in the development of his theory. I am able to summarize this in short with the aid of Martin Bergmann's book *The Anatomy of Loving* (1987). The book in its entirety deals with the history of man's search for knowledge about love.

The initial stage of Freud's theory was a by-product of his discoveries about juvenile sexuality, and it appears in *Three Essays on the Theory of Sexuality* (Freud, 1905d). In that, Freud said that, for the child, the mother or her substitute is its first sexual object as well as its first object of love. Freud noted our loss of the primal object (in lieu of which the mother already constitutes a substitute) and that suckling from the mother's breast has become the prototype of every kind of loving connection, so that the discovery of the object is actually its rediscovery (Freud, 1905d). As Lacan put it, love comes from the belly—which is to say, from the breast. Thus Freud went further than St Augustine: love is, indeed, directed towards an object, but an object that had already been ours in the past. This refers to the same object that Lacan said is to be found in a person who is loved, but which is loved more than that person. In regard to this, Freud said some five years later in 1909 in his "Five Lectures on Psycho-Analysis", given at Clark University in the United States:

> It is inevitable and perfectly normal that a child should take his parents as the first objects of his love. But his libido should not remain fixated to these first objects; later on, it should merely take them as a model, and should make a gradual transition from them on to extraneous people when the time for the final choice of an object arrives. [Freud, 1910a (1909), p. 48]

This is the normal love that he speaks of. In neurotic love, however, the complete opposite happens, as he set out in "On the Universal Tendency to Debasement in the Sphere of Love": if the currents of affection and of desire do not intersect, the desire as a whole will not focus upon one object. This failure to combine the two currents triggers neurotic symptoms: where they love they do not desire and where they desire they do not love (Freud, 1912d).

This came at a period when Freud discovered that there are specific preconditions for love and the awakening of sexual passion. An example can be found in part of Freud's description of the Wolf Man case of 1914 (Freud, 1918b [1914]). Freud constructed the case of the Wolf Man, who had seen his parents having sex when he was 1½ years old. His mother had been penetrated from the rear. Freud saw a connection between the way he supposed the child had gazed then and the way he gazed at the age of 2½, as he watched his nanny's behind when she was scrubbing the floor. The Wolf Man remembered that when he saw her, he had urinated.

Freud interpreted this memory as male identification with the father. As an adult, the Wolf Man would fall hopelessly in love with bending-over peasant girls. Freud noted that he would fall in love with them in a flash, uncontrollably—without even having glanced at their face.

* * *

The second stage of Freud's theory on love was based on the discovery of narcissism. He formulated an antithesis between the libido of the I and the libido of the object. He said that the state of love is the highest attainable level in the development of the libido of the object. This is the stage when the subject is ready to sacrifice its personality for the object of love. Excess libido on the part of the object impoverishes narcissism (Freud, 1914c). There are two sorts of fixation that threaten the love for another: incestuous fixation (sexual love towards either one of the parents) and narcissistic fixation. In 1914, Freud began to term the first sort *anaclitic love* and the second *narcissistic love*. In his paper "On Narcissism: An Introduction" (1914c), he classified the different types of love:

1. *Narcissistic love* (love of the identical or similar). In this category, there is love for:

    a. Oneself—that is, one's reflection in the mirror.

    b. What was—that is, an older person's love for a younger person or a lover's love of his beloved (as described and discussed in Plato's *Symposium*).

    c. What one would like to be—in this case, the object occupies the position of the ego ideal. If such love is reciprocated, it means that one is loved from the place where one would like to see oneself.

    d. Somebody who was once a part of one—in this kind of love, we love what we have previously repressed within ourselves. For this category, Freud gave the example of the love of men who give up their own narcissism in favour of narcissistic women—love for a *femme fatale*. However, I prefer to point out how frequently examples of the opposite occur—where women fall in love with men who are entirely devoted to their own narcissism, men who graciously allow women to adore them or to play a role in that narcissism.

2. *Anaclitic love* (love for another):
   a. Love for the woman that nourishes one.
   b. Love for the man that protects one.

* * *

By 1914 Freud was using economic terms more and more in referring to love. In *Group Psychology and the Analysis of the Ego* (1921c), he said that the object devours the I—that is, the I becomes the object of love. In it he differentiated between love for another and love of the I.

In his article "Fetishism", Freud pointed out the difference between erotic investment in an object and the state of being in love. In the latter, there is far more investment in the object while the I empties itself, ostensibly in favour of the object. However, in the case of erotic investment, one invests in another in order to satisfy one's own needs (Freud, 1927e).

While Freud's first theory concentrated more on the genetic angle by emphasizing the past, his second theory turned to economy by emphasizing the transition of hypothetical quantities of libido from the I to the object. In Freud's opinion, falling in love occurs at the moment when narcissistic libido becomes the libido of the object. Now, why does that transition occur and how does it happen?

As was mentioned above, Lacan dealt with this in his XIth seminar (1973) in the section entitled "From Love to Libido". He adopts the opposite approach, saying that love, as a kind of imaginary screen (*semblant*), constitutes a kind of link between the subject and the Real, which is intended to veil the fact that such a link does not really exist at the level of the drive. According to him, the subject has a constructive link to the Real, a link confined to the narrow borders of the pleasure principle, which is not compelled by drive. Within these borders appears the object of love. The question is, how can this object of love fulfil a role that is parallel to the object of desire? Upon what equivocations could the possibility rest of the object of love becoming an object of desire? (Lacan, 1973).

* * *

The third stage of Freud's theory of love can be found in his article "Instincts and Their Vicissitudes" (1915c). When Lacan spoke of Freud's contribution to the theory of love, he was referring chiefly to this work. How does sex drive turn into love? The question remains unsolved. Freud said in the same article that the matter of love and hate take on particular interest because of the fact that they refuse to fit in with the way we perceive drive. There is no doubt about the close connection between the two opposing emotions and sex life, but naturally we do not want to think of love as just a component of the sex drive, similar to other components that have been discussed. We would prefer to relate to love as an expression of the combined emotional and sexual current, but this concept does not clarify everything. Still, we cannot see what significance should be attached to an antithetical meaning (hatred) in this current (Freud, 1915c).

* * *

In the case of love this refers to three antitheses, rather than just one. Beside the love/hate antithesis, there is also the loved/beloved antithesis and the love/apathy antithesis, as opposed to love/hate.

The first category is of the opposing love and apathy, which belong to the Real order. Lacan terms this "real antithesis". Following Freud, who attributed the auto-erotic trait to this antithesis, Lacan explained that in the case of auto-eroticism, this does not mean that a baby is not interested in things outside itself; rather, it means that objects would not appear at all if the subject did not have a use for them. Narcissistic love of this type is located in the Real. First the I appears, defined by its function as an apparatus of the central nervous system that maintains tensions at the lowest, homeostatic level. Apart from this role, the only sensation is of apathy, and at this level apathy means non-existence.

The rule according to which auto-erotic interest functions is not the non-existence of objects but, rather, their function solely in relation to pleasure.

* * *

Lacan termed the love/hate category the "economic category". In psychoanalysis this antithesis is not considered to be real since at the level of the unconscious the power of the affect is what determines things, even when a minus sign is added to it.

In this context, Lacan said: "Here, then, is constituted the *Lust-Ich*, and also the field of the *Unlust*, of the object as remainder, as alien. The object that one needs to know, and with good reason, is that which is defined in the field of *Unlust*, whereas the objects of the field of the *Lust-Ich* are lovable" (Lacan, 1973, p. 191).

* * *

Lacan termed the third category—the loved/beloved antithesis—the "biological antithesis" or the "passive/active". He said that this is the only category entered by the problem of non-existent sexual connection. Following Plato's *Symposium*, Lacan refers in the VIIIth seminar, *Le Transfert* (1991b), to the significance of the love that is generated when the function of the lover (Eronemus) as the lacking subject is replaced by the loved object (Erastes). In an essay entitled "Mazes of Love", Jacques-Alain Miller (1992) said that this perception introduces the castration complex into love. The basis of deceit in love is located in the place of the ideal of the I, from which the subject sees itself as others see it, in a kind of illusionary vision. Such love is directed not at what the Other has but, rather, towards what it is lacking in—a phallus. This is focused on the point of the ideal, which is located somewhere in the Other—the point from which the Other sees me in the way I like to be seen (Miller, 1992). Regarding this, Miller added that loving the Other means establishing it as a phallus, but wanting to be loved by it means that one wants the loved to be the lover—that is, lacking, which in effect means castrating it. Loving, therefore, is in essence wanting to be loved. This lack of symmetry is what differentiates between love and drives. The entire theory of transference can be considered within the context of this definition.

* * *

In "Instincts and Their Vicissitudes" (1915c), Freud contended that love is not a drive. The total I is the lover of its objects (just as fishermen tend to like fish—though in this case, it is the fish that eat the fisherman rather than the opposite: the objects devour the I). For Freud, love stems from the I's ability to satisfy some of its compulsions in an auto-erotic way by achieving the pleasure of the organ. Narcissistic love is thereby transferred to the expanded I, from objects that have been assimilated.

In "The Subject and the Other: Alienation" in the XIth seminar, Lacan related to the myth of Aristophanes. In this myth, love is seen as a way of finding that which makes us whole. He saw this as identical to our quest for our other sexual half. The experience of analysis replaces this mythical presentation in regard to the mystery of love as the quest of the subject not for the entity that will complement him sexually but, rather, the other part of himself that he lost forever, precisely due to his being a sexual mortal (Lacan, 1973). Perhaps, like the woman in the Song of Songs: "I opened to my beloved; but my beloved had withdrawn himself, and was gone: my soul failed when he spake: I sought him, but I could not find him; I called him, but he gave me no answer" (Song of Songs, 5:6).

By noting the connection between love and knowledge in the XXth seminar, Lacan shed more light on the question of transition from love of narcissism to love of the Other (Lacan, 1975a). The connection is made not just in the context of "What can be known of love?" but also in the sense of "To love means loving what the Other knows of me". Lacan said that all love is based on a kind of link that exists between two subjects, through the unconscious knowledge of each of them. In this context, transference to the subject-that-is-supposed-to-know [*sujet supposé savoir*] constitutes only one specific application.

It appears that through the mechanism of transference the psychoanalyst can strip love of its uniqueness and mystery. That is because psychoanalysis generates a kind of non-specific, one-off love. The love of transference in psychoanalysis is directed towards a particular locus—where the analyst and his or her supposed knowledge is, irrespective of who is in that place. Thus the imaginary dimension of love (*semblant*) is emphasized—but is it so?

Falling in love is a contingent affair. Lacan characterized this contingency saying that unconscious knowledge "stops not being written" or registered, while "sexual relationship doesn't stop not to be written". He adds that there is nothing but an encounter, an encounter with the partner of the symptoms, of the effects, of everything that marks within us the traces of its exile, not as a subject but as a speaker, its exile from the sexual context (Lacan, 1975a).

* * *

As creatures of speech we find ourselves interminably in exile, even within our own homes. Love serves as the illusion of coming home, the illusion of redemption through the impossible bonding of two beings. In relating to the illusion of love, Lacan continued in dramatic style reminiscent of Albert Camus. The illusion of love registers in every one of our fates, and with its help—for a while at least—what should have established a sexual relation finds its way, like in an imaginary vision, to the speaking being. Lacan said that this stage of delay can perhaps be likened to delaying the tragic fate of love and that it is located in the transfer of negation from "ceasing not being written" to "not ceasing to be written"—from contingency to necessity.

* * *

In "Mazes of Love", Miller (1992) also spoke of the contingency of love, of the chance meeting. In referring to this he used the Greek term *tuché*, which Lacan also used—but is love, in its essence, really a random phenomenon? What are the conditions for love if not necessity?

Miller said that in love the subject meets with the conditions for his love, as if chance suddenly intersects the path of necessity. If there is choice, it is imposed and predetermined (Miller, 1992), but the imposition of choice does not mean that there is no choice at all. Choice is both offered and denied in one fell swoop, but a gesture so empty may be considered to be subjectiveness, much as in the way highwaymen would offer their victims the choice of "Your money or your life!" We are offered choices that have been predetermined—and in choosing we experience loss.

Imposed choice is always connected with love in its various forms. We must opt for love, thereby surrendering freedom of choice. As Kierkegaard maintained: if we opt for freedom of choice, we lose both. Mladen Dolar developed this approach in reference to erotic love, saying that love and the autonomy of the subject do not coexist and that this is illustrated by all melodramatic love stories (Dolar, 1996a). Most familiar romantic melodramas do indeed follow a similar pattern—a chance meeting between a young hero and a young woman in exceptional circumstances. But that which appears to occur randomly and unintentionally eventually turns out to be the fulfilment of the "young man's" wishes and his most primal and deepest desires.

I believe there is also similarity in the way female heroines relate to young men that they meet. Chance turns marvellously into the deepest place of truth of the two lovers—a kind of sign of fate awarded by the Other. In retrospect, it becomes apparent that it was the Other that made the choice rather than the helpless young man or girl.

* * *

The introduction of the unexpected became vital, *tuché* turned into an automaton. The moment of subjectivization comes when subjectiveness is put aside in favour of the Other, which reveals itself as pure contingency of the Real. The only choice individuals have is to recognize that choice has already been exercised irrespective of their freedom of choice. All that's left for them to do is to accept what cannot be avoided as part of their being, thereby adopting and ratifying the decision of the Other. To put it another way, choice here has to be perceived in a retroactive context, always in the past—but a past that has never been the present. It moves directly and immediately from "not yet" to "since always". These terms were used by the poet Paul Celan in referring to the nature of poetry. Similar perception, perhaps, led Lacan to state that poems are the love letters of the unconscious.

* * *

So falling in love is nothing but surrender to necessity, to the moment when the Real begins to speak. Its opaqueness becomes transparency. The meaningless sign becomes the embodiment of the highest meaning, and the subject makes do with recognizing such after the fact. Thus comes the moment of the lauded miracle of love that we all desire. This sudden recognition—the *tuché*—hints that, in a sense, even the first time is always a repetition. In retrospect, we realize what we have always known. The Real looks back, even if the other individual did not respond, was not affected, and even if they weren't aware at all. Perhaps Lacan was basing himself on this line of thinking when saying that thing that we all yearn for so much—love is always mutual (1975a).

There is knowledge that is connected with sexuality. In biblical Hebrew the term "to know" is a euphemism for sexual intercourse. This is knowledge of the flesh or perhaps knowledge of the Real. Knowledge of love is not knowledge of the Real, although it does touch on it. It is knowledge relating to necessity, which finds expression in the wake of the chance encounter. Lacan queried whether love is connected with the attempt to become "one". Are we back at the myth of Aristophanes? We can use this myth as long as we employ the term of discourse and signifiers. "Love that is connected with the one never causes someone to leave themselves behind", Lacan wrote (1975a, p. 47).

* * *

Love is indeed narcissistic in essence and connected with the image (*semblant*) of the one, but it is directed at the remainder, at *objet á*—which is within you more than it is of you. Unlike desire, love is directed towards being rather than towards its lack—towards what is rather than towards what is not, even if such being already existed or is just about to exist. It could even be said that love invents being in that it somehow constitutes recompense for the non-existence of a sexual relationship. What is meant by the word "love" is the subject—that same subject that is an effect of the unconscious knowledge held by the object, which resides within the subject and is dearer. The subject is not well connected with *jouissance*, with the exception of *jouissance* of speech—speaking of what? Of love, as well as *jouissance*, when the knowledge of that love is revealed.

* * *

Towards the end of the XIth seminar, Lacan has a surprise in store for us. He discusses the conclusion of analysis and mentions another kind of love—love without boundaries, which is connected with the generation of new knowledge. This is love for what is left of the object once all the imaginary and symbolic contours have been stripped away (Lacan, 1973).

In the XXth seminar, Lacan continued differentiating between love and sexuality by saying that the *jouissance* of the Other does not signify love. Love itself is a signifier or sign indicating mutuality, demanding nothing other than love, love, and yet more love.

Perhaps this is the "love powerful as death", unequalled even by all the wealth in the world.

* * *

At the beginning of this essay, I showed how Freud and Lacan link love with need rather than drive. At this point, considering the connection between love and knowledge, love is characterized as a sign rather than a signifier, thereby deviating once again from the fields of imagination and symbolism. Like the letter, it is also located at a kind of intermediate juncture between the symbolic, the imaginary, and the Real (more on this in chapter 8 herein, "The Letter as Place and The Place of the Letter"). The sign is a form of registry in the Real, registry that can become symbolic as it plows a furrow in *jouissance*. That is the function of love—the role of inscribing the body. That is why poetry knows what to do with it whereas visual art, such as cinema, only knows how to use passion and sexuality to indicate love, rather than how to show love itself. In this context, we may wonder whether art really deals with the visual aspect of love or whether it makes do with displaying some other aspect or sign that then requires interpretation.

What, then, is unlimited love? "Love powerful as death"? "The Fire of God"?

I contend that in psychoanalysis, love, like death, constitutes an impassable boundary—a boundary that simultaneously leads to the desire for knowledge, and suicide.

The very same thing that both generates knowledge and annihilates its significance as soon as it is formulated into words. Furthermore, we desire and insist that it stays that way. All we can do is meekly revert to the realm of poetry, just as Freud and Lacan did. Thus I shall conclude with Shakespeare's Sonnet 116 , since *he* certainly knew a thing or two about love:

> Let me not to the marriage of true minds
> Admit impediments. Love is not love
> Which alters when it alternation finds,
> Or bends with the remover to remove:

O, no! it is an ever-fixed mark,
That looks on tempests and is never shaken;
It is the star to every wandering bark,
Whose worth's unknown, although his height be taken.
Love's not Time's fool, though rosy lips and cheeks
Within his bending sickle's compass come;
Love alters not with his brief hours and weeks,
But bears it out even to the edge of doom.
    If this be error, and upon me proved,
    I never writ, nor no man ever loved.

CHAPTER THREE

Phantasy— from Freud to Lacan and from Lacan to the artist

"The moon that is in the water.
The water does not break.
The moon does not get wet."

Y. Raz (1995, p. 67; translated for this edition)

The short haiku above defines, accurately and concisely, I believe, everything that will be written in many words in the rest of this article. The first line defines an existential condition: the moon that is in the water. Not: the moon reflected in the water; nor: the image of the moon in the water. The moon really is in the water, but in a different manner, a different essence—an essence that does not create changes in the "real world"—and yet: the moon is in the water. Absent and present at the same time. This, as will be seen later on, is the essence of the connection between phantasy and the Real dimension in the world.

* * *

Previously published in English as *Phantasy* [Catalogue of the exhibition *Phantasy*] (Herzlia: The Forum of Art Museums, 1996).

At the beginning of the last chapter of *The Interpretation of Dreams* (1900a), Freud relates a dream of a father who lay down to rest, while in the next room lay the body of his dead son, left in the care of another man. In the dream, the son comes to the father, grabs him by the arm, and whispers to him reproachfully: "Father, don't you see I'm burning?" The father wakes in panic and discovers that the guard had fallen asleep and, indeed, that one of the candles burning by the body had fallen and set fire to the deathbed.

If, as Freud claims, the function of the dream is to prolong sleep, what is it that wakes the father, asks Lacan (1973)? Beyond the realistic detail of the candle setting fire to the bed, is it not, in the dream, a different reality, worse than the waking reality—a reality in which a father stands helpless confronting the death of his child? What is the reality and what is the phantasy in this dreadful event? Do not the child's words in the dream express a deeper reality, more real, exposing itself in the dream, and from which it is better to wake into a reality where the consoling phantasy is possible?

* * *

Indeed, the term "unconscious phantasy", or *phantasme*, appears for the first time when in *The Interpretation of Dreams* Freud speaks about the role of the ego as guardian of sleep. Anything that belongs to the dimension of the ego as an alert, watchful agency occurs at the level of the secondary processing of the dream. However, according to Lacan, Freud cannot differentiate between this dimension and the fantasizing function in which the ego is intertwined. Lacan talks about a series of relations that were meant to differentiate between phantasy, dream, and daydream according to the types of mirror relations—namely, the relations with an imaginary object. The primary body image is created when the baby looks in the mirror and his mother (the Other) points at it and tells him: "It is you." There is a big gap between the reflection in the mirror, on the one hand, and the degree of maturation of the baby's body and his bodily experience, on the other. Therefore, the body image is basically imaginary. (Lacan regards this illusory body image as the primary basis for the formation of the ego.)

* * *

In their dictionary of psychoanalysis, Laplanche and Pontalis define phantasy as an: "Imaginary scene in which the subject is a protagonist, representing the fulfilment of a wish (in the last analysis, an unconscious wish) in a manner that is distorted to a greater or lesser extent by defensive processes" (Laplanche & Pontalis, 1973, p. 314)

Phantasy has different modes: conscious phantasy or daydream, and unconscious phantasy, or *phantasme*. *Phantasme* is uncovered by analysis as the structure underlying the manifest content. There is also a primal *phantasme*, around which the subject constructs his identity as an answer to the question he poses to the Other ("What does he want from me?"), but to which he does not receive an answer. (I elaborate on this later.)

* * *

Freud began to speak about *phantasme* after abandoning in 1897 the theory of the symptom (the seduction theory), which was wholly explainable by a primary sexual trauma that was repressed. If at first he assumed that traumatic childhood memories exposed during analysis are realistic pictures, later on he withdrew from this recognition, claiming that the reality of these memories is a "psychical reality". Yet, if we return to the dream I described at the beginning of this chapter, we can say that the notion of "psychical reality" is more complex than first meets the eye, and it also embeds the dimension of the Real, or, as Freud puts it,

> Whether we are to attribute *reality* to unconscious wishes, I cannot say. It must be denied, of course, to any transitional or intermediate thoughts. If we look at unconscious wishes reduced to their most fundamental and truest shape, we shall have to conclude, no doubt, that *psychical* reality is a particular form of existence not to be confused with *material* reality. [Freud, 1900a, p. 620]

Freud notes that the source of the libidinal drive could be found in *phantasme*, when the same drive is located in the imaginary dimension. Lacan finds in the imaginary nature of the "mirror stage" the primary channelling of the libidinal energy, which will affect all the phantasies to follow. That is to say, the body image establishes a dimension of the human that structures the world of phantasy.

Freud attributes great significance to the relationship between phantasy and time. Every phantasy is simultaneously marked by three times: (1) In order for phantasy to occur we need an actual impression, a cause in the present that may evoke one of man's basic wishes. (2) This cause connects to a memory of a past experience, usually from childhood, where this wish was fulfilled. (3) Thus, we get a situation where there is a projection on the future that appears as a wish fulfilment—that is, the daydream or the phantasy—in which we can identify the traces of its origin from the cause and the memory.

* * *

In psychoanalysis, the paradigm of a basic *phantasme* is described in "'A Child Is Being Beaten'" (Freud, 1919e). Freud describes a phantasy that reappears in the stories of several of his patients. They think "A child is being beaten" and feel *jouissance*. Freud, naturally, explores what underlies this sentence. He discovers the earlier version of this phantasy, being: "The father beats the (other) child." Something has happened between the first sentence and the second. The active became passive. Freud structures an unconscious intermediary stage in which this transformation occurred. This stage gives the phantasy its erotic spin. The patient does not articulate the intermediary stage; Freud reaches it through analytic research and reconstructs it as: "I am being beaten by the father." This is a formula that has never received verbal expression, never risen to consciousness. It is a construction of the analyst. It is a sentence that expresses the truth about castration—namely, being beaten equals being castrated. It is a masochistic form, where the cause of castration is the father. In a regressive manner, the drive becomes anal-passive; "The father beats the child" turns into "My father is beating me (I am being beaten by my father)." The being beaten becomes a meeting-place between a sense of guilt and sexual love. It is not only the punishment for the forbidden genital relation, but also the regressive substitute for it.

Jean-François Lyotard and Rosalind Krauss refer in length to the structure of *phantasme* when discussing modern art (Krauss, 1988). Lyotard is impressed by the logic of ambivalence, as it is expressed in the structure of the *phantasme*. Just as the beating is not only a punishment but also a source of pleasure, every other element is similarly ruled by this ambivalence, through a simultaneous holding of two wholly contrary positions—that is, a structure of "but also". One "stage" does not progress beyond and thus supersede another: on the contrary—the meaning of every stage remains suspended within it. Lyotard calls this a "difference", which confuses the structuralist rule of opposition. The structure of "A child is being beaten" brings together active and passive, genital and anal, sadism and masochism, gazing and being gazed at. It overlays contradiction and creates a simultaneity of logically incompatible situations.

Nevertheless, according to Lyotard, there is a constant variable in all this, and it is the action "to beat". The contents of the *phantasme* may be in continual flux from one form to another, but underlying these contents is a form: a rhythm, a pulse of beating. It is this form that works to secure the identity of the *phantasme* such that in each of its obsessional repetitions it always returns the same. Lyotard contemplates on Freud's essay *Beyond the Pleasure Principle* (1920g) and the two different pulses Freud describes there. One is charge and discharge as the pleasure principle operates towards the release of tension and the maintenance of low levels of excitation. It is the rhythm of a pulse (on/off +–+–+–+–), or presence and absence of contact—the form of beating. This pulse is demonstrated in the game played by Freud's grandson with a cotton-reel, which he throws away and pulls towards him in alternation, while uttering the words *"fort/da"* [gone/here], a game aimed at dealing with the anxiety of the mother's absence. The *phantasme* has a role similar t o that of the game. Namely, to derive pleasure from a situation of anxiety. The child of *fort/da* operates the "machine" when the desire of the Other—in this case the mother (who desires something or someone else more than being with her child)—is revealed. In order for the desire to be exposed, there must be absence or inconsistency.

The *phantasme* is therefore a kind of a machine that starts working when the desire of the other is revealed, a desire that stimulates anxiety. It can be said that the *phantasme* is the defensive answer of the subject confronted with the desire of the other—that which was called by Lacan the Other [*Autre*] and which is represented in this case by the father but can equally be represented by the mother. That is the answer to "What does he want?" Indeed, what does this Other, who is everything to me, want? What does Mummy want when she yells at me? She wants me to be a good girl when I go wild—but when my younger brother goes wild she kisses him. So what does she want? There is a point where the Other cannot answer, because he himself does not know what he wants. The subject then finds a phantasmic answer, which makes him what he is, which constitutes him.

* * *

The second type of pulse is not a principle of recurrence guaranteeing that an "on" will always follow an "off", but a principle of interruption, cessation, a pulse that can be described as $+/0$—that is, existence followed by total extinction. It is a beat that does not promise the return of the same thing, but only a return per se, a return of nothing. This second pulse is not a good form, says Lyotard. On the contrary—it is a transgression of form. The anxiety that is part of the effect of "A child is being beaten", combining with its erotic pleasure, arises precisely from the force of rupture that is recurrent in the rhythm of the figure, a rupture that is not experienced as the onset of yet another contact but as an absolute break—that discontinuity without end, which is death. Thus it is the death drive, operating beyond the pleasure principle, that dictates this rhythm—as it beats with the alteration between pleasure and extinction, into a compulsion to repeat. And indeed, we know that the *phantasme* of one's death, of one's disappearance, is usually the first manipulation a child uses in his love relations with his parents—for instance, when hiding behind a curtain: "Can they separate from me? Can they lose me?"

* * *

Back to the dream of the burning child: the terrible thing that is revealed in this dream is precisely the Real, which is exposed like a bleeding wound; the horrifying Real from which we awake to phantasy. Thus, *phantasme* protects the Real and the Real in turn supports *phantasme*; they are closer to each other more than to the symbolic dimension, the dimension of language and culture. The *phantasme* serves as some sort of screen that protects the Real. According to Lacan, the subject cannot enter the Real but through *phantasme* (Lacan, 1973, p. 41).

* * *

In the case of his patient, the Wolf Man (1918b [1914]), Freud powerfully deals with the essence of the first encounter—the Real that lies behind the *phantasme*—and comes to a construction of the primal scene (the parents' intercourse) the child saw when he was 1½ years old. Freud strongly insists upon exposing this Real, leading Lacan to assume that this insistence could have later driven the Wolf Man to insanity.

One of the Wolf Man's phantasies occurred at the age of 5. He said he was playing in the garden near his nurse and was carving with his pocket-knife in a bark of a tree:

> "Suddenly, to my unspeakable terror, I noticed that I had cut through the little finger of my hand, so that is was only hanging on by its skin. I felt no pain, but great fear. I did not venture to say anything to my nurse, who was only a few paces distant, but I sank down to the nearest seat and sat there incapable of casting another glance at my finger. At last I calmed down, took another look at the finger, and saw that it was entirely uninjured." [Freud, 1918b [1914], p. 85]

According to Freud, the fear felt by the child is the fear of castration as a punishment for the forbidden *jouissance*.

* * *

Lacan wrote about that when he compared Kant's philosophy to that of the Marquis de Sade: the *phantasme* is anchored in perversion. The pervert thinks that if the lost object—according to which the drive object is constructed—is, for example, a lizard's tail, he will turn himself into a lizard's tail. He occupies the place of the visible factor—the object—which he thinks will allow him to be the subject of pure desire (Lacan, 1962).

In *phantasme*, the subject is frequently unperceived, but he is always there. "The moon that is in the water", says the haiku, yet the wise men of Chelem tried to capture that same moon inside a barrel of water, and how disappointed were they when they opened its lid the next morning.

* * *

In the dream or daydream, the subject situates himself as determined by the *phantasme*. *Phantasme*, says Žižek (1993), in its most basic dimension, suggests the choice of thought over being, in contrast to the symptom, which suggests the choice of being, since what emerges in the symptom is a thought that was lost, repressed, when we selected being (p. 64). In *phantasme* I find myself reduced to the point of thought that refers to the events occurring while I'm absent, not present. In the *phantasme* of "A child is being beaten", the ego is seemingly absent, out of the picture. The structure of the phantasmic gaze includes a self-doubling of the gaze, as though we are watching the "primal scene" from behind our very own eyes, as though we are not wholly identified with our own gaze but, rather, stand somewhere "behind it"—as though the gaze is concealed by the eye. In his optical research, Descartes talked about a man who has put between himself and reality the eye of a dead animal. Instead of watching reality directly, one watches the images that emerge at the back of a dead animal's eye.

* * *

Normally, the person who comes for treatment talks a lot about his symptoms: he complains about his suffering. As to phantasies, the opposite is true: the patient does not come to complain about them; if he does depict them, he is usually ashamed. It can be said that through *phantasme* he derives *jouissance*. It has a role of consolation, and there is a connection between it and what Miller (1987) calls "the philosophical consolation", which is masturbation. The *phantasme* usually draws its content from the discourse of perversion; it is the treasure of the subject and his most intimate and unique possession.

According to Žižek, the *phantasme* is the "absolute particular", that part which we will never be able to share. In Kant's words: we do not respect the other on the basis of the universal moral law that is embedded in each and every one of us, but on the basis of its "pathological" nucleus, the particular way in which each one "dreams his world", devises his way of deriving *jouissance* through his own *phantasmes* (Žižek, 1993, p. 64).

* * *

In essence, the *phantasme* resists universalization; it is the unique way in which each of us structures his "impossible" connection to the traumatic or Real Thing (*das Ding*). It is the way in which each of us, by an imaginary scenario, conceals the inconsistency of the Other, the one who does not know what he wants. The Other stands for the symbolic order, the field of the law, of culture, of rights and duties—only it apparently has cracks and holes. It is precisely at this point of absolute particularity that the artist belongs: as connector between this unique, intimate world and the general culture.

The haiku cited at the beginning of this chapter consists of four elements—the moon, the water, the sight of the moon in the water, and the poet who turns the phantasy into a poem. Freud dedicated to this an article entitled "Creative Writers and Day-Dreaming", where he compares the creative writer and the child: both create a world of phantasy and take it very seriously. There are things that being realistic about can cause us suffering, but when transferred into the realm of imagination can become a source of pleasure, like war games, for instance. In this article, Freud (1908e [1907]) formulates one of the most amazing truths about man's psyche: "Hardly anything is harder for a man than to give up a pleasure which he has once experienced. Actually, we can never give anything up; we only exchange one thing for another"(p. 145).

It can be said that for all our lives we are in pursuit of an object that once gave us pleasure and was lost to us. All phantasies are substitutes for that object and at the same time represent it. A common feature in the works of story writers is that each of them has one hero who is the centre of their interest, a person for whom the writer tries to win our sympathy by doing everything in his power. It is very easy to recognize in this hero what Freud calls "his majesty the ego"—the hero of all daydreams, novels, and romances alike.

The daydreamer is ashamed of his phantasies, and if he does agree to share them, he will often find out that the phantasies of others repel the listener:

> But when a creative writer presents his plays to us or tells us what we are inclined to take to be his personal day-dreams, we experience great pleasure . . . the essential *ars poetica* lies in the technique of overcoming the feeling of repulsion in us. . . . the writer softens the character of his egotistic day-dreams by altering and disguising it, and he bribes us by the purely formal—that is, aesthetic—yield of pleasure which he offers us in the presentation of his phantasies. [Freud, 1908e (1907), pp. 152–153]

To such a yield of pleasure, which is meant to allow the release of greater pleasure arising from deeper psychic sources, Freud applies the term "incentive bonus", or "fore-pleasure". Freud believes that all aesthetic pleasure rendered by the writer is characterized by such fore-pleasure, and that the true pleasure derived from the aesthetic work of art springs from the release of tensions in our mind. A large part of this success may be attributed to the fact that the creative writer creates for us the ability to enjoy our own phantasies from now on, without feeling self-reproach or shame.

* * *

What we get in the painting (or in any other artistic medium) resembles the final formula of "'A Child Is Being Beaten'", which is a more legitimate formula than the unconscious version. Like in *phantasme*, the painting is a substitutional object that, in fact, raises the phantom of the subject. However, we have to be careful not to mix art and *phantasme* or to say that what the artist does while painting is simulating one *phantasme* or another. A painting, even if its content is fantastic, functions as a substitute for misrepresentation. A painting does not even represent the model it resembles; rather, it represents the movement of appearance and disappearance, which records the misrepresentation—namely, it represents the misrepresentation: the lost object.

In conclusion, regarding painting, I would like to pose a few questions: Are the portrayed phantasies a final version like "A child is being beaten", phantasies in which the subject is absent, yet according to which we can reconstruct previous sentences and structure a basic *phantasme*? Do we have here a game of presence and absence, or a veiling of the Real by the portrayed? Is the painting a bribe or enticement, as Freud says, to advance pleasure? Can we observe a phantasmatic structure that is beyond the visual content, which is expressed by the process of painting and protects the absolute uniqueness of every painting? Is the moon in the water (the painting) an empty reflection on the surface, as in the story of the wise men of Chelem, or can we trace a unique mode of truth that the moon in the water conceals and at the same time attests to?

PART II

JOUISSANCE, WOMAN

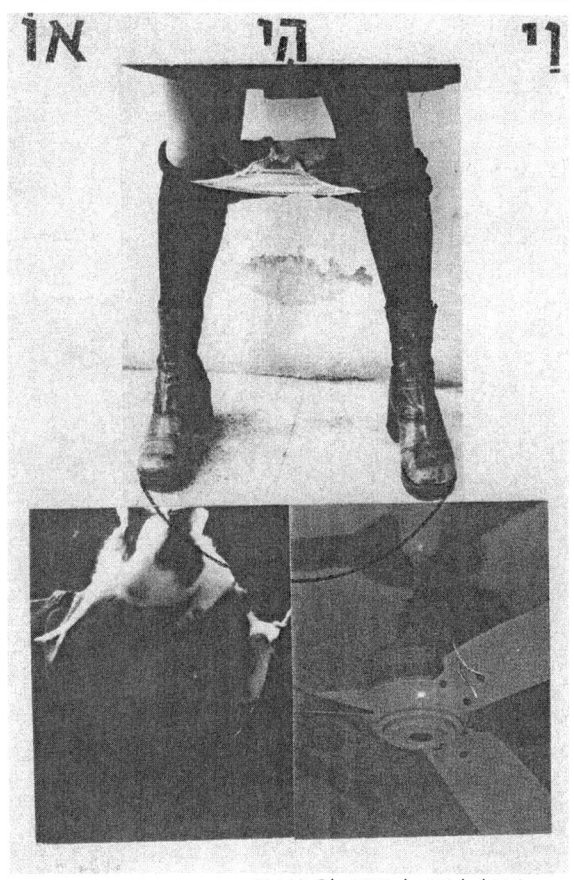

Vai Hi Oh, 1975, by Michal Na'aman

CHAPTER FOUR

Paul Celan and the question of feminine *jouissance*

"So powerful was his love for her that it would have pushed open the lid of his coffin—were it not for the weight of the flower she had placed there."

Paul Celan (1986)

Paul Celan is considered one of the most important European poets of the post–World War II period. Celan, a Romanian Jew born in Czernowitz, survived the Holocaust and settled in Paris. He wrote in German. In 1970 he committed suicide by jumping into the Seine. Celan is frequently discussed in academic and psychiatric circles, which attribute various diagnoses to him. For example, he is thought to have been a psychotic, paranoid, depressive patient who bore symptoms typical of Holocaust survivors.

What can psychoanalysis learn from Paul Celan, based on the testimony of his poems and the sparse accounts by the people who were acquainted with him?

***

Having read his poems, some thoughts occurred to me that may perhaps shed light on the Lacanian psychoanalytic approach to the concepts of *jouissance* and the Real, two concepts that Lacan developed out of Freud's concept of the death drive.

In his article *Beyond the Pleasure Principle* (1920g), Freud distinguished between the pleasure principle—a principle relating to every action that aims to discharge tension and attain balance—and "beyond the pleasure principle", which is connected with what he later called the death drive. Lacan called this connection between the libido and the death drive *"jouissance"*. *Jouissance* does not necessarily involve feelings of pleasure. In fact, it is usually connected more with pain.

Lacan spoke of two types of *jouissance*: "phallic *jouissance*", the *jouissance* of the male sexual function, and, connected with this, the *jouissance* resulting from cultural achievements, of speaking and language. As for women, according to Lacan they do not fall entirely under the authority of "phallic *jouissance*" but have an additional *jouissance* that cannot be expressed in words, if only because every act of speech entails a demand of sorts and every demand is on the phallic level. Therefore, women have a surplus value of *jouissance*, which perhaps only mystics and poets know how to touch. For men, women therefore constitute the radical Other. I would like to emphasize that when psychoanalysis refers to the differences between the sexes, it is not referring to biological differences. Psychoanalysis tries to distinguish the differences between the sexes on the symbolic level—that is, to formulate the different functions, the masculine and the feminine. And since there is no signifier in the unconscious for the difference between the sexes, beyond the social aspect the boundary separating men and women is very nebulous, and it is crossed in endless ways.

* * *

Paul Celan's poems and fate have led me to think that this poet was one of those who crossed this boundary, since, in my opinion, he touched upon feminine *jouissance* and knew something about it. What he knew was apparently insufferable for him and was connected in an inescapable manner with the death drive. By means of the following autobiographical details, I shall attempt to make a partial list of the symbolic world in which he grew up. The way he was brought up and educated should not necessarily be perceived as a direct causal link with his poetic world. However, through study of the poet and his poetry, I do hope to learn more about the riddle of feminine *jouissance*.

The name, the father, and the mother

The biographical information presented here about Paul Celan is based primarily on conversations with people who grew up with him or lived near him (Chalfen, 1991). This is, therefore, Celan as seen through the eyes of others, who constituted part of the cultural-symbolic field of his youth.

* * *

From the little that has been told of his family, it seems that the female, matriarchal line was dominant.

At birth Celan was called Paul, but he was also given the name of his grandmother's father—Pesach. This name represents the concept of Jewish freedom, where God passed over [*pasach*] the homes of the Hebrews and did not kill their first-born sons.

Celan's mother Fritzi lost her own mother when she was young, and she took over the running of the household and the care of her younger brothers. Once her father had remarried, there were actually two women running the household.

Celan's father Leo had a rather complicated surname, so he chose to bear his mother's—Antschel. Paul's grandfather had arrived from the countryside and had entered the wealthy Antschel household as a stepson who spent his days studying, while his wife ran the store by herself. Pesach Antschel had no sons and left all his property to his daughters.

For several years, Fritzi and Leo lived with Leo's father and two unmarried sisters. Fritzi was a good-looking woman and was apparently both educated and strong minded. After she married, she managed the affairs of the house, as in her childhood, and seems to have played a maternal role towards her husband, Leo. Recognizing her husband's lack of confidence and resolve, Fritzi saw herself as solely responsible for making important family decisions. As far as is known, the Antschel couple had almost no social life.

* * *

Paul Celan was an only child, brought up in an authoritarian manner. A relative testifies that the father, not an endearing character, enforced strict discipline in the home and made heavy demands on his son. He employed extreme methods of punishments and often hit the boy, more often than not with no good reason.

* * *

Leo Antschel was a short man, shorter than his wife, and it seems that he would sometimes try to compensate for his small stature and economic failures by terrorizing his household. However, he almost never fought with his wife and showed devotion to her. It was his sensitive son Paul who suffered from him. Any warmth and love that Paul received came from his mother. His father forbade anything that might "spoil" the child; from a young age Paul learned to behave obediently, in accordance with his parents' concept of "good upbringing". He had to adhere to extreme physical hygiene, he was not allowed to leave anything on his plate, he was forbidden to ask any unnecessary questions. If he answered back, rebelled, or was simply stubborn, his father would scold him soundly or hit him. If his "transgression" was deemed particularly severe, his father would lock him in an empty room. Fortunately for Paul, the room had a window facing the backyard, and after Leo left the house, Fritzi or the other women would release the crying child from his cell.

* * *

Paul spent his first years in the company of adults. His grandfather was old and sick and remained shut in his room. Paul saw him only infrequently but was required to maintain the quiet so as not to disturb him. Every way he turned the young boy ran into restrictions on his freedom: closed doors that he was not allowed to open, the front door through which he was only allowed to exit when accompanied by an adult. He was therefore a sad child, his childish spontaneity constrained by "suitable behaviour" and gaiety repressed. His cousin relates how in their childhood they would play together when his parents were away, and Paul would sometimes shout: "I'm afraid that Death is searching for me. I must hide from it!" He would then quickly crawl into his bed (which stood in his parents' bedroom until he was 12 years old!) and hide under the blankets.

* * *

In photographs from that period, Paul appears compulsively stiff. His parents had very ambitious plans for him, quite out of accordance with their financial means. When he was young he was considered a quiet, well-behaved boy, but he did not excel in the Hebrew school to which his parents forced him to go. Paul felt himself bound by restrictions, and the stronger they were, the more his need to rebel grew.

In elementary school Paul was a lonely boy—he was not allowed to invite friends home, and since he was constantly under the supervision of adults, he could not initiate visits of his own. In school he was awarded the job of teacher's helper and would report every act of mischief. For this reason he was unpopular among the other pupils, who looked upon him as an ambitious teacher's pet, although Paul was sure that his behaviour was utterly correct.

* * *

Paul's first rebellion against his father arose due to his heavy study load. As a result Paul was released from Hebrew studies. His mother supported him in this respect.

Paul's parents only moved away from Leo's father's family into a house of their own when Paul was a teenager. According to his biographer, even though relations between the parents remained outwardly harmonious, they grew further and further apart. Fritzi Antschel became more and more devoted to her son and bestowed all her love on him. When his friends came to visit, she would sit with them, take part in their conversations, or listen enthusiastically to Paul. She made a great effort to make the guests feel comfortable, and she tried to behave in a young manner, adapting to the age of her son's friends. It was obvious to all his friends that

Paul worshipped his mother. When he was a teenager, his childish love for his mother developed and turned into an intense relationship that took over his emotional life. Everything sexual was repressed or turned into an ideal, romantic tie with his mother. A perfect symbiotic relationship formed between them. Paul cut his emotional ties with his father. He saw him as a marginal presence in the household. He rejected the man's bourgeois Zionism and despised his "dirty" financial work.

In high school the tables turned, and Paul became very popular and respected among his friends.

* * *

During World War II, the Jews in the city would hide on the days when Jews were deported to concentration camps. Fritzi refused to hide, claiming that one's fate cannot be avoided. Paul objected to this and, for the first time, came into severe conflict with his mother, but he could not convince her. When the hour of curfew grew near, Paul decided to act without his parent's consent. He left the house and went into hiding, assuming that his parents would follow. They, however, did not. Several days later, when he returned home, he found the front door sealed. His parents had been deported.

It seems, therefore, that it was not so much the hard physical labour, hunger, or cold that led Paul to sink further and further into melancholy but, rather, the sense of guilt he bore in regard to his parents. In 1943 he wrote: "What would it be, mother: growth or wound—/ if I should also drown in the snow drifts of the Ukraine?" (in Chalfen, 1991, p. 157).

And when in the course of the winter he heard that his mother had been shot in the back of the neck, he wrote: "Oh stone masts of melancholy! Oh I among you and alive! Oh I among you and alive and beautiful, and she cannot smile at me . . ." (in Chalfen, 1991, p. 157).

Paul Celan and the encounter with the feminine

Ilse, Paul's first female friend, wrote:

> "as he approached me, an icy shadow fell over everything and stayed. His presence burdened me. . . . In his whole being there was something effeminately weak and self-pitying . . . I found myself the more masculine . . . I think it was this . . . confusion of gender which . . . gave rise to a deep antipathy. In later years I realized . . . that this is one of the ingredients, the curse and property of the poet, the creator: to stand between the sexes or to be of both. I also remember that he once acted out Ophelia's madness scene and Juliet's balcony scene for me. . . . he had a surprisingly lively and critical eye, something of Hölderlin's capacity for premonition. . . . In fact, in these years he had a sense only for the extraordinary." [in Chalfen, 1991, pp. 75–77]

* * *

Another female friend reports that Paul was a very handsome, intellectual, delicately built, almost girl-like boy who took no interest in boy's games. He took great care with his looks and could not bear a single stain on his clothes. His biography emphasizes the love he had of flowers, once even risking his life during the Nazi curfew to steal out to pick a stalk from a bush in blossom. He gathered a reading circle around himself comprised mainly of women, and he had many female companions. Not one of them, however, was romantically attached to him—he was afraid of girls, as one of his friends related. It would seem that he was captivated by his mother's love alone.

A female friend from the university related:

> "It is strange that his infinitely rich and emotional inner life was never mirrored in his features. . . . His face was inscrutable. It was a face that wanted to reveal nothing. . . . No close friend knew much about his inner life. . . . His judgment—whether it dealt with teachers or colleagues—was severe and mercilessly just. . . . He despised everything amateurish. . . . One had the feeling that Paul wanted to speak to people, rather than *with* them." [in Chalfen, 1991, pp. 107–109]

* * *

56   *JOUISSANCE*, WOMAN

The poems that he wrote in his youth dealt with blood, death and riddles:

> ... or just earth
> and a silver strip of water
> better were it
> blood ...
> do I solve, do you solve
> the rusty riddle of the earth
> with a bloody cut of the spade?
>
> [in Chalfen, 1991, p. 85]

Ruth Lackner, Paul's girlfriend, relates that

> "Although entirely unconventional in his social relations and friendships, Paul was very sensitive and easily hurt. ... Paul despised presumption ... and superficiality. He made the toughest demands especially on himself, but he also imposed his imperative standards on the people around him. One got the impression, even then, that he was not prepared to accept compromise, that he strove exclusively for the absolute." [in Chalfen, 1991, p. 120]

* * *

When he fell in love, Celan sank into a dream world. Love was experienced by him as something so precious that one is almost forbidden to touch it. Love is, in essence, "silent, beautiful, light". According to the biographer, the 20-year-old Celan still repressed the sexual urge.

Among his friends, he often played the joker. Social relations held the threat of jealousy and suspicion for him, and since he wanted to keep his beloved woman to himself alone, he began to suspect her. These feelings led to despair and non-serious suicide attempts; he even wanted his loved one to die along with him. One day he appeared at her house with the veins in his wrist bleeding. "I wanted to die last night", he said. Celan would not understand love as a reality, and in this sense he could approach the beloved only as a sister. He failed to abstract himself from his mother, so that until her death everything feminine remained taboo to him. Celan seemed to have been drawn by death: he identified with the suicide attempts of his friends and acquaintances, especially the female ones. In 1951 he wrote: "wherever one went the world was blooming. And yet despair gave birth to poetry" (in Chalfen, 1991, p. 192).

It was only after his mother's death that he could free himself of his inhibitions regarding women, since the taboo seems then to have lost its power, or perhaps it underwent repression and displacement, as we shall see later on.

Celan and language

We have already seen that Leo Antschel wished to raise his son according to Jewish tradition and tried to force him to read the Bible and keep Jewish customs, whereas Fritzi wanted the members of her household to speak German, and she made sure that they did all her life. It should be noted that the "mother-tongue" in the family was Hebrew. Because of his problematic relationship with his father, Hebrew became a "father-tongue" for Paul, and later he tried to reject it, just as he tried to reject his father's entire heritage.

* * *

Celan knew various languages and was also interested in linguistics. A linguist who met him relates how he noticed him mostly because of his precise use of language. Till the day he died, German remained the language of Paul's inner life, his poems, which at first he wrote in secret.

* * *

Celan testified that after the Holocaust his life grew dark, and the only thing that remained important to him were his poems. His name, however, has become meaningless to him. His work is to bear witness to that "unspeakably great" thing that had moved him.

Having survived the Holocaust, Celan decided to change his name by using an anagram of Ancel, which he used because Antschel sounded too Jewish. This was done when he published his first book of poems. At that time he also said: "If only my mother could have seen this book! I think she doubted my abilities" (in Chalfen, 1991, p. 183).

To those who complained that he wrote in German he replied: "Only in one's mother tongue can one express one's own truth, in a foreign language the poet lies. . . . Poetry is a fateful and unique instance of language" (in Chalfen, 1991, p. 184).

From these partial details, related by people who knew Celan and his family, one can gauge the extent of the dominance of the maternal line in Celan's experience: the maternal name, already chosen to be the surname by his grandfather, and the mother-tongue, German, preferred over the father-tongue, Hebrew.

* * *

Freud, and following him Lacan, placed great emphasis on the place of the paternal function in the structuring of the subject's symbolic field. The paternal function represents culture and law. Its role is to separate mother and child and to penetrate their dual system as a third factor. The child enters the world not as a subject, but as an object of love or hate, wanted or rejected—yet always as an object. Therefore, at the outset of every subject there is always the Other. The primary Other is the mother. Only by means of the signifier that is called the "Name of the Father" can the subject change its initial position. In general terms, this means that a part of the body—the penis—undergoes symbolization and becomes a signifier—the phallic signifier. The role of the "Name of the Father" is to represent the meaning of the phallus. This significance is imaginary because the phallus does, in fact, signify lack: the fact that both the male and the female are lacking. Since the significance of the phallus relates to castration, the phallus simultaneously changes the relation of the subject to the Other.

Note that according to Freud, castration always alludes to castration of the mother (the child has to deal with the fact that the mother does not have a phallus—a fact that gives rise to anxiety, because he concludes that if she had been castrated, it could happen to him as well)—or, to be more precise, to the representation of the mother in the child.

* * *

The significance of castration is separation between the mother and her object—in other words, the Oedipus complex. Lacan called the shift in the position of the child in relation to the Other, and the entrance of a third factor into the system, the "paternal metaphor". The following formula can be used to express the link between the initial position of the subject and the "Name of the Father": belief in the signifier must be stronger than any *jouissance* that the child might gain by remaining in his original position; if the subject does not sacrifice some of the original *jouissance*, there will be no change.

However, this formula should not be seen as quantitative. The signifier's effectiveness depends mainly on the credibility of the individual personifying the phallic signifier. Therefore, the question is not whether the father is strong or weak, pleasant or unpleasant; rather, it is whether he is credible or not in relation to the symbolic function that he has to fulfil. Since the Other is the mother—the essential figure of the Oedipus complex—the question arises whether the mother's connection to the symbolic law is credible or not. After all, the mother's recognition of the father is what emplaces the paternal metaphor and the paternal law. The mother is the one who can identify the father and grant him a name. On the other hand, the psychotic structure is built upon foreclosure of the paternal function.

* * *

In Celan's case, it seems there was no such recognition of the father's place on the part of his mother. From the time of her childhood, Fritzi Antschel had been the dominant figure who made the decisions. She did not acknowledge the "Law of the Father", and her passion was directed towards her son. Thus, the relationship between mother and son remained dual, and the third factor—the paternal function that was to enter as representative of the law—was missing. Moreover, a false condition prevailed in this structure: the weak father tried to represent himself to his son as master by means of rigid educational methods employing fear and terror, while in fact he was defenceless against the women in the family. This fact led Celan to an even greater rejection. The question should therefore be asked: Can one say that in Celan's case there was indeed a rejection of the "Name of the Father"? We have already seen that Celan identified with female figures, above all with his mother. This identification was deep, and his mother's traumatic death, for which Celan felt perhaps responsible, only served to intensify it.

* * *

Upon studying Celan's poems, a number of signifiers recurred in a manner that caught my attention: water and drinking, flowers, death, and women's hair. For instance, in the poem "The Years From You To Me":

> Your hair waves once more when I weep. With the blue of your eyes
> you lay the table of love: a bed between summer and autumn.
> We drink what somebody brewed, neither I nor you a third:
> we lap up some empty and last thing.
>
> [Celan, 1972, p. 57]

And in the poem "Corona":

> ... we love each other like poppy and recollection,
> ... like the sea in the moon's blood ray.
>
> [Celan, 1972, p. 59]

The thing that stands out in the recurrence of these themes is the way Celan linked women to death drive. To me it is reminiscent of the figure of Ophelia, the object of Prince Hamlet's desire. Adorned with garlands of flowers, Ophelia drowned in water.

According to Lacan, she was the one responsible for Hamlet's fall because of the sudden way in which she revealed Hamlet's secret (Lacan, 1977a). Perhaps Shakespeare was aware that it is with the woman that one fails, just as one fails in the encounter with the Real—the Real as a dimension not given to symbolization. Ophelia revealed that Hamlet, having already lost the faculty of his desire, was trapped in his relationship with his parents. He would never again be able to love Ophelia as a desirable young woman. In Lacan's opinion, Hamlet would only be able to love her once more after her death—only then would she be as a shrouded phallus. According to Lacan, the phallus's signifier can only appear when it is covered, because it actually signifies the lack, the fact of castration. As a woman, Ophelia both covers and reveals the *jouissance* beyond passion, *jouissance* that indicates the pleasurable aspect of

Hamlet's suffering—that is, the woman is the one who reveals the incest taboo with which Hamlet struggles.

Shakespeare describes Ophelia's death with these words:

> There is a willow grows askant the brook,
> That shows his hoar leaves in the glassy stream.
> Therewith fantastic garlands did she make
> Of crowflowers, nettles, daisies, and long purples,
> That liberal shepherds give a grosser name,
> But our cold maids do dead men's fingers call them.
> There on the pendent boughs her crownet weeds
> Clamb'ring to hang, an envious silver broke,
> When down her weedy trophies and herself
> Fell in the weeping brook. Her Clothes spread wide,
> And mermaid-like awhile they bore her up,
> Which time she chanted snatches of old lauds,
> As one incapable of her own distress,
> Or like a creature native and indued
> Unto that element. But long it could not be
> Till that her garments, heavy with their drink,
> Pulled the poor wretch from her melodious lay
> To muddy death.

Celan was also to die in a river.

In "The Aspen Tree" he wrote:

> Aspen Tree, your leaves glance white into the dark.
> My mother's hair was never white.
> Dandelion, so green is the Ukraine.
> My yellow-haired mother did not come home.
>
> [Celan, 1972, p. 39]

In his first poem after the Holocaust, "Death Fugue", there are recurring themes:

> Black milk of daybreak we drink it at sundown
> We drink it at noon in the morning we drink it at night
> We drink and we drink it.
>
> [Celan, 1972, p. 61]

And:

> ... your golden hair Margaret
> your ashen hair Shulamith. . .

and, to my taste, the strongest line:

> ... death is a master from Germany...
>
> (Celan, 1972, p. 61)

I contend that death, together with its German agents, held a kind of fascination for Celan. In this context the connection between women and the death drive, which can be found as a central theme in the poems, may have been a replacement for the spurned "Name of the Father". Women's hair constitutes a partial object that signifies feminine *jouissance*, which leads to death.

* * *

In the XIth Seminar, Lacan (1973) related to the Holocaust, stating that in order to examine it honestly, one must confront our fascination in the sacrifice of the victim. In other words, there is almost no escape from the enchantment with which the victim captivates those who sacrifice him, because it is the sacrifice that provides proof of the desire of the Other, whom he refers to in this context as the dark god.

It is hard to face the fact of the lack in the Other without feeling anxiety or panic. The act of sacrifice proves to the individual that he knows what the Other wants and that he can satisfy that desire. In this context the victim may be the Other, the object of love, or even the self. When Kant wrote of "practical reason" and of a universal moral law, he was actually referring to pure desire—objectless desire (which may be one of the aspects of the dark god). Such desire is achieved by sacrificing anything that is regarded as an object of love. In Lacan's opinion, Kant's moral law, in its very structure, is indecent to the extent that the structure is the driving force that leads man to obey its injunctions—that is, it is indecent as long as man observes moral law due to it being law, not because it represents a system of positive reasons. Kantian ethics are characterized by the need to be rid of all the objects that create *jouissance* or suffering as the focus of moral activity. However, concealed in Kant's theory is that there is *jouissance* in the actual relinquishing, and therefore Lacan wrote an article called "Kant avec Sade" (1962), in which he drew a parallel between Kant's theory and that of the Marquis de Sade, who also claimed that ultimate *jouissance* lies in the sacrifice of the love object (more on this in chapter seven herein, "The Secret Bearers"). For both, the law is absolute—beyond the question of life and death. There is no room for exceptions.

* * *

The annihilation that Celan strove for in his own death (total eradication, not even a grave) is similar to the annihilation to which the Marquis de Sade aspired.

In this context, Shimon Sandbank wrote of Celan's poems "No One's Rose":

> Celan took the phrase from Rilke, who requested that on his grave be written: "Rose, oh pure contradiction, joy/ of being no-one's sleep under so many/ lids." The eyelids suggest poems: *lider–lieder*. Rilke's metaphor is sophisticated and suggestive—though perhaps more amusing than serious—and the rose petals covering an empty center are the poet's poems covering the impersonal poet that eludes exposure even in the sleep of death. In Celan's hands this phrase takes on grave seriousness: a mystical sunrise of beauty, arising out of an empty world: "A nothing/ we were, are, shall/ remain, flowering:/ the nothing-, the/ no one's rose."
>
> Rilke intended for his beautiful words to adorn the tomb of a great poet, while Celan made no provision for his own grave. He cast his body into the waters of the Seine.
>
> Celan yearned not only for death, but also for total annihilation; he was to have no grave, like his parents who were never buried. [Sandbank, 1983, p. 14; translated for this edition]

In a eulogy to Celan, Schocken quoted:

> "The skin wants to rupture. The flesh below it asks to be devoured, consumed, corrupt. The bones beneath the flesh want to be exposed and scattered. The marrow wishes to be spilled from the scattered bones. The bones want to be hollow and cracked for a while, until the waves and pebbles grind them down to nothingness." [Schocken, 1970, p. 20, translated for this edition]

Researchers who write about Celan tend to attribute his depressions and suicide to his experiences in the Holocaust and his conflicts in relation to his Jewishness. According to the trauma theory, it is clear that external conditions alone do not lead to trauma. Trauma is only caused in conjunction with inner conflict—repression connected with sexuality—even in an event as horrifying as the Holocaust. In this sense, Judaism for Celan was part of the "Name of the Father", which he rejected. Therefore, it is possible that the mother is the same Margaret who made sure that she only spoke pure German and later turned into Shulamith. I contend that the trauma was caused by Celan's fascination and enthrallment with the *Meister* from Germany—his attraction to the realm of the insufferable death drive, to the eroticization of death, the death drive that he associated with art as well as women and feminine *jouissance*. Actually there was no art in that murderous machine—only monstrous bureaucracy. It was the personal "emptying"—that is, the death of the subject (in particular in this context, turning human beings into numbers)—that was the most horrifying aspect of the Holocaust. We must remember that it was the *Meister* from Germany that severed the most significant and problematic relationship in his life—the one with his mother.

* * *

It seems as though Celan was attempting to cross the boundary. Using language he was trying to reach beyond it without recognizing the necessity of castration. Perhaps he was seeking pure desire, but through the symbolic dimension he again and again encountered the same unbearable dimension that touches the death drive and that Lacan refers to as the Real.

In that place where the "Name of the Father" should have been, setting down limits, there is actually a terrible void that is sometimes filled by death and sometimes by the haunting eye. And as the poet cannot pass through this void, he seeks salvation through language and poetry as substitutes for the "Name of the Father". But the substitutes cannot withstand the void—language cannot imprison it within itself.

* * *

Shimon Sandbank quoted the poem "Once": "Once/ I heard him,/ he was washing the world,/ unseen, nightlong,/ real./ One and Infinite,/ annihilated,/ ied./ Light was. Salvation" (Celan, 1972, p. 271).

Sandbank wrote that "ied"—not a real word—is composed of void and light. *licht*—light, *vernichtet*—annihilated. Celan used *ichten*, also not a real word. There was the archaic *ihten* of the Middle Ages which means "to turn something into", but that word is also derived from *ich*, meaning: "I". the void here, inside the forming I, turns into light. The potential paradoxical salvation of the poem is not proclaimed, but takes place before one's eyes (Sandbank, 1983).

* * *

This matter is reminiscent of the second stage of the *phantasme* in Freud's article "'A Child Is Being Beaten'" (1919e), where he discusses the *phantasme*'s structure (chapter three herein, "Phantasy"). According to his line of reasoning, the first stage of thought is: "A child is being beaten." The second stage is: "I am being beaten by my father." The third, conscious stage is: "A child is being beaten." The second stage is the stage that is unconscious, the part that does not exist. The unconscious is the thought that should have been there but is not.

* * *

I believe that, for Celan, that which was inexpressible in words was not the Holocaust, as literary researchers assume, but feminine *jouissance*, embodied in the attraction to death. If Celan tried to break the words, to go beyond language, then he did so in order to reveal the living-dead Real that lies beyond the phallus and the "Name of the Father". In this sense, therefore, Celan can be seen a tragic hero. He searched for the Word that would save him, but it was not to be found. It could not be found because it did not exist and there was no "Name of the Father" to denote boundaries for him.

Schocken (1970) wrote: "Celan's fate forced him to penetrate beyond the realm of the language of negotiation, expressions of happiness and sorrow and contact between ordinary people, and to be thrown again and again onto the barrier of language." And he quoted: "a language devoid of mouth, say,/ that still are things happening/ not far from you" (p. 20, translated for this edition).

A few months before committing suicide, Celan visited in Israel and even considered settling there.

> I came to you, to Israel, because I needed you. I have rarely felt as strongly as now, after all I have seen and heard, that I have done the right thing. . . . Here, in your inner and outer landscape, I find much of the compulsion toward truth. . . . I believe I have encountered the calm and confident resolution to hold on to what is human. [Celan, 1986, pp. 57–58]

The same Celan—the one who changed his surname and rebelled against everything that his father represented, who married a French Catholic from an aristocratic, anti-Semitic family and who baptized his son—complained that he was writing poems for Jew-hating Germans and teaching French to German-hating Frenchmen. What meaning did this visit to the land of his forefathers—the country that his father had dreamed of, the land that Celan had tried to deny and erase his every connection to—hold for him? Was it a desperate attempt to find the foreclosed "Name of the Father"? A desire to re-adopt that which he had never received? To connect with a father? There is no doubt that it was an attempt doomed to fail and that it did indeed fail. "I am losing you to you", he wrote about Jerusalem (Sandbank, 1983, p. 14).

* * *

The poet Esther Cameron, whom Celan met in Israel, wrote: "He related to me like a symbolic creature, expecting some Word from me that would descend on him. I sat petrified, exhausted by the burden of the guilt that was to rest on him." Many years after her meeting with Celan she admitted (Cameroon, 1988, p. 17): "if I had tried to find the Word he would have mocked me, and his scorn would simply have killed me."

It is not by chance that Celan sought the Word from a woman, because women and their *jouissance* were a substitute for the missing "Name of the Father". But the paradox lies in the fact that it was exactly that, which could not be expressed in words. It was precisely the attempt to seek that which cannot be written, the need to hold on to "what is human" (i.e., to hold on to the heritage of his father), that led to his annihilation.

When the poet Manfred Winkler read from Celan's poems in Jerusalem, he said:

> Celan spoke in the words of the German language and in words that are no longer words, he spoke with the sounds of

> experience that still awaits words—yet already stands on the border that cannot be traversed without harm—a lonely place somewhere between earth and sky. And the loneliness grew in him and around him and became concrete and abstract at the same time. Perhaps the mystery of creation is indeed embodied in language—and can be revealed through language. If not, at least part of the veil might be removed. [Winkler, 1970, p. 26]

However, the phallus signifies only when it is covered, and removal of the veil reveals the lack, the void, the Real of the *jouissance*, which leads to madness and death. As it is written in the poem "Mandorela":

> In the almond—what dwells in the almond?
> Nothing
> What dwells in the almond is Nothing.
> There it dwells and dwells.
> In Nothing—what dwells there? The King.
> There the King dwells, the King.
> there he dwells and dwells.
> Jew's curl, you'll not turn grey.
>
> [Celan, 1972, p. 189]

Within the nothing dwells the king, the phallic, jouissant Other, and opposite him—death.

The meridian—partitioning line—the uncanny side of art

Upon receiving the Georg Büchner Prize in 1960, Celan gave a speech presenting his position on art and poetry. He called his speech "The Meridian"—the latitude of high noon: "I find something as immaterial as language, yet earthly, terrestrial, in the shape of a circle which, via both poles, rejoins itself and on the way serenely crosses even the tropics: I find . . . a meridian" (Celan, 1986, p. 55).

The tropics are both the tropical regions and the tropics of rhetoric, like metaphor. Sandbank (1983) says of this: "The Meridian is the embodiment of paradox for Celan, the nothing out of which everything grows" (p. 14). Celan claimed that he found this imaginary line of partition. It may be said that through words Celan tried to attain pure desire, the same desire that lacks an object.

Over and over again he tried and failed. In his speech he speaks of Büchner, who wrote about a poet that went mad and tried to walk on his head. Celan said: "A man who walks on his head, ladies and gentlemen, a man who walks on his head, sees the sky below as an abyss." When speaking of poetry, he added:

> the poem clearly shows a strong tendency towards silence . . . the poem holds its ground on its own margin. In order to endure, it constantly calls and pulls itself back from an "already-no-more" into a "still-here" . . . the poem has only this one, unique, momentary present. . . . [Celan, 1986, pp. 48–50]

Sandbank added:

> At the end his poems were competing with silence. The laconic syntax, the comprehension of compound neologisms, are already standing on the average of something which is beyond language. "A flower—a word of the blind", the flower, "missing from all the bouquets." [Sandbank, 1983, p. 16]

In the poem "Silence", Celan wrote:

> Silence! I stab the thorn into your heart,
> for Rose, the rose
> with its shadow stands within the mirror and shall be soundless!
> already silenced as we devoured the yes with the no,
> as we sipped,
> for a cup, as it fell from the table, rang out:
>
> . . . most avidly did we imbibe:
>
> . . . Silence! The thorn penetrates into your heart more deeply:
> for it is in alliance with the rose.
>
> [Celan, 1988, p. 29; translated for this edition]

* * *

The impossible here-and-now of this poem connects with feminine *jouissance*. The structure of this *jouissance* is not comprised of words and does not form a language. The words are only to be found on its margins.

In his speech Celan related to another Büchner story:

> As I was walking in the valley yesterday, I saw two girls sitting on a rock. One was piling up her hair, and the other helped.

> The golden hair hanging down, and a pale, serious face, so very young, and the black dress, and the other girl so careful and attentive. Even the finest, most intimate paintings of the old German masters can hardly give you an idea of the scene. Sometimes one wants to be the head of Medusa—to turn such a group to stone and gather the people around it. [Celan, 1986, p. 42]

Up to this point Celan quoted Büchner. Then he added:

> Please note: ... "One would like to be a Medusa's head" to ... seize the natural as the natural by means of art! *One* would like to, by the way, not: *I* would. This means going beyond what is human, stepping into a realm which is turned toward the human, but uncanny—the realm where the monkey, the automatons and with them ... oh, art, too, seem to be at home. ... here, ... art has its uncanny side. [Celan, 1986, pp. 42–43]

Celan adds further that it is a challenge that all poetry must turn to face if it wants to question further:

> Art makes for distance from the I. Art requires that we travel a certain space in a certain direction, on a certain road. And poetry? Poetry which, of course, must go the way of art? Here this would mean the road to Medusa's head and the automaton! ... perhaps poetry, like art, moves with the oblivious self into the uncanny and strange to free itself. Though where? in which place? how? as what? This would mean art is the distance poetry must cover, no less and no more. [Celan, 1986, pp. 44–45]

* * *

In his poetry Celan tried, perhaps, to be the head of Medusa that would capture feminine *jouissance* and turn it into stone. In his poem "There, Where the Ice Lies" he wrote:

> There, where the ice lies, there is coolness for two
> For two: therefore I asked you to come.
> A breeze like a fire's was surrounding you—from the rose
> you came to me.
> I asked you: how did they call you there?
> You said to me, that same famous name:
> A flickering like an ember was laying on it—
> From the rose you came to me.
> There, where the ice lies, the chill is for years,

> I gave you the double name
> From beneath it you opened an eye
> Above the opening in the glistening ice
> And behold, I shall close mine, and say
> Take this word—which my eye has anointed your eye with!
> Take it and hone it after me
> Hone it slowly, slowly after me
> Hone it slowly, slowly, anoint with it
> And open your eye for as long as it lasts.
> [Celan, 1988, p. 34; translated for this edition]

* * *

In his poetry, using language and with the aid of sublimation, Celan tried to do the impossible—to capture the drive of the object. It could therefore be said that sublimation failed, leaving Celan to stand exposed before the object that gives rise to such dread.

In his seminar "The Ethics of Psychoanalysis" (1986), Lacan pointed out that individuals seeking pleasure must circumvent the object.

Sublimation is connected with death rather than with the "desexualization of the object".

The kind of charm radiated by the sublimative image always has a threatening aspect to it, too. Celan tried to encapture the object and ossify it, but it seems that, instead, he fell into the imaginary trap of idealization of the object—the woman.

According to Lacan, idealizing includes the subject identifying with the ideal object. Subjects try as hard as they can to identify with their ideal, while sublimation provides drive in a way different from what was originally intended. Sublimation separates drive from the object so as to facilitate its exchange with an object of social value. However, Freud said that it is paid for with the living flesh and is never perfect. Celan was trapped between his identification with the feminine object and the quest for that which must always remain shrouded—a quest that contains fatal *jouissance* within it.

In his "Poem in the Desert" Celan wrote:

> with interweaving blackish leaves the wreath was around
>   Accra:

where I rode my black horse and with my sword tried to lunge at death.
from a wooden bowl I drank ashes from the well of Accra:
... they destroyed the crescent and the flower by Accra:
... and thus I utter the name and sense the heat of the conflagration on my cheeks.

[Celan, 1988, p. 5; translated for this edition]

Lacan (1986) said that all art is a form of organization around emptiness. As an example he mentioned that most ancient of art forms, pottery—the art of moulding jugs (more on this in chapter nine herein, "The Act in Psychoanalysis and Art").

In any form of sublimation, as in art, the emptiness is the determining factor. He claimed that the sublimation of the creator is in the death drive.

The moment one deals with a chain of signifiers, something is to be found beyond the chain, the "ex nihilo on which it is based"—the emptiness.

In "Jugs" Celan wrote:

By the long tables of time
The jugs of God sit down to drink
They drink up the eyes of the seeing and the eyes of the blind.

[Celan, 1994, p. 12; translated for this edition]

* * *

The boundary that deters the subject from penetrating a field that cannot be expressed in the language of pure desire is the field of absolute destruction. Lacan identified this phenomenon with the experience of the beautiful. Beauty, which is the envelope of truth, is also that which halts passion. The phantasy is beauty, which may not be touched. The beautiful is the boundary of death, and its effect is blindness. The function of the beautiful is to reveal to us the location of man's connection to his own death (Lacan, 1986).

To me it seems that beauty was to Celan the image of a woman who died in water, a long-haired woman adorned with flowers. Using this image he tried to connect through drinking (water, wine, black milk, the void, and the ultimate), and through death.

To this woman he gave the "double name"—her name and his. Thus in "In Pairs" he wrote:

> The dead float in pairs,
> in pairs, the wine washes round them,
> in wine, which they poured on your body,
> the dead float in pairs.
> Their hair they wove into mattresses
> lying with one another, legs entwined,
> throw the dice once more
> and dive into one eye of the twain.
>
> [Celan, 1988, p. 37; translated for this edition]

And in "Night Ray":

> Most brightly of all burned the hair of my evening loved one:
> To her I send the coffin of lightest wood.
>
> [Celan, 1972, p. 55]

CHAPTER FIVE

One eats—the other eats "no"

After Rachel's grandmother passed away, the family observed the traditional week of mourning. It was during this time that Rachel's family first *noticed* how thin she was becoming. Her father was the first one to *notice*. Rachel has a twin sister, an older brother, and an older sister. She was 15 then. Previously her family had been fully occupied in caring for her ailing grandmother, so "no one had really *looked* at what Rachel had been eating".

Rachel had begun to lose weight, and she had stopped menstruating. Her mother hadn't actually *noticed*, despite the fact that for several months, the one twin had not been asking her for the tampons that both twins always needed.

It is evident that in this family's case, *noticing* and *paying attention* are important signifiers—signifiers relating to knowledge, knowledge about "something is wrong".

Rachel was the one who used to go shopping and bake the special *halla* bread for the Sabbath. She used to be a "partner" to

---

Previously published in English as "One eats, the other eats 'no'." *ERR: The Journal of Affiliated Psychoanalytic Workgroups*, 2 (2002) <http://www.apwonline.org/journal.htm>.

her mother in long walks and a "partner" to her father and brother in playing football.

Her relationship with her twin ("normal") sister had been good, but when Rachel started receiving more attention, Leah got annoyed. "We both have the same I.Q.", says Rachel, "The same clothes, we share the same room and we both paint".

Partnership also constitutes an important signifier and demand in this family. I believe that in this family there is collusion (partnership) against knowledge concerning differentiation and particularity, and Rachel uses her anorexia to sabotage this collusion.

Now, the subject of what Rachel does or does not eat has become the cause of ongoing discussion and argument in her home. "The body needs food, the muscles need food!" say her parents. "Eat this and nothing will happen to you." "It all depends on what you do—it's just a question of what you decide." "No", she replies, time and time again.

The demand of the mother

The mother and her husband share mutual admiration. The husband is one of eleven brothers and sisters who "All serve for the glory of Israel".

"This family is like a nation state," says her mother, "It has its rules and regulations."

And what of Rachel? "She's very organized and has a strong character—like me," says mother. "She wouldn't let herself slip up without first considering it. There's a lot of thought behind what she's doing, some special reason—otherwise she would never let herself fall, never get carried away".

So what could be the special reason for Rachel's refusal?

Could her "No" be a reaction to her mother's cliché-laden style of discourse?

Rachel refuses to ignore subjective knowledge. Perhaps she is seeking some lost desire. Could her way of solving things be to position herself as an exception to the family rules of need and demand?

While mother is always quoting and generalizing, Rachel seeks her own personal form of expression.

Mother observes: "she gulps her food down like someone from the Holocaust, as if she's afraid it will be gone".

"They say that I've ruined the whole family!" Rachel sobs.

"I don't want my child to be finished!" says mother.

The desire of the father

Rachel insists on her "no". What does she really want? We find a clue in the desire of her father, who works in the field of education. "My dream (my wish)", says father, "is to reach the point when she says 'yes'."

In Israel there was once a popular song that went: "When you say 'no', what do you mean?" This was a song about what women desire. Its message is that when women say 'yes', the meaning is clear, but when they say 'no', it is ambiguous—it requires interpretation.

The problem with Rachel is that she eats during meals, but not between meals. There are some foods that she does like (low-calorie ones). "You do say 'yes' to some foods," says her analyst.

But "There's a part of me that always refuses. I have a little and they get angry with me. Perhaps I've lost the part of the brain that desires. Perhaps it will never come back."

What is it that Rachel is refusing? In refusing, could she be asking for recognition as a subject?

The stumbling stone

Her mother views Rachel as a partner to the ongoing Jewish history: to the Holocaust—since the entire family of the maternal grandfather was exterminated (remember the mother's complaint that Rachel eats like someone from the Holocaust)—and to the State of Israel (an enlarged model of the family that one should glorify) gaining independence. She is also a partner to the family (she cooks for them, is very concerned about what they eat), and to her twin sister ("They're both exactly alike" says mother—"Both brilliant").

Saint Catherine of Siena also had a twin sister. Catherine's mother chose to breastfeed her. She sacrificed the other sister by giving her to a stranger to wet-nurse her. The sister died. Catherine was the Chosen One (as her mother repeatedly told her). Yet another sister died in childbirth. Eventually, against her mother's wishes, Catherine chose to devote herself to Jesus rather than marry the husband of the dead sister. Anorexia constituted her own peculiar form of devotion. In one of her letters to her mother she wrote: "I would very much like to see you as a spiritual mother and not just as the mother of my body. If you would have loved my spirit more than my body, all your affection for me would have disappeared, and you would not have suffered so much if you missed my physical presence. . . ."

Rachel's anorexia also started during the period between two deaths. Information about the first death only came to light at a late stage of her analysis. Her father's youngest brother had died a year earlier than her grandmother, from a fatal disease that nobody *noticed* until it was too late.

Rachel is also a sister, and her anorexia distinguishes the boundary between herself and her sister. She tries to awaken in her family the desire for knowledge about death as well as about birth—birth of a subject who is also a twin—before it is too late.

Rachel is not a Christian like Catherine, and Jews only have prophets—no saints. Prophets are crazy, aren't they? Out of their madness emerges the truth. By refusing, she becomes the family's stumbling stone. By saying "no", she forces the family to *notice*. She eats just a few morsels in order to leave room for desire to emerge, through the holes in the web of this *jouissance* of universal glory.

More recently a subjective symptom has emerged. It seems that not only is it the family that is concerned about what Rachel does or does not eat—Rachel, too, is concerned about what her family eats. When the analyst asks her why, she doesn't know the reason but nevertheless she does *notice* what they eat.

"Just a little"

In expressing his desire that Rachel say "yes" (not just in regard to eating but also in regard to speech)—her father is actually saying something about his own desire. By recognizing desire rather than need, he indicates his affirmation in the symbolic order. Perhaps he is opening up a new way. Perhaps this is a breakthrough. He desires her not to eat, but to speak.

The analyst's interpretation is also oriented towards desire. "You do say 'yes' to some foods"—to some of it, not to all of it.

When Rachel says "no", sometimes she means "yes" and sometimes "no"; however, because she is not aware that she is entitled to her own desire, she does it by means of her body. She declares: "I am not the same as my sister (my country, my religion). She eats. I eat 'no'. When I say 'yes' it is a gift of a particular love in response to my father's desire."

CHAPTER SIX

"A woman's voice is *erva*":
the feminine voice and silence—
between the Talmudic sages
and psychoanalysis

with Admiel Kosman

The subject of this chapter is a comparison of psychoanalytic theory as it was formulated by Freud, and has been interpreted by Lacan, with Jewish culture as it is expressed in the Talmudic texts concerning the unique and problematic issue of man's relation to the female voice and speech, in particular two central sayings: "Talk not much with a woman" (Mishna, Avoth 1:5), and "A woman's voice is *erva* [nakedness, sexual incitement]" (Babylonian Talmud, Ber. 24a). In this chapter we concentrate on studying and understanding the meanings and the consequences of the latter saying.

What, then, is the link between the feminine voice/speech and sexuality? Why was it often so important, even outside Jewish culture, to warn men about the dangers of the feminine voice and

---

Reproduced by permission of Brill Academic Publishers from A. Kosman & R. Golan, "'A woman's voice is erva'": The feminine voice and silence—between the Talmudic sages and psychoanalysis." In: M. Poorthuis & J. Schwartz (Eds.), *Saints and Role Models in Judaism and Christianity* (Boston: Brill, 2004), pp. 357–376.

Admiel Kosman, a poet, is a Professor in the Faculty of Philosophy at Potsdam University and the Academic Head of Geiger College in Berlin.

to try to repress it, as Sophocles concisely formulated, "Women's glory is silence—and it is their beauty"? What can the Talmud teach contemporary psychoanalytic research concerning this issue?

"A woman's voice is erva" in the Jewish tradition

The scriptures do not exclude explicitly women's voices from the general life of the community circle and do not limit such manifestations in any way. In the few references that deal with this question in biblical literature, we find that women probably sang in the presence of men, and probably also sang along with them, as in the canticle of Miriam (Exod. 15:20) and in that of the prophetess Debora (Judg. 5:1). However, these texts appear in a wholly different light in rabbinical interpretation. Our research concentrates on the later rabbinical interpretation of these texts, from the time of the Second Temple period and afterwards.

* * *

Philo of Alexandria, the great first-century Jewish philosopher, believes that there is no promiscuity in women and men chanting together. On the contrary, he sees in the combination of voices a spiritual virtue of grace and harmony. Philo describes not only the communal chant of both sexes, but also a communal dance, and he reveals his position, according to which the harmonic blending of the voices of men and women is a "friendship with god". Philo asserts that this chant is religious by nature and leads to the sublime, as well as to a closeness to god.

The position of Philo meets opposition in the strict view of the fourth-century CE Babylonian sage Rabbi Yoseph Bar-Hiya, who states: "When men sing and women join it is licentiousness. When women sing and men join it is like fire in tow."

* * *

So, according to Rabbi Yoseph's interpretation, one should forbid women to participate together with men in a choir, because, in his opinion, neither of the two possible consequences that arise agrees with Jewish sexual moral rules, even though the second possibility is worse. Either way, he does not even think it possible that the chanting of women and men together could have the quality of spiritual sublimation, as does Philo. Rashi (*Rabbi Shlomo Itzchaki*) supposes—a perfectly logical supposition—that this determination, which was stated in the Babylonian's Amoraim of the fourth century, is based on more ancient ways of behaving. This is how, for instance, Samuel in the third century determined that "a woman's voice is *erva*" (Babylonian Talmud, Ber. 24a).

In any case, this is a very interesting assertion from a cultural point of view and is not an obvious one, so we shall cite the entire Talmudic paragraph. In this paragraph there appears a list of different things, which are called *erva*, in the sense of exciting sexual provocation.

> Rabbi Isaac said: An [exposed] handbreadth in a woman constitutes *erva*. In what circumstances? Shall I say, if one gazes at it? But has not Rabbi Shesheth said, "Why did scripture enumerate both the ornaments worn outside the clothes and those worn within them? To tell you that if you gaze at a woman's little finger—it is as though you gazed at her genitals!"—No, it means [an exposed handbreadth] of one's own wife—when he recites the *Shema*. Rabbi Hisda said: A woman's leg is *erva*, since the bible says "Uncover the leg, pass through the rivers" (Isa. 47:2), afterwards it adds, "Thy nakedness shall be uncovered, yea, thy shame shall be seen" (Isa. 47:3). Samuel said, A woman's voice is *erva*, as it says "For sweet is thy voice, and thy countenance is comely" (Cant. 2:14). Rabbi Shesheth said: A woman's hair is *erva*, as it says "thy hair is as flock of goats" (Cant. 4:1).
>
> [Babylonian Talmud, Senh. 45a]

Rashi explains Samuel's statement thus: from the fact that the Bible is praising the beauty of woman in that way, we can deduce that this beauty is passion. That is to say, the fact that the paragraph in the Canticles sees the voice of the beloved as a pleasant voice, and compliments it, means that this pleasantness can arouse sexual passion.

This statement, which identifies completely aesthetic pleasure with sexual arousal, is not obvious, and it is not common to all ancient civilizations. Philo's position mentioned above, for example, reflects a completely opposite position—one that maintains that the chanting of men and women together is not prostitution but even holds an element of sacredness and religious sublimation. Later we will try to understand this duality, which passes through all of the different views in Judaism regarding a woman's voice.

"A woman's voice is erva" in the post-Talmudic tradition

From discussions of this subject in the Gaonic period (8th to 10th centuries CE), it seems that Samuel's statement that "A woman's voice is *erva*", was not interpreted as a prohibition on hearing a woman's voice in general. This prohibition was asserted only in the context mentioned earlier, and according to which it is forbidden for a man to recite the *Shema* (the Jewish Pledge of Allegiance, a testimony to His grace that is commanded to be recited twice a day, beginning with "Listen Israel, The Lord our God, the Lord is One!") while listening to a woman's voice, especially her singing voice. It should be noted that a woman's voice is thought of as disturbance during the recital of *Shema*, not because it contains an element of lasciviousness in it, but by the mere fact that it attracts and distracts the mind from concentrating on the words at the time of the prayer.

Only in fourteenth-century Provence do we find a more strict position regarding the woman's voice. Rabbi Abraham Ben David probably interpreted the prohibition regarding the hearing of a woman's voice as not related specifically to the recital of *Shema*, but as a general prohibition regarding women's modesty. However, the analysis of his interpretation brings us to the conclusion that he did not think that there was any element of seduction in the feminine voice itself. Rather, he meant to say that only when a woman sings to a man songs that are directed at him is there an element of seduction—and thus the prohibition of hearing a woman's voice is similar to the prohibition of greeting her. A surprising and more unusual interpretation of Samuel's saying may be found in Sefer Hassidim from twelfth- to thirteenth-century Germany: "From everything that is written in Cant. about beauty, it appears that one must avoid hearing the voice of a woman. The same thing applies to a woman who must avoid the voice of a man" (Margaliot, 1960, p. 407).

* * *

From the development we have studied so far, the following general picture arises: The sages of Europe thought that the sayings of Samuel in the Talmud prohibit only the recitation of *Shema* prayer while a woman is singing, whereas the sages of North Africa and Spain (and some of the sages of Germany) thought that the prohibition is related only to greeting a married woman, for fear that this would lead to fornication (Berman, 1980). And among the sages of Provence the opinion was also expressed that both greeting a woman and praying while her voice might be heard should be prohibited.

"A woman's voice is erga [craving] "— Signs of conflict and different positions concerning the woman's voice in rabbinical literature

One has to admit that opinions such as Philo's, which look upon the singing of men and women together as a sublime means for devotion to God, do not exist at all in rabbinical tradition. One should also remember that this tradition was subject to the strict Talmudic judgements we have noted above, concerning the singing of men and women together—so that even if we find in this literature signs of conflicts, it is clear that the possible room for interpretation will be extremely narrow. This is why the sources that look indulgently upon the singing of women can surprise us. So, for instance, was written in the *Zohar*:

> "Then Miriam the prophetess, Aaron's sister, took up in her hand the hand-drum" (Exod. 15:20)—And all those pious people in paradise listen to her pleasant voice, and several holy angels thank and praise with her the holy name of God."
> [Bamidbar, Shelakh 167b]

* * *

And in the Bible itself, we will find (as was mentioned earlier) that women probably sang in front of men, and sometimes even together with men. As Miriam and her friends sang about the miracle at the Red Sea (Exod. 15:20), so Deborah the prophetess sang with Barak the song on the victory over Sisera and his army (Judg. 5:1). And in the same way the women sang and danced when receiving King Saul, after David had beaten Goliath (I Sam. 18:6). The writer of Ecclesiastes tells us that among other pleasures of life, which he prepared for himself, there were choruses of "male and female singers" (Ecclesiastes 2:8). And even in the time of Ezra a group of people is mentioned in the list in Ezra, Chapter 2: a group that immigrated to the land of Israel in the first immigration, thanks to the permission of Cyrus, included "two hundred singing men and singing women" (Ezra 2:65).

Of course, these sources were difficult for those interpreters who tried to harmonize the Bible with the Talmudic Halakhah, although such harmonization may even appear in Tannaic literature. Thus we find in Mekhilta De-Rabbi Ishmael: "'And Miriam sang unto them'—Scripture tells that just as Moses recited the song for the men, so Miriam recited the song for the women: 'sing ye to the Lord . . .'" (Lauterbach, 1933, p. 83). The interpreter probably understood that Miriam sang only for the women, and that her chanting was not directed at men, neither by herself nor within a joined chorus of the women with that of Moses', as was understood by Philo. But, as was stated before, our aim is to accentuate the opinion that saw the women's voice as a spiritual voice, even if the halakhic texts cited above made this possibility quite limited.

These opinions, as we later show, have a common denominator that can be defined as a spiritual–utopian direction.

* * *

We would like to state that since it was not possible to legitimize the feminine voice in society and law, interpreters and commentators described the spiritually provocative power of this voice in utopian terms. This is how, for example, they could claim that a woman's voice is actually very spiritual for men—but it can be grasped only when certain conditions render it possible. These conditions will dominate man's world only in the future, when the sexual drive that serves now as a blurring screen will be cancelled. A blur prevents men from appreciating the spiritual vitality of a feminine voice. The blur is caused by the sexual phantasies men have upon hearing a woman's voice.

Rabbi Azaria of Pano, for example, assumes that this uplifting moment when Miriam and the women sang before the men on the edge of the Red Sea was an exceptional moment of "the world beyond" that penetrated into "this world" and made it possible to transgress the law that prohibits women's singing before men (Azaria, 1884). The woman's voice was therefore, in that special moment, a prophetic and divine one, resulting in unique spiritual uplifting. This is what he means when he writes: "since her intention was only for singing" (Azaria, 1884, no. 36, 99b). By using the expression "singing", he refers to the spiritual revelation that this singing made possible. Nevertheless, it should be pointed out that he does not speak about a unique feminine quality of this singing but, rather, about a general prophetic quality of singing, which can be either male or female, and it seems as if in this singing the distinction between male and female is completely annihilated as the singing becomes perfectly divine.

Another possibility suggested by Rabbi Azaria is that only Miriam sang in front of the men, and the rest of the women joined in only by playing various musical instruments but did not sing. Why was Miriam's singing permitted here? His reason is that the rest of the women were simply ordinary women and therefore could not possibly "turn their minds to God". But Miriam, as a prophetess, could know that at that moment the will of God is close to her, and therefore she can sing in front of the men, even if the law forbids it completely.

* * *

Rabbi Efraim of Lonshitz explains it in another way. In his view, the change was brought about by the women changing in this brief moment, as their spiritual level rose to reach the level of men in "perceiving the prophecy". This is why at that moment there was no danger of sexual arousal.

It seems that the principal difference between Rabbi Azaria's position and that of Rabbi Efraim is that according to the former, the emphasis in this miraculous moment is placed on the transformation of the interior male world and its sublimation on the spiritual level, to a level at which men could sense the spirituality of the female voice without being sexually aroused; whereas according to the latter, the transformation should have taken place in the women themselves, so they might be sublimated to a higher spiritual level—the level of men—and hence make the seductive element disappear from their voice.

Several later halakhic commentators expressed a very liberal position regarding practical issues, and they reduced the prohibition as much as they could. For instance, in the nineteenth century, Rabbi Hayim Hizkiyahu Medini stated that if the voice is not *kol agavim* [a sexual voice] it is not prohibited (Medini, 1963). In the twentieth century, some of the Rabbis in Germany allowed ensemble singing of men and women, on the condition that it would be limited to sacred music (Weinberg, 1999; Wolowelsky, 1986).

* * *

We must point out here that sometimes we can find various "male" traditions that clearly evoke the argument (as we later discuss) that the spiritual level of women is higher than that of men. This was, for instance, noted by the Maharal (Rabbi Yehuda Lev ben Betzalel), who sought to explain the fact that women were not commanded to study the Torah. According to his interpretation, this is an expression of their spiritual superiority over men. In the Talmud it is even said that they are rewarded equally as men (who studied the Torah) merely by helping men—so why was this Sisyphean effort to study the Torah day and night demanded of men in order to heal their soul, while the women did not need it? He answers (in reference to Babylonian Talmud Ber. 17a) that women are better "prepared" than men for that spiritual reward, so they can obtain it more easily by the help they give to their husbands so they may study. Men have to invest much more effort than women in order to reach this spiritual level (Lev, 1971).

The threat of the "feminine" voice and music to "male" language and law

In the fascinating book she edited on the history of women, Pauline Schmitt Pantel comments on the fact that almost no texts written by women in the Middle Ages have come down to us (Schmitt Pantel,

1992). Schmitt asks whether women had access to the recognized and common language. Furthermore, in the second volume of *A History of Women*, Danielle Regnier-Bohler shows how women's voices in the Middle Ages were scorned. Behind this rejection of the feminine voice stood the philosophy that considered the sins of the tongue to be a source of lust and pride. Women who talked in public were thought to be diffusers of the poison of sins and were condemned for it (Regnier-Bohler, 1992). In the Middle Ages, if a quotation of a woman's speech was introduced in a man's text, it was often in order to emphasize its evil.

According to Regnier-Bohler, one must understand that feminine voices were seen not as the basis of significant speech, but as something that transgresses the language boundaries. This point links us to a long-standing and general problem: the continuing struggle with regard to music and voice, present among different cultures throughout history. This struggle focuses on the demand that music and voice should not deviate from the words that give them meaning, lest the voice becomes meaningless and threatening, especially due to its power to seduce and intoxicate the spirit. Moreover, the voice "beyond meaning" is identified with "femininity", whereas the "meaningful" text is identified with "masculinity". The voice "beyond words" is considered as a meaningless, sexual and seductive instrument. It has an attractive and dangerous power, although it was also considered to be empty and frivolous.

* * *

In a study that focuses on such phenomena, Dolar (1996b) cites a few examples that demonstrate that the voice was considered to threaten "the male order" of society and that music—like that of a voice without words—is considered to be feminine.

Already for Plato—as for most of the Greeks—the gender differentiation passes through music. In Greece, only girls were allowed to play the flute, and the right audience for hearing this kind of music was women, because when one plays the flute it is not possible to pronounce words. Men, however, were expected to engage in philosophy. An early example is from the saying of the Chinese emperor Chun (ca. 2200 BC): "Let the music follow the sense of the words. Keep it simple and ingenuous. One must condemn pretentious music which is devoid of sense and effeminate."

We see later that the Christian tradition shared this conception. St Augustine, for example, writes that the voice is a source of danger and decadence and that the cure for it is to adhere to the word—the divine word, of course—in order to make sure that the word will rule, and to get rid of the voice of that which is not connected to words.

Music in Christianity is considered something that elevates the soul to the divine but can also lower it to sin—*Delacatio Carnis*. In many texts, music represents the flesh in the most concrete way.

* * *

Opposing this rejecting conception, which sees music or voice without words as sinful and seductive, some of the medieval mystics suggested a contrary paradigm. Music, for them, was conceived of as the only adequate way to attain devotion, because it aspires to God beyond words. This is the way to a limitless, eternal being. If God is the musical principle *par excellence*, and if the word of God attains its true register only through the singing voice, then the radical result is that the word alone belongs to Satan. Hildegard von Bingen, a nun and composer of the twelfth century, proposed this extreme conclusion.

These conclusions raised a heated discussion in the Church (Dolar, 1996b). Does music come from God or from the devil? There were those who thought that what is "beyond" the word leads to the highest spiritual level, while others emphasized the danger of seduction. Music can be the element of spiritual sublimation beyond this world and its representations, but it can also release, by the same token, the uncontrollable meaningless *jouissance* beyond the sensual pleasures that can be represented. The voice, according to this conception, undermines every certainty and every institution of established meaning. It is limitless and is found, of course, on the feminine side.

The voice as objet á in Lacanian theory

Our discussion until now clearly presented the fundamental tension existing between those ancient philosophers who saw the woman's voice as spiritual and even divine, and those who were afraid of this voice and thought of it as a seductive and dangerous instrument. It must be emphasized repeatedly that even those who held the former position had to eliminate the "danger" of female sexuality in order to be able to make this position tenable for them (even Philo speaks of the voice of women only as part of a vocal harmony that combines the voices of women with those of men). Now we can ask whether psychoanalytic theory will be able to help us arrive at a better understanding of this tension.

Throughout all its history, one can discern discontent in psychoanalysis, especially relating to the enigma of what can be called "the particular place the feminine holds in our culture". One possible way of dealing with it is to learn from discontent in culture—that is, from the conflicts that are inherent to it, its gaps and fissures, through which the drive returns and erupts, threatening to destroy it. Observing the basic tension that we saw in the Jewish and general sources presented above is one way to understand the meaning of the "feminine" better from a contemporary psychoanalytic point of view.

On jouissance and feminine jouissance

The drive can achieve satisfaction in two main ways. The first is within the framework of the "law", and in this way it does not transgress the pleasure principle; the second is by combining the two drives in such a way that leads to transgressing the law, going "beyond the pleasure principle". In this second way, the death drive is stronger than the libido, and this combination leads to taking chances and defiance of rules, law, and language.

Desire and drive have an inverted logic. Desire is connected fundamentally to the law and to the transgression of the law, for it seeks always something forbidden or unavailable. On the other hand, the drive could not care less about law or prohibition. While the drive always obtains its satisfaction one way or another, desire stays forever unsatisfied and passes from object to object. The forbidding of *jouissance* itself creates the desire to transgress. In this sense, the death drive is the drive to transgress the symbolic law towards the Real—what Lacan calls, following Freud and Kant, *das Ding*, "the Thing" (Lacan, 1973, 1986). To the Thing itself we do not have an immediate access. Instead, we put supplementary objects, which we invest with the energy of the libido. The Thing is, in a way, a hole.

In his seminar, *The Ethics of Psychoanalysis*, Lacan described it thus:

> No doubt the question of beyond the pleasure principle, of the place of the unnameable Thing and of what goes on there, is raised in certain acts that provoke our judgment, acts of the kind attributed to a certain Angela de Folignio, who joyfully lapped up the water in which she had just washed the feet of lepers—I will spare you the details, such as the fact that a piece of skin stuck in her throat, etc.—or to the blessed Marie Allacoque, who, with no less a reward in spiritual uplift, ate the excrement of a sick man. The power of conviction of these no doubt edifying facts would vary quite a lot if the excrement in question were that of a beautiful girl or if it were a question of eating the come of a forward from your rugby team. In other words, the erotic side of things remains veiled in the above examples. [Lacan, 1986, p. 188]

* * *

The innovation in Lacan's arguments is that although in these cases the erotic side is veiled, there is a veiled erotic energy. It should be emphasized that although this side is hidden and we cannot see it at first, nevertheless it exists.

Jouissance does not relate to the Other. The Other is nothing but an object for the subject to enjoy. But in his XXth seminar, *Encore* (1975a), Lacan developed his radical claim concerning two kinds of *jouissance*. He claimed that there is phallic *jouissance* but that not all *jouissance* is phallic. While the law that is linked in our culture to desire is the "Law of the Father", and *jouissance* in our culture is essentially phallic, Lacan claimed that since the woman is not wholly subject to the phallic law, feminine sexuality has a possibility of experiencing a kind of *jouissance* that is not phallic—a *jouissance* that cannot be expressed in words that are essentially subject to the paternal law. Lacan called this other *jouissance* feminine *jouissance*. This kind of *jouissance*, usually experienced by women, can also be experienced by artists and male mystics. But the problem is that one cannot speak about feminine *jouissance*, since it exists outside language and law. This is an asexual *jouissance*, says Lacan: *jouissance* of the body as such.

* * *

It is the element of *jouissance* of the symptom, connected to the body, that Lacan places as linked to the order of the Real. The "gravity force" of *jouissance*, explains Lacan, is intensified as one approach this nucleus, similarly to what we find in the physical world, in the gravity that attracts the electrons to the nucleus of the atom. This is why we observe in the praxis of psychoanalysis that patients find it very hard to renounce their symptoms, even when they become aware of their symbolic meaning. The human being is attached to his or her suffering.

The analytic consequences of these observations are that subjects can renounce their symptoms only if they are willing to pay the price of renouncing part of their *jouissance*. In other words, this is an equivalent description of castration in Freud's teaching. And now there is a possibility to understand this point in a new way: acceptance of the mere fact of one's own castration is probably the key for renouncing the symptom. Therefore, we suggest that the distinction between the feminine inner position that cannot accept castration, and that psychological fact, is the cause of the "penis envy"; against that stands the feminine sexuality, the feminine possibility that comes from a real inner acceptance of castration—and that makes room for the "infinite".

Voice and speech

Lacan counts the voice as one of the primal lost objects, among other objects such as the breast, the excrement, and the gaze, around which the drive circulates in an attempt to attain satisfaction.

In his XIth seminar Lacan explains how the drive, which is connected to the voice, is bi-faceted (Lacan, 1973). On the one hand, there is the desire to hear the voice, but on the other, the drive is to be heard, or, in Lacan's words, "making oneself heard" (p. 195).

* * *

As in the "mirror stage", which is linked to the gaze (when the baby sees himself in the mirror and receives a message from his mother that this reflection is he, his ego), one can look at the event of "hearing oneself speak" and be recognized, because it is also an elementary formula of narcissism that is needed in order to be able to crystallize the minimal ego (Lacan, 1966a). Recognizing his own voice has the same effect on the baby as recognizing oneself in the mirror. The voice of the mother that answers the cry of the baby turns this cry into a call, and this becomes the primary relation to the other.

In this context, the myth of the love story between Narcissus and Echo is relevant. This myth proves that the Narcissistic saga consists of an element of voice as well as of gaze. The myth is of a tragic love and a failed narcissism, because the nymph Echo could only reiterate Narcissus' words, since she did not have a voice of her own. Narcissus preferred to die in his narcissism (to drown in the pond) rather than to give himself to another, to Echo's love. After Echo died, only her voice remained and became his voice's echo. It is a bodiless voice, nothing but a trace of the lost object. If Echo had had her own voice which could have said, like the mother to the baby, "How beautiful you are!"—and if Narcissus had listened to her (namely, had seen himself as an ideal in the eyes of the other and had adopted her point of view, i.e. that "inner split" that is created in the "mirror stage" and creates in the normal child the ability to look at himself from the outside)—a sensation of the ego would have been created in him that could have cut him off from his extreme narcissism, this unawareness of himself that is represented in his drowning in the pond.

* * *

Miller (1988) explains thus the contribution of Lacan to an understanding of the status of the voice as an object: if Freud discovered the primal objects—the breast and excrement—in his study of neuroses, Lacan adds the objects "gaze" and "voice" in his study of psychosis. The voice appears as an object when it is the voice of the Other. The voice is the element of language that cannot be assimilated into a part of the I, so it is subjectively referred to as Other. This is the haunting voice that represents surplus *jouissance*. Castration means that one does not hear a voice in the Real, which is to say: it is a situation of "deafness". So where is the intention of the voice when I speak? Not in the tone of speech. The voice lies precisely in what cannot be said. It inhabits language, it haunts language. It is enough to say something in order for it to become as uncanny as something that cannot be said. If we talk, chat, sing, and listen, it is connected, according to Lacan, to the fact that we try to hide what we can call "The voice in its function as *objet á*. The voice contains the craving for the lost object, and it reveals what the words, which are part of the symbolic order, try to cover.

* * *

Linguistic researchers in our modern epoch, especially the structuralistic school inspired by Ferdinand de Saussure and Roman Jackobson, ignored the voice and its materiality and only dealt with the structural characteristics of speech and the chain of signifiers that are characterized solely by differentiation, the difference existing between signifiers. In opposition to them, for Lacan, there is a "leftover" remaining from the signifying chain. This leftover is the voice, which is why the voice is meaningless by itself, because meaning arises only from the oppositions existing between signifiers. A voice represents a leftover that cannot be signified—and singing and music are nothing but sublimative attempts to domesticate this pure voice, this leftover, and turn it into an object of aesthetic pleasure. Singing and music throw a screen that hides what is unbearable and threatening in this leftover of the symbolic order, since in its purity it belongs to the Real. In the paradigm where the symbolic logos creates meaning, it stands in opposition to the voice that is considered as a pure voice, a penetration of "otherness", mysticism and femininity.

The meaning of the threat embodied in the singing of the Sirens

The myth of the singing of the Sirens is a suitable metaphor for the voice as *objet á*. Their voices represent on the one hand pure desire, and on the other pure death. The Sirens' song binds its listeners in an obsessive way to the fascination of death. The *jouissance* derived from listening to it is lethal *jouissance*. Renata Salecl (1998) analyses the myth of Odysseus in his encounter with the Sirens. As opposed to the function of the Muses in Greek mythology—to arouse past memories directly linked to forgetfulness—the knowledge of the Sirens is of past secrets that will never arise in the memory of future generations.

* * *

For Lacan, following Freud, memory is linked with the forgetting of trauma. The function of memories is to screen primal trauma. This is the Real around which the subject constructs its being. So the Sirens make those who listen to their voice receive knowledge in the Real, the kind of knowledge of which the listeners do not want to know anything—knowledge that exists in the Real is linked to the drive that seeks satisfaction. According to Salecl, a paradox is created here: that which cannot ever be memorized, symbolized by way of its inclusion into the narrative frame, is not some fleeting moment of the past, forever lost, but the very insistence of drive as that which cannot ever be forgotten in the first place, since it repeats itself incessantly.

* * *

Trauma is not something that happened in the past; rather, it is something that goes on happening, like in the nightmares of shell-shocked soldiers. That is why, Salecl emphasizes, the paradox lies in the fact that on the one hand "we don't remember it", but on the other this non-remembering is present and significant at all times. In the case of the voice, the leftover, the excessive *jouissance* that is linked to it is what turns it into a fascinating and deadly element.

In the Odyssey we have, on the one hand, the promise of limitless *jouissance* through surrender to the siren's singing and, on the other, the prohibition of hearing this singing and the threat of death.

The relation between the "Voice of the Father" and the feminine voice

At the end of our discussion, which has concerned mostly the female voice, we would like to comment upon the relation between this voice and the male voice, the "Voice of the Father". In opposition to the feminine voice stands the voice of the "Primal Father", the voice of God. This is a voice that stresses the word, the logos; a commanding voice, which ties a bond and signs a pact. Lacan raises this issue in his seminar *On Anxiety* (1963a), where he takes the sound of the *shofar* (a Jewish ritual instrument) as a metaphor. According to Lacan, the sound of the *shofar* is the "Voice of the Father"—the cry of the primal father of the herd, the leftover that pursues and that also stands as the foundation of the Law and seals it. The sound of the *shofar* is the sign of the pact with the Lord that the community of believers signs. This is how it declares its recognition of the Lord, its surrender and its obedience to the Law. "Pure Law", before it commands specifically, is embodied in the "Voice of the Father", the voice that commands total obedience even though it is meaningless by itself. The voice is a substitute for the impossible presence of the Lord, a presence that covers a substantial absence.

* * *

The struggle is not between the word, or logos and voice, but between "voice" and "voice"—the "Voice of the Father" against the "Feminine Voice". Is the "Voice of the Father" inherently different from the "Feminine Voice"? Is the pursuing voice inherently different from the pursued voice? Dolar (1996b) suggests the possibility that perhaps they are both identical. The most significant sound of the *shofar* in Jewish tradition is the one that was blown on the occasion of the Sinaitic Theophany. The *shofar* in this establishing moment is what testifies to the presence of God for His people, because all they could hear was this terrible commanding voice, and only Moses could speak with the Lord and understand His words. The voice that is described in the Sinaitic Theophany is a Real voice: "And all the people saw the thundering, and the lightning, and the noise of the trumpet, and the mountain smoking, and when the people saw it they removed, and stood after off" (Exod.

20:18). *Objet á* in this instance was constructed in this impossible way from voice and gaze—the auditory drive and the specular drive blended together. To see the voices means that the voice has materiality, which is the Real. There is only one voice object that attaches itself and splits the other from the outside and from the inside. And why not interpret the face of the Other, the face of God, as supported by the feminine *jouissance*, asks Lacan in his late teachings (Dolar, 1996b).

And so, feminine and masculine positions are perhaps two ways to approach the same impossibility—two related versions of the same voice that guards deliberate dimness.

Conclusion:
a psychoanalytic view of the relationship
to the woman's voice in Jewish sources

The encounter between the interpretative and halakhic study and the psychoanalytic study presented above can teach us how completely different methods of thought can enrich each other. It is possible to realize now, after specifying the psychoanalytic sources and ways of conceptualizing, to what extent the tension between different approaches in Jewish thought is a case study of the general psychoanalytic discussion relating to *objet á*, which is the voice (these examples of different interpretations clarify in a definite way the meaning of the relationship to this *objet á*).

The psychoanalytic insights of Freud and Lacan concerning the object of the drive can help us understand how this tension between the different interpreters in Jewish tradition relating to the woman's voice was created—a tension that we called "a woman's voice is *erva*" as opposed to "a woman's voice is *erga*". As we have seen, this tension is not unique to Jewish sources, but rises to the surface in different times and different cultures.

However, the Jewish sources, in referring directly and clearly to the woman's voice as carrying a seductive sexual quality, help us understand the psychoanalytic assertion on the sexual quality of the search for *objet á*—in this case, the voice.

* * *

Another issue that has become clear to us here, and was at the centre of our discussion, is related to the Lacanian assertion about the tension existing between the symbolic order and the order of the Real. Lacan claimed that the symbolic order falls under the phallic function, which is why it is more closely linked to the male position in culture. As opposed to that, the woman is closer to the Real, because she is not totally subject to the phallic function. That is why there is a threatening aspect to the feminine voice, a threatening element to the symbolic order in traditional Jewish society, represented by the prohibitions related to the performance of the rituals while hearing this voice. So, for example, we saw that even the liberal interpreters in the Talmudic issue in Ber. 24a, perceive the woman's voice as a disintegrating factor that undermines the ability of men to concentrate on "masculine" rituals of holiness, such as the recital of *Shema* and so forth.

* * *

However, we also saw that many traditional sources relate to the woman's voice as carrying a "sublime" quality, even if only in a utopian way. Our claim is that precisely because women do not fall completely under the "Law of the Father", they can represent a possibility of "liberation" that makes the contact with the Real possible, a contact without which the artist cannot create and without which the religious man cannot attain devotion to the Lord. The psychoanalytic conception of feminine *jouissance* as "an-other" *jouissance* also links the feminine voice and the artistic and mystical voice (Lacan, 1975a).

This element in the woman's voice is threatening for the symbolic masculine world quite as much as the sexual seduction, because it presents a kind of transgressive craving to disintegrate the accepted symbolic order. It is important to remember that even those interpreters who are ready to recognize a spiritual quality in the woman's voice had to work to cancel its sexually seductive aspect.

* * *

At the end of this discussion we would like to present here a Talmudic story that expresses, in our opinion, the full power of the

"A WOMAN'S VOICE IS *ERVA*" 97

tension between the symbolic order—the one belonging to the masculine world—and the order of the Real. It is revealed in the following story as an almost materialistic power of light emanating from the woman's sexuality, which threatens to disintegrate the masculine order. In this case, it appears in the most symbolic form one could possibly imagine, as it represents the Law—the legal court.

> Homa, Abaye's wife, came to Raba [after Abaye's death] and asked him, "grant me an allowance of board", and he granted her the allowance. "Grant me", she again demanded, "an allowance of wine". "I know", he said to her, "that Nachmani [*lit.*: my comforter, a name in which Abaye was often referred to] did not drink wine". "By the life of the Master [I swear]", she replied, "that he let me drink from horns like this". As she was showing it to him, her arm was uncovered and a light shone upon the court. Raba rose, went home and solicited Rabbi Hisda's daughter [his own wife]. "Who has been today at the court?" enquired Rabbi Hisda's daughter. "Homa, the wife of Abaye", he replied. Thereupon she followed her, striking her with the straps of a chest until she chased her out of all Mahuza. "You have", she said to her, "already killed three [men], and now you come to kill another?" [Babylonian Talmud Ktubot 65a]

* * *

We have shown above the relation existing between *objet á*, which is the object of the drive, and the Other, which represents the Law, the ideal—and, one can say, that which represents the "masculine" God. The craving after the ideal, the belief that the Other has it (he knows, he is potent, he determines), is responsible for most of the human suffering expressed in symptoms or in negative emotions such as envy and hatred.

In opposition to this Other, feminine *jouissance* represents the psychic fact that the Other does not exist (and to the extent that he exists, it is perceived as not whole)—an idea that Lacan developed in his XXth seminar.

Feminine *jouissance* is seen in this context as the signifier of the lack in the Other, as in Lacan's matheme $S(\cancel{A})$. So when one makes room for feminine *jouissance* and does not silence it, the Other—as a whole, as an ideal—falls and a possibility is opened for liberation from paralysing negative emotions.

* * *

So, in light of these findings, it is clear that the "utopian" description existing in the interpretative texts that we have presented, of the possibility that women's voice will lose its threatening quality in the eyes of men, has a potential to be realized. It may be that the time will come when men will be able to see (through the screen of the phallic search after *objet á*) its spiritual quality—the "infinite".

This interpretation represents the masculine craving for that same "utopian" situation—a situation where listening to the "Feminine Voice" will teach men other spiritual possibilities, which those who are under the phallic function are usually barred against.

Our claim—in its last essence—is therefore that both sides of this coin are identical. This is because without feminine *jouissance* (the "infinite"), there can be no contact with the divine.

PART III

TESTIMONY

CHAPTER SEVEN

The secret bearers—
from silence to testimony,
from the Real to *phantasme*

I wish to share with you parts of a journey, a journey that passes through several intersecting paths. I begin with a quotation from an interview given by Claude Lanzmann concerning his film *Shoa:* "It is like a black sun, and you always have to struggle against yourself in order to go on. It's what happened during the process [of the making] of the film. I had to struggle against my own irrepressible tendency to forget what I had done" (in Felman & Laub, 1992 p. 252).

My work on the Shoa (Holocaust) is a psychoanalytic research as well as a personal journey. The struggle Lanzmann referred to is also my struggle. In this journey I was helped by a small study group as a symbolic frame of reference in order to be able to plunge into this unbearable Real and yet avoid drowning, to elude the horrible fascination that lies within this black sun or the heart of darkness, or these dark gods, as Lacan called them at the end of his

---

Previously published in English as "The secret bearers—from silence to testimony, from the real to phantasm." *Israel Psychoanalytic Journal,* 1 (2003, No. 2): 247.

seminar *The Four Fundamental Concepts of Psycho-Analysis* (Lacan, 1973).

This, to me, is psychoanalytic work *par excellence*, both in the way of thinking and in the nature of the encounter with the traumatic Real, the way this work touches the core of the Real, that impossible and unbearable place, an *extimité* place—internal and external at the same time.

* * *

I would like to share with you one of the personal outcomes of this work, which was like a rite of passage for me, or a testimony. When I started my Lacanian analysis with a Parisian non-Jewish analyst, I wanted to explain my symbolic background to her, so I said, quite proudly, that because my father was also born in Israel, I was a second-generation Sabra. Here in Israel, a country of immigrants, that implies a higher status. I was always certain that my only connection to the Shoa was through the fact of my being Jewish. After about a year, when I started working with this group on the Shoa, I began, for the first time in my life, to ask questions about my family—not my immediate family, but cousins of my parents, the families of my grandfathers and grandmothers, and so on. I broke the silence. I spoke, and mainly listened, to some of the members of my family concerning their experiences in the Shoa. For the first time in my life, I heard from my mother's cousin the story of my family in the Shoa, a story even my mother was unfamiliar with. Again for the very first time—after participating in all the memorial days and watching the film *Shoa* as well as other films—I recognized a fact that I had never admitted to myself: that I have a personal connection to the Shoa. After countless years of therapy and analysis, it came as a revelation to me, an uncanny revelation. I went to my analyst and told her about it, horrified. "But," she answered, quite surprised, "you said it in the first meeting. You said you are second generation!" This formulation refers to the emergence of the unconscious, that I have always "known", but never thought of.

Now I am working, breaking my inner silence as I go deeper. This subject holds a strange fascination—more and more I understand the difficulty and the necessity of this research. The journey, parts of which I am going to share with you, passes through the problems of giving testimony, the different kinds of testimony, and the question as to the place of subjective truth. Through psychoanalysis and art, particularly in reference to the fascinating book *Testimony* by Shoshana Felman and Dori Laub (1992), as well as to Primo Levi's last book, *The Drowned and the Saved* (1988) and the enigma of his suicide after the book was published, I shall try to unravel this problem.

From silence to testimony

The twentieth century was characterized as the period that elevated the culture of bearing witness to the highest rank. Elie Wiesel noted two major events that are responsible for this all-important status of the testimony: the Shoa and the invention of psychoanalysis. Beyond the physical annihilation of the Jews, it was the testimony about the Shoa that the Nazis tried to annihilate. Primo Levi quotes Simon Wiesenthal on this subject:

> "Many survivors . . . remember that the SS militiamen enjoyed cynically admonishing the prisoners: However this war may end, we have won the war against you; none of you will be left to bear witness, but even if someone were to survive, the world would not believe him. There will perhaps be suspicions, discussions, research by historians, but there will be no certainties, because we will destroy the evidence together with you. And even if some proof should remain and some of you survive, people will say that the events you describe are too monstrous to be believed. They will say that they are the exaggerations of Allied propaganda and will believe us, who will deny everything, and not you. We will be the ones to dictate the history of the Lagers.
>
> "Strangely enough, this same thought ('even if we were to tell, we would not be believed') arose in the form of nocturnal dreams produced by the prisoners' despair. . . . In the most typical (and cruelest) form, the interlocutor turned and left in silence. . . . both parties, victims and oppressors, had a keen awareness of the enormity and therefore the noncredibility of what took place in the Lagers. . . .
>
> "It did not matter that they might die along the way; what really mattered was that they should not tell their story. . . .

> The Lagers had become dangerous for a moribund Germany because they contained the secret of the Lagers themselves, the greatest crime in the history of humanity. The army of ghosts that still vegetated in them was composed of *Geheimnisträger*, the bearers of secrets who must be disposed of . . ." [Levi, 1988, pp. 11–14]

The secret bearers—this was the name given to potential witnesses from both sides.

In the eyes of Levi and others, the secret bearers were also the guilty ones, the privileged, those with special rights. In most cases, as Levi tells us, those were the only ones who survived. And he adds:

> We, the survivors, are not the true witnesses. . . . we are those who by their prevarications or abilities or good luck did not touch bottom. Those who did so, those who saw the Gorgon, have not returned to tell about it or have returned mute, but they are the "Muslims", the submerged, the complete witnesses, the ones whose deposition would have a general significance. They are the rule, we are the exception. . . .
>
> We who were favored by fate tried, with more or less wisdom, to recount not only our fate but also that of the others, indeed of the drowned. . . . The destruction brought to an end, the job completed, was not told by anyone, just as no one ever returned to describe his own death. Even if they had paper and pen, the drowned would not have testified because their death had begun before that of their body. Weeks and months before being snuffed out, they had already lost the ability to observe, to remember, to compare and express themselves. We speak in their stead, by proxy.
>
> I could not say whether we did or do so out of a kind of moral obligation toward those who were silenced or in order to free ourselves of their memory; certainly we do it because of a strong and durable impulse. [Levi, 1988, pp. 83–84]

On the limitations of memory

Shoshana Felman defines the concept of testimony as follows: "Testimony is . . . a discursive *practice*, as opposed to a pure *theory*. To testify—to *vow* to tell, to *promise* and *produce* one's own speech as material evidence for truth—is to accomplish a *speech act*, rather than to simply formulate a statement" (Felman & Laub, 1992, p. 5). For Felman, testimony of this kind consists of strips and fragments of reminiscence brought to the surface by events that were inconsistent with understanding or memory, acts that cannot be fully comprehended cognitively.

Primo Levi, referring to the limitations of memory, says:

> The memories which lie within us are not carved in stone; not only do they tend to become erased as the years go by, but they often change, or even grow, by incorporating extraneous features. . . . This scant reliability of our memories will be satisfactorily explained only when we know in what language, in what alphabet they are written, on what surface and with what pen. . . .
>
> Nevertheless, even in normal conditions a slow degradation is at work, an obfuscation of outlines. . . . Doubtless one may discern here one of the great powers of nature, the same that degrades order into disorder, youth into old age, and extinguishes life in death. . . .
>
> A memory evoked too often, and expressed in the form of a story, tends to become fixed in a stereotype, in a form tested by experience, crystallized, perfected, adorned, installing itself in the place of the raw memory and growing at its expense. . . . The memory of a trauma suffered or inflicted is itself traumatic because recalling it is painful or at least disturbing. . . . the injury cannot be healed. [Levi, 1988, pp. 23–24]

* * *

Levi quotes Jean Améry, an Austrian philosopher who was tortured by the Gestapo and deported to Auschwitz:

> "Anyone who has been tortured remains tortured. . . . Anyone who has suffered torture never again will be able to be at ease in the world, the abomination of the annihilation is never extinguished. Faith in humanity, already cracked by the first slap in the face, then demolished by torture, is never acquired again." [Levi, 1988, p. 25]

For Améry, torture was an interminable death, and he killed himself in 1978. The distinction between good faith and bad faith is optimistic, says Levi:

> There are . . . those who lie consciously, coldly falsifying reality itself, but more numerous are those who weigh anchor, move off, momentarily or forever, from genuine memories, and fabricate for themselves a convenient reality. The past is a burden to them; they feel repugnance for things done or suffered and tend to replace them with others . . . initial bad faith has become good faith. The silent transition from falsehood to self-deception is useful: anyone who lies in good faith is better off. [Levi, 1988, p. 27]

Testimony—from the Real to phantasme

The aim of narrative, literary, and poetic testimony was to grapple with the crisis of truth. Especially during the past twenty years, we "witness" how the practice of testimony has become the dominant form of expression in every aspect of our life connected to language—in literature, the plastic arts, cinema, the media, the internet— the deluge of words that strive by any possible means to capture "the whole truth", in speech and in writing. Isn't this the same as we do in psychoanalysis and free association?

Levi harshly criticizes the position of psychoanalysis as he knows it, saying:

> I do not believe that psychoanalysts (who have pounced upon our tangles with professional avidity) are competent to explain this impulse [to give testimony]. Their knowledge has been built up and tested "outside", in the world that, for the sake of simplicity, we call civilian: psychoanalysis traces its phenomenology and tries to explain it; studies its deviations and tries to heal them. Their interpretations, even those of someone like Bruno Bettelheim, who went through the trials of the Lager, seem to me approximate and simplified, as if someone wished to apply the theorems of plane geometry to the solution of spherical triangles. The mental mechanisms of the Häftlinge were different from ours; curiously, and in parallel, different also were their physiology and pathology. Gastric ulcers and mental illnesses were healed (or became asymptomatic), but everyone suffered from an unceasing discomfort that polluted sleep and was nameless. To define this as a "neurosis" is reductive and ridiculous. Perhaps it would be more correct to see in it

an atavistic anguish whose echo one hears in the second verse of Genesis: the anguish inscribed in everyone of the "tohu-bohu" of a deserted and empty universe crushed under the spirit of God but from which the spirit of man is absent: not yet born or already extinguished. [Levi, 1988, pp. 84–85]

* * *

Today, in fact, the bulk of verbalization is concerned with bearing witness to the awful events that have occurred and still occur on our planet; through personal stories we confess to ever more atrocities, and the media have contributed greatly to the deluge of grisly information, to the flood of testimony. The media are more adept at this than literature, for today we "know" almost everything—even transmitted live. But what is this knowledge? What is this "intolerable truth" whereby we derive *jouissance* from the horror that it causes us? Does this knowledge have any effect on the subject? Do we thereby come into contact with any Real? As with everything that seeks to capture truth in a net of words, it seems that the more testimonies there are about a particular event, the more the truth connected to the Real succeeds in escaping.

* * *

As I write this essay, an animated discussion is going on in the newspapers about the destiny of Adolf Eichmann's memoirs, the notes he wrote during his trial and before his execution. The question is whether they should be published, and whether they belong legally to his son, as an inheritance. Among other things, Eichmann wrote:

> "I did not set to work like a mindless animal. On the contrary, I derived endless happiness from this work. I was fascinated by the fact that it fell to me to take care of these things. . . . The main thing was to solve once and for all the entire Jewish question. This thing was part of me. Otherwise I would have been a mere apprentice, a cog in the wheel, a soulless creature." [in Shatner, 1999; translated for this edition]

Can these memoirs of Eichmann be considered testimony?

I would submit that this form of narrative testimony is coming to its end in our time, also as a result of psychoanalysis and its impact on culture and the assimilation of its concepts in the cultural discourse. Passing from the field of history to that of the clinic or to psychoanalysis, we discover, following Freud, an unconscious testimony, a testimony conveyed more by what remains unspoken than what is said openly. It is not necessary to recognize truth in order to testify effectively about it. Speech is in itself unintentionally testimonial, and the speaking subject bears witness to the truth within himself while it continues to elude him. The subject eludes the consciousness in the end like the closest relative going away in the dream of the secret bearers.

For psychoanalysis to survive as a living science, it must henceforth proceed along a different path. Bearing witness has not lost its importance, but it has become reoriented to what can be called "eyewitness testimony", or testimony that issues from the Real and not from the narrative.

Repetition and trauma

In psychoanalysis, we are therefore witnesses to unconscious testimony, apparently by way of the repetition compulsion, which, in psychoanalytic theory, originates in the death drive. Precisely because of the impossibility of constructing the event in memory, there is constant repetition of the same painful process in a vain but obstinate attempt to seize the object that escapes in the net of the symbolic register. The compulsion to repeat is an attempt to recall what was forgotten by means of movements or actions, and thus it is not connected to tangible, empirical realism but, rather, to the Real. The repetition actualizes the dimension that is present by virtue of its absence—that is to say, which cannot be described in words—and arouses in us the feeling of the uncanny (more on this in chapter ten herein, "The Return of Orpheus").

* * *

Regarding the psychoanalytic theory of trauma, Freud thought at the beginning of his research that through memories the hysteric reached the sexual trauma of her childhood (the so-called seduction theory). Later, he noticed that through remembering, one reaches the basic *phantasme*—the imaginary texture of the structure that is used as a screen. The Real is there not in the remembered trauma but, rather, in that which is not remembered.

The encounter with the Real is always a missed encounter. In this *tuché*, where the subject tries to deal with the trauma through *phantasme*, the Real is the sign—the trace of that part of the trauma that is indigestible. The subjective knowledge in the Real is the sign of the traumatic signifier.

The trauma of the victims of sexual seduction that Freud studied happened suddenly, because their shock "happened" when they were not ready for it. They "missed" the event by not having time to put on their defensive armour against it—that is to say, it passed directly into their unconscious without being registered consciously. Freud speaks of two events required for the formation of trauma, when the second event registers the first retrospectively, thereby making it traumatic.

Therefore, in their attempt to prepare themselves for the event, in order to be witnesses simultaneously to what they were experiencing and what they had missed, their destiny was to repeat the trauma and relive their paradoxical absence over and over again.

One can say that the Real has two faces. As Galliano puts it:

> There is the Real as destructive to the subject, threatening him with annihilation, focusing on the things that cannot enter the unconscious—the Real that goes beyond the symbolic. . . . On the other hand repetition enables the Real to fix itself in the phantasmal scene, and it shows the other side of the Real. When the trauma appears as a sign it holds the subject in the signifying chain where he can organize himself. [Galliano, 1998, p. 6; translated for this edition]

* * *

If we read the trauma as a form of absence, we see that it brings up one of the impossible sentences that a living subject cannot say and mean when he says it: "I am dead." We can feel it again in the trauma, where a personal testimony is emptied of meaning by the subject's absence from the event that he experienced most deeply. This is the rhythm of the shock: an outburst of extreme violence to the organism, who experiences in advance its annihilation even while it compels infinite repetition.

* * *

As an example, I shall refer to the dream that Freud writes about at the beginning of the last chapter of *The Interpretation of Dreams*, a dream that Lacan analysed in his XIth seminar (Lacan, 1973). This is a dream about trauma and a traumatic dream, a dream that horrifies me whenever I read about it. Freud reports it as follows:

> A father has been watching beside his child's sick-bed for days and nights on end. After the child had died, he went into the next room to lie down, but left the door open so that he could see from his bedroom into the room in which his child's body was laid out, with tall candles standing round it. An old man had been engaged to keep watch over it, and sat beside the body murmuring prayers. After a few hours' sleep, the father had a dream that his son was standing beside his bed, caught him by the arm and whispered to him reproachfully: "Father, don't you see I'm burning?" he woke up, noticed a bright glare of light from the next room, hurried into it and found that the old watchman had dropped off to sleep and that the wrappings and one of the arms of his beloved child's dead body had been burned by a lighted candle that had fallen on them. [Freud, 1900a, p. 509]

While sleeping, the father probably sensed the light emanating from the fire but did not wake up immediately. Instead, he incorporated this perception into the dream. Freud asks why the dream appears instead of the father waking up. According to him, the dream has two aims: to lengthen the child's life by a few minutes and to lengthen the father's sleep for those same few minutes. What, then, woke the father up?

Lacan claims that it could not have been an external physical stimulus that woke up the father, and he asks: "What is it that wakes the sleeper? Is it not, in the dream, another reality?" (Lacan, 1973, p. 58). The answer, according to him, is the desire not to wake up and confront the message of his child's death:

> The awakening shows us the waking state of the subject's consciousness in the representation of what has happened—the unfortunate accident in reality, against which one can do no more than take steps! But what, then, was this accident? When everybody is asleep, including the person who wished to take a little rest, the person who was unable to maintain his vigil

and the person of whom some well intentioned individual, standing at his bedside, must have said, *He looks just as if he is asleep*, when he knows only one thing about him, and that is that, in this entirely sleeping world, only the voice is heard, *Father, can't you see I'm burning?* This sentence is itself a firebrand—of itself it brings fire where it falls—and one cannot see what is burning, for the flames blind us to the fact that the fire bears on the *Unterlegt*, on the *Unterträgen*, on the real. [Lacan, 1973, p. 59]

The man awakens from this dream or nightmare, says Lacan, precisely so as to continue not to see. The awakening comes in order for him to continue sleeping and not meet the Real that appears in the dream. The Real is not only the death of the child. If the reality of the unconscious is sexual reality, then the thing the father cannot stand is that the child represents the burning of sexual desire. So the dream makes the father encounter his sin.

The purpose of the awakening is to put to sleep the unbearable desire. In reality one can repress, forget, or deny, but, says Lacan, this desire is irreducible. That is why it continues to vibrate, appearing and disappearing in the rhythm of a pulse.

* * *

The father hears in his dream—*father, don't you see*? And who is the father of the father? And what about an era where there is no father? To whom will this fire turn, and what will happen to it? The father is a gaze one turns to, a gaze that is missing in the encounter. The missed encounter is that the gaze is not there, the Other does not answer. If the father sees consciously, the inverse angle of vision is that unconsciously he does not see, because a father is not an entity that can answer from the same angle of vision. What remains is the reproachful voice of the child—a voice and an appeal for a gaze. The gaze represents the impossible representation. When the encounter with the Real situates what cannot be represented, cannot be spoken, then silence appears. Giving testimony is the only solution for the subject, but an interval of time is needed for speaking. One needs to disengage from deadening *jouissance*, from the horror riding on the back of repetition.

Arbeit macht frei—*entropy*

Entropy is the constant and irreversible degeneration of energy in every system, leading to a situation of progressive disorder and undifferentiation in matter (more on this in chapter twelve herein, "There Is No Such Form"). Entropy is negative movement towards formlessness, or, as Bataille calls it, *l'informe* (Bataille, 1985).

If we cancel the dichotomy between form and content, life and death, and relate to that element in the libido that is not given to annihilation, then entropy is indeed an element of erosion, an element of extinction that works within existing form, an element that, although it opposes change, leads in the end to disintegration of the existing order and to the possibility of creating a new order.

The quest for information breaks the silence, but if entropy is loss of information, then the process of narrative testimony on the Shoa entails the danger of generating an inverse process: one can use historical knowledge in order not to know. By accumulating information about more and more small details, we may lose the general picture. In terms of information theory, entropy in language means that the words become more like clichés, to the point where they almost lose meaning, like hot and cold water mixed together until it becomes lukewarm. To be in touch with truth or with the Real, a different kind of process is needed. Perhaps, as Adorno (1962) claims, we need art in order to transmit them.

* * *

The work of the *l'informe* liberates culture from testimony associated with death and makes it possible to organize towards new meanings and new bodies. The operation of *l'informe* shatters metaphor, figure, subject, morphology, meaning—anything that resembles something, anything that is gathered towards the unity of the concept. The entropic movement floods the field of vision in the absence of a subject. It shows that in the automatism of endless repetition, the disappearance of the shifter (I) is a mechanism that evokes formlessness.

We can bless the law of entropy because it shows that truth will always elude us. There will always be a place of erosion—of loss of information, a place for the possibility of chaos.

Out of the shattered madness

The incident referred to in the testimony, which seeks to comprehend and capture it, is both historical and clinical at the same time. If this is so, asks Felman (Felman & Laub, 1992), is the testimony simply a medium of historical transmission, or can it also serve, by unseen paths, as a medium of therapy?

Felman, a student of culture, derives clinical results from literature and poetry. In her analysis of Camus's *La Peste* [The Plague], she reaches the following conclusion: what impels and arouses the attention of the witness, and what calls for his testimony, is basically always, in one way or another, the scandal of the disease, a metaphoric or literal legacy, and the imperative to bear witness, which becomes more urgent here with the contracting of the plague—the outbreak of an illness that is radically incurable is, in itself, an ethical and philosophic parallel to an incurable human condition of exposure and vulnerability. What generates change? Is the story itself the remedy?

* * *

Miller (1996) analyses the attitudes of Freud and Lacan towards the ways in which the symptom is produced. He specifies the two ways in which the libido can move, and, following Freud, he terms them the *Holzweg* ["forest paths"—a concept borrowed from Heidegger]. The forest paths are those paths that woodcutters blaze for themselves in the course of their work, paths that do not lead from one point to another, but to a certain place, where movement desists and the libido has the option of either getting stuck or returning. The symptom comprises "sense" [*Sinn*], which Lacan calls the "formal envelope of the symptom", and there is also the "meaning" [*Bedeutung*] of the symptom. As long as we hold on to the core of the *jouissance*, it will be difficult for us to renounce the symptom. But the symptom is only one path to which the libido has recourse. The second path that Freud mentions is art. The artist, he says, can play with the symptom. This, according to Miller, is an artificial symptom, which is willing to suspend our *jouissance* as observers and release us from afflictions associated with our unconscious knowledge.

But if one takes into account the unconscious testimony given in the psychoanalyst's clinic, a question arises: is it really possible to bear witness only by speaking or writing? Only through the narrative? Or can it be that the unconscious testimony arises more from structure—the structure of fracture and repetition?

Thus, when we speak about non-narrative testimony, we refer to unconscious testimony arising from compulsive repetition—repetition that attempts to grapple with anxiety while itself arousing anxiety. The constant recurrence of the motif speaks and betokens. It is testimony not of content, but of form, or, rather, the dissolution of form, as in Celan's disarticulated language. Testimony of this kind is connected with the unconscious, in that it can be construed.

This is a testimony that is both pursued by the artist and is pursuing him; he is like a captive to the exigency of giving it expression. Celan writes in a marvellous poem:

> Out of the shattered
> madness
> I arise
> and contemplate my hand
> as it draws
> the one and only
> ring.
>
> [Celan, 1976, p. 118; translated for this edition]

* * *

The event is paradoxically "known", but only after the fact—by means of its effect. It is known to the extent that it pursues the witness, and the witness, in turn, pursues it.

If the event pursues the witness, what is revealed is the testimony's compulsive character: the witness is pursued, and, at the same time, he is compelled and bound by something, whereby the event's unexpected impact is simultaneously incomprehensible and unforgettable. The event does not abate: it is one from which the witness can no longer release himself. But if, in a manner even more unpredictable, the witness becomes the pursuer of the event, this is perhaps because the witness has realized that it is from the event itself that unexpected deliverance might flow. Coincidence may become a liberating factor.

It is already possible to speak of the post-narrative epoch of the testimony, in which all the important information is available to us but truth continues to elude us. In this case, what does testimony represent for us? It is precisely that obstinate return to the place where information is already known to us—the place where anxiety, the uncanny, and the comical converge.

Eyewitnessing

In the last chapter of Lacan's book *The Four Fundamental Concepts of Psycho-Analysis*, based on a seminar he gave in the year 1963, he claims that we tend to avert our gaze from the Shoa, and that to turn a courageous gaze towards it means to see the fascination that the act of sacrificing holds for us (Lacan, 1973).

The fascination stems from the fact that the sacrifice gives us evidence of desire in the Other, a desire that he calls the "dark god". Comparing the positions of Spinoza and Kant on this question, Kant's is the more tenable for the human experience. According to Lacan, Spinoza's position states that desire is the essence of man, and he locates this desire in the dependence of the subject on the universality of the divine attributes through the function of the signifier. In so doing he succeeds in detaching himself from human desire and postulates instead *Amor Intellectualis Dei*.

Kant's position is that universal law stands above everything and one has to sacrifice to it even the loved object, which he calls the pathological object. Kant ignores the fascination, the *jouissance*, derived from such a sacrifice, and in so doing his position is not far from that of the Marquis de Sade. Indeed, Lacan writes "Kant with Sade". In the act of sacrifice, we "know" what God wants, and in the presence of His gaze we become the object. The gaze determines our being.

One cannot face the fact of lack in the Other without anxiety, or even panic. The incongruence in the Other is unbearable, and the aim of sacrifice is the fantasy of filling the lack with an object. If this Other is the dark god, the sacrifice is of the love object that produces pure desire.

A clinical example:
The averted gaze and the sacrifice of womanhood

This is an example of the unbearable connection between gaze as an object and the object of sacrifice—the fascinated frozen gaze that immobilizes life, and the testimony on this gaze in the body itself. The case is that of an anorexic girl, 18 years old, who was hospitalized in a mental hospital.

When this girl's father was 14, he saw his own father shot in front of his eyes in Auschwitz. When he came to Israel (which was then Palestine), he said he did not want to look back, since he was afraid of becoming "petrified like Lot's wife". So he became an active member of the developing community, fought in the War of Independence, established a new kibbutz, and never mourned the past. He said that no one noticed his façade. I would say that there was no gap that left room for desire.

* * *

The story of Lot contains a few elements that are relevant to this story. First, the people of Sodom wanted Lot to hand over the messengers to them so that they could commit sodomy. Lot offered them his two virgin daughters instead. By this act of sacrificing his daughters he still observed the symbolic laws of heterosexuality and hospitality. Then the sinners were punished, as was Lot's wife when she looked back. In the end, Lot committed incest with his daughters. The law was broken. That biblical portion that is called "and God saw," contains the offering of Isaac as a sacrifice, and in the end Abraham called the place of sacrifice "God will see," because on this mountain "God shall be seen" (Gen. 22:14).

* * *

I met Or (the word in Hebrew means "light") when she came to our adolescent ward. She was a tall, slender, boyish girl. At the age of 14, the age when her father's gaze was frozen, she began suffering from severe anorexia. After four years of endless therapies and therapists, as a last resort she was sent to the hospital by her therapists and the kibbutz. Her parents were ambivalent at the thought of their "bird", as they called her, being locked in a cage, but Or herself wanted to be hospitalized. During my first meeting with the parents, Or's father said that she was his only daughter, who compensated him. (The Hebrew word *tmura* means both compensation and exchange); she was the one he loved. The mother, a slender, very feminine woman, said that she had watched Or closely from birth because there were complications with her birth and she was afraid something was wrong with her. Both parents are survivors of the Shoa.

* * *

Or says that she feels *transparent* and that people can see her insides. When she was a small child she had an imaginary world of an orphanage, where she was the only girl who was adopted. The orphans were her friends, and their home was in the walls and in the floor. The description was similar to a ghetto. She got rid of them at the age of 15 after she became anorexic, because "they" didn't agree to the anorexia. She wanted to become a *muselmann* weighing 27 kg, as her father had been. She still wishes for it. It may be said that her concentration on her body was a substitute for the orphanage. She went inside the walls (her body) and became *transparent*. After telling me of this phantasy, she dreamt of stepping on dead birds wherever she went.

* * *

Here we can see three moments of the gaze:

1. The gaze of the father—seeing his own father being killed. It is possible to say that Death gazed at him and determined his being.
2. The disavowed gaze—he sacrificed his truth as a subject in order to survive. What the unconscious thought was we don't know—perhaps it was the pleasure of staying alive that he couldn't bear. He said that the most important thing for him was staying alive. He was in the death line with his mother and sister, and somebody he knew by chance moved him into the line of life with his father. So his unconscious question may be—am I dead or alive? or, why am I alive while he is dead? Alternatively, the fear could be that there was nothing there except the gaze of death—his father looking at him looking at him, and what did the father say? Nothing. In all those years

there are no signifiers to symbolize that event, only the unbearable Real.

Lacan says that the gaze is the *objet á* that best evades castration. In this case, there was no lack and no symbolic law. Does this mean that everything is possible, like incest in the case of Lot?

3. The third moment is when Or has to fulfil the symbolic function of womanhood. She is caught between the anxious gaze of her mother and the disavowed gaze of her father, and she refuses to let the gazes encountering her derive *jouissance*. She refuses to become the object of sacrifice. She tries to become transparent. She poses the question to her father—"Father, can't you see?" But in the place of the father's name there is this avoidance, so she simultaneously incarnates the lack that the father does not want to acknowledge. The father used to say to her: "If the Nazis couldn't break me, you will not be able to break me either." Or told me she was angry with him for not breaking. She wanted him to break down.

In refusing to eat, she opens the dialectics of desire. The last time Or looked at herself in the mirror, she hated herself so much for being fat that she cut herself under the eyes.

* * *

Or's leading *phantasme* about her anorexia is seeing herself on her deathbed, connected to transfusions, while everybody around her is worried. Thus she responds to the father's unconscious wish to sacrifice his love object. At the same time that she poses the question of looking for desire, she is in danger of rejecting the symbolic law of the phallus as a lack—she is in danger of becoming the phallus.

A few years ago Or's father went back to Auschwitz, to the same spot where he saw his father being shot. He placed some stones on the spot, symbolically burying his family, and said the *Kadish* prayer. He thought that maybe that would help him understand the death of his parents and his sister.

Inasmuch as it can be stated that he was there, he feels that he wasn't there. Of course, this attempted repetition was a failure—one can never be at the spot where one is gazed at by the Other and still save the gaze. But after that, something happened: he broke down, and he became obsessed by his daughter's anorexia as though he knew the answer was there. The daughter's transparency helped him.

* * *

In looking for her desire he is looking for his own, which was petrified. The lost appetite for food indicates that the appetite is for desire. Or's father has ceased all his activities and has almost stopped living; he is on the verge of depression. Freud said about the melancholic subject that the latter knows whom he has lost but not what he has lost in him. If Or's father can allow the truth in the unconscious to come forward, if he can talk and recognize his desire, maybe his daughter can be freed from her lot as Lot's wife and be a woman again and, through her discourse, enter the field of the symbolic.

Primo Levi's suicide

In my opinion, Primo Levi's suicide symbolizes the end of narrative testimony. The question that bothered me while reading his last book, *The Drowned and the Saved*, was why he committed suicide when he finished writing this book, 40 years after his first book on the subject, *Ecce Homo*. Why, after 40 years of being a survivor, did he decide to succumb? (And he was not the only one: there were others, like Romain Gary, Jean Améry, Paul Celan, Bruno Bettelheim, and many more.)

In *The Drowned and the Saved*, Levi refers many times to his friend, the Jewish philosopher Jean Améry. Améry was also sent to Auschwitz. He gave his testimony and years later, in 1978, committed suicide. Levi argues with him in his book, as though struggling with his teaching, but perhaps that argument led to the identification. He admits that "To polemicize with a dead man is embarrassing and not very loyal, all the more so when the absent one is a potential friend and a most valuable interlocutor: but it can be an obligatory step" (Levi, 1988, p. 127).

To Améry—the young assimilated Jew whose real name was Hans Meier, whom only Nazism forced to return to Judaism—to be

Jewish was simultaneously impossible and obligatory. Here, says Levi, begins the split that will accompany him until his death and will be its cause. Améry accepted his Jewish identity out of dignity and not for any other reason, but as a Jew, quotes Levi, "[he will travel] through the world as a man afflicted by one of those diseases which do not cause great suffering but are certain to have a lethal end" (Levi, 1988, p. 129).

All of his book, according to Levi, is simultaneously a summary, a paraphrase, a discussion, and a critique of an essay by Améry, "The Intellectual in Auschwitz and at the Mind's Limits". The book in which it appears also has two titles, *Beyond Guilt and Reparation: An Attempt to Overcome by One Overwhelmed* (Améry, 1977).

* * *

When Levi argues with Améry's postulations, it sounds like a painful discussion with his inner self:

> This surrender before the intrinsic horror of the past could lead the scholarly man to intellectual abdication, furnishing him at the same time with the defensive weapons of his uncultivated companion: "It has always been like this, always will be like this".
>
> ... by his very nature the intellectual ... tends to become an accomplice of power, and therefore approves of it. He tends to follow in Hegel's footsteps and deify the state, any state; the sole fact of its existing justifies its existence. [Levi, 1988, pp. 144–145]

* * *

The believers withstood better the experience of the *Lager*, and more of them survived. Levi tries to show us, as Jorge Semprun says in his book *L'écriture ou la vie* (1994), that in the end nothing was true except the *Lager*; the rest simply was nothing but a short vacation, an illusion of the senses, a doubtful dream. That's it.

What was the hidden motive behind the suicide of the intellectuals? Was it the repeated missed encounter with the Real of silence that stood before them every time they tried to testify? Was it the presence of *jouissance* in the heart of testimony that only suicide can save from its horror?

* * *

After the war, a religious friend told Levi that his survival was not accidental, that he was a chosen man. Levi says: "I, the nonbeliever, and even less of a believer after the season of Auschwitz, was a person touched by Grace, a saved man. And why me? It is impossible to know, he answers. Perhaps because I had to write, and by writing bear witness" (Levi, 1988, p. 82). Testimony legitimizes the survival of the guilty, a legitimization that does not suffice. Levi responded to this decidedly:

> Such an opinion seemed monstrous to me. It pained me as when one touches an exposed nerve, and kindled the doubt I spoke of before: I might be alive in the place of another at the expense of another. . . . the "saved" of the Lager were not the best, those predestined to do good, the bearers of the message: what I had seen and lived through proved the exact contrary. Preferably the worst survived, the selfish, the violent, the insensitive, the collaborators of the "gray zone", the spies. . . . The worst survived, that is, the fittest; the best all died.
> . . . My religious friend had told me that I survived so that I could bear witness. I have done so, as best I could, and I also could not have done so; and I am still doing so, whenever the opportunity presents itself; but the thought that this testifying of mine could by itself gain for me the privilege of surviving and living for many years without serious problems troubles me because I cannot see any proportion between my privilege and its outcome. [Levi, 1988, pp. 82–83]

***

What is the result? The result is this incongruence, this gap between all the years of testimony and the silence of the *Geheimnisträger* [secret bearer], and maybe that was unbearable for Levi. The limit of narrative testimony, testimony that tries to tell "the whole truth", is not catharsis or liberation but suicide and death.

Shoa testifies through us

Before the end of this journey, I would like to refer to the function of art as a vehicle for transmitting testimony—the other kind of testimony that encircles the Real.

122   TESTIMONY

The art that "liberates" is that of contemporary artists who investigate the Real by means of repetition. The art from which testimony arises is not narrative but, rather, structural art, form-giving, that which I term "eyewitness testimony".

This is testimony that is connected to entropy, that deconstructs existing forms and encircles another place, another knowledge, knowledge that emanates from the Real, and so opens the possibility of breaking through a new *Holzweg*.

* * *

Let us take as an example Christian Boltanski, one of the most important artists of our time. In his exhibitions he collects old photos, clothes, and personal effects, presenting them as archetypal artefacts that trace an individual's life. Boltanski frequently uses documents of everyday currency—passport photos, class photos, and family albums, to evoke ordinary people: unidentified children who died in the Shoa, the burghers of a Swiss city, or the workers in a carpet factory. The spaces he creates, filled with flickering lights and shadows, and located somewhere between small theatres and churches, evoke a sensation of silent wonder and arouse a keen sense of loss.

Semin writes of Boltanski:

> We might suggest that a number of artists have answered Adorno's question (can we write or paint after Auschwitz?) by allowing images into their work, probably not in a concerted way, which confront the reality of the camps. . . . All of Christian Boltanski's work deals not with the memory of the Holocaust—then it would have been completed with the emergence of explicit pictures of the camps—but with the extraordinarily complex mechanisms that have made horror possible, with that which enables us to conceive the inconceivable.
>
> These complex mechanisms include what we might call the bankruptcy of language. [Semin, Garb, & Kuspit, 1997, pp. 82–85]

From an interview with Boltanski:

> "At the beginning of all the work there is a kind of trauma: something happened. This might be a psychoanalytic problem. All your life you can be telling the same story, but then you can tell it in different ways—through poetry, through song, etc. . . .

I only do what I do now because I used to be crazy. Art for me is one way of talking about problems and about the past; sometimes, as with psychoanalysis, you are a little better for having done so. . . . When I do a large piece with used clothes some people talk about it in relation to the Holocaust and say how sad the piece is. But children find it fun, it makes them happy because they can try on all the clothes. I never speak directly about the Holocaust in my work, but of course my work comes after the Holocaust. You know, at the end of the nineteenth century people believed that science was going to save us. Now we can see that things have gotten worse. . . ." [Semin, Garb, & Kuspit, 1997, pp. 8–19]

* * *

When Benigni, in his film *Life Is Beautiful*, is playing with his son and the boy says that perhaps the Germans are really making soap and buttons from the Jews, he laughs. He takes the seemingly "impossible assertion" to its absurd extreme. It is funny, and we laugh, but choke in the midst of our laughter, for we know that the son is right. Truth is revealed by way of its very impossibility. And, if so, this touches us in the Real, not the symbolic place. This is the testimony that bears witness not to knowledge, but to another place.

* * *

While working on the subject of Shoa I interviewed a relative of mine who was a partisan with Tito in Yugoslavia. One of the uncanny, horrifying stories he told me was the following: at some point in the war a group of partisans was captured and put in a concentration camp. The commander of the camp was a particularly cruel, sadistic person, who murdered prisoners in cold blood and abused them. One day the prisoners rebelled and managed to defeat the guards and take the commander captive. My relative's role was to keep watch of the commander all night in a wooden cabin up on the mountainside until the partisans came in the morning to try the man and punish him. The man did not stop talking all night. My relative remained silent. What did the commander speak about? Music. It happened that he was a music teacher by profession. At dawn he asked my relative what was going to happen to him. My relative answered: "The partisans will come and try you." "And what will they do to me?" asked the man anxiously. "They will probably kill you," answered my relative. "Me?" asked the man, totally overwhelmed and surprised, "It is not permitted to kill me, it is impossible to kill me, I have a family, I have kids!" And he took out his wallet and showed pictures of his wife and children to my relative, who had lost all his family.

His argument was completely logical—it was made inside the frame of the law, but it was really no better than tautology. His basic argument was that it was forbidden to kill him because: "I am me." And this deadly innocent argument evokes horror in us, horror that testifies through us.

I would like to conclude by quoting Paul Celan's poem once again, because no one can say it better than the poet:

"Out of the shattered
madness
I arise
and contemplate my hand
as it draws
the one and only
ring."

[Celan, 1976, p. 118; translated for this edition]

Out of the fracture, out of the loss of meaning, man arises and looks around; he liberates his gaze from the freezing death, he studies his hand drawing a unique and particular circle—it is drawn through the medium of himself.

PART IV

ART, LETTER

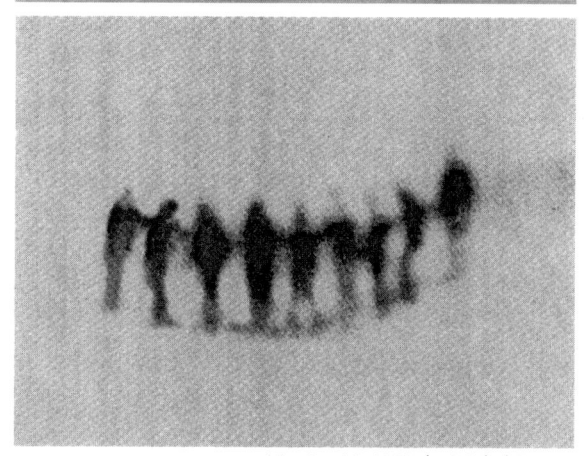

Merging 11, 1997, by Michal Rovner

CHAPTER EIGHT

The letter as place and the place of the letter

A Lacanian analyst says to his analysand who writes poetry: "The problem is that you are in love with the poems rather than with the unconscious." After some time, the analysand failed to find her place and left the analysis.

What does it mean to be in love with the unconscious? It means to want to know something about it. And a poem—is it not a love letter of the unconscious? (In French and in English, "letter" is an ambiguous word denoting both the text and the character that is its building block.) Does it not set the stage for a question regarding the unconscious?

Discussing ethics and knowledge, Kierkegaard asserts that:

> All knowledge has something captivating about it; but on the other hand it changes the state of the soul of the one who has it. The objectivity, the lack of interest, with which a psychologist counts a person's pulse-beats, or studies his nerves, have no relation to ethical enthusiasm ... the ethical is hostile to a body of knowledge which, after having consumed a man's whole life, ultimately ends in his not being able to explain the most important. [Kierkegaard, 1990, p. 100]

* * *

Žižek (1991) is surprised to learn that Lacan, in his later seminars beginning with *Encore* (1975a), rehabilitates the notion of the sign, after years of giving precedence to the notion of the signifier. While a series of contingently interdependent signifiers creates, a-posteriori, an effect of meaning, the sign preserves the continuity with the Real (Žižek, 1991).

In the case of signifiers, every element exists only in its "difference" from the others, without any support in the Real. Lacan tries to indicate the status of that letter that cannot be reduced to the dimension of the signifier—that is to say, that is pre-discursive, still permeated with the substance of *jouissance*.

In Hebrew, the word designating letter (in the sense of character), *ot*, also denotes sign: a heavenly sign, an omen; a sign from the Other. God in Hebrew is also called *Makom* (place). In the Kabbala, it is said that in order to create the universe, God had to reduce Himself—to make room, place, so to speak. He created the universe out of 22 letters. Hence, one may say that reduction allowed the letter to occupy a place. Although the sign's place is in "heaven", it is directed towards human beings.

In his seminar *Encore*, Lacan maintains that one letter can serve as a description of a place, the place of the Other (Lacan, 1975a). Lacan creates a word game, wishing us to hear the word "*signe* as *thing*"—the Thing, *das Ding*—thus emphasizing that the sign is closer to the Real order than to the symbolic.

* * *

Therefore, I claim that the letter is a primary element. It is located within a twilight zone. It does not yet belong to the symbolic order, being meaningless in itself, but does not belong to the Real order either—being, as Lacan says, an effect of discourse: pre-discursive on the one hand, an effect of the discourse on the other. This may sound paradoxical, but if we take the interlocked circles of the Borromean Knot, then the letter is located at the juncture point between the circles, for the Real is not the "natural", the "biological", just as the drive is not an instinct. It is located as a concept in-between the physical and the psychic. One may perhaps say that the letter is a threshold—threshold in the sense of edge, border.

Lacan takes as an example the common sign of smoke, which cannot exist without fire. Smoke is a sign of fire, but also a sign

The Borromean Knot

of the smoker. Everyone knows, says Lacan, that if you see smoke when approaching a deserted island, there is probably someone there who can light fire. According to Lacan, a signifier may become a sign. If the signifier represents a subject for another signifier, then it may be said that the signifier is a sign of the subject (Lacan, 1975a).

The letter is, thus, a type of sign. From the moment of its formation, the necessity to decipher—the division between the material and its decoding—emerges. Hieroglyphic writing is perhaps the first instance of writing being a pictographic script, but it is already a sign script that requires decoding. Lacan discusses the Phoenician writing that was found before the time of Phoenicia on Egyptian potshreds, which were used for marking jugs. That is, letter emerged from the market, which is in itself an effect of discourse.

* * *

That brings me back to writing. The sign renders signs. It is a type of drawing, drawing in the Real. In the sixteenth century, a scholar named Zucceri called drawing *disegno interno*, implying that:

> Drawing is not merely another projection of foreknowledge onto paper. . . . The way in which the hand and the pencil conceive the form, uncover it through inquisitive roaming, the way in which a body materializes, crystallizes on the paper. Unrepresented, not projected from the outside, rather formed somehow from the chaos of reflection. . . . [Geva, 1994, p. 42; translated for this edition]

* * *

Aristotle defines the individual merely as a body—body as an organism; one that is sustained as such, rather than multiplies. Lacan asks: Is the body not the knowledge of the "one"? And he replies: the disclosed knowledge of the "one" does not come from the body. It comes from the signifier "one" (Lacan, 1975a).

Are letters akin to signs of drawing on the body, which render the sexual difference? The letter, being meaningless, like matter, belongs to the feminine function, but it is no longer matter. Writing already has a phallic value; it is a division (between the object and the meaning) and a union at the same time.

In *Encore*, Lacan states that writing does not belong to the same order as the signifier. Freud maintains that the aesthetic pleasure offered by the writer possesses the nature of foreplay.

Hence, the effect of the letter is a beginning of drawing, a continuation of the movement of thought from the outside inwards. This drawing can become the symbolic that ploughs a furrow in the enjoying Real. In the case of the psychotic, the letter as sign can become a burn in the Other's body.

Psychotics write. Writing can organize them around themselves as a kind of symptom, around which an identity can be stabilized. Lacan calls this *"sinthome"* (a word play between "symptom" and *"saint homme"*), as he affirms with regard to Joyce's writing. But one can ask whether, in their writing, there is something of the drawing—whether it is not an attempt to avoid the control of the Other, who marks the psychotic?

* * *

When the ten plagues are described in the Passover *Hagadah* (the tale of the Exodus read by Jews on Passover Eve), it is said that "Rabbi Yehuda gave abbreviations . . ." (in direct translation from Hebrew: "Rabbi Yehuda gave them signs . . ."), signs in the sense of characters in mathematics. Lacan says:

> I based the analytical discourse on a precise articulation which is written on the board in four letters . . . this writing is part of a primary reminder, that the analytical discourse is a new type of relation relying only on that which functions like speech, within something that may be defined as a field. . . . In order to explain the functions of this discourse I used a number of letters. First, *a*, which I called "object", yet it is but a letter. Then *A* . . . I described that which is first of all a place. I said, the place of the Other. . . . [Lacan, 1975a, pp. 27–28]

* * *

The ten plagues are but signs. The object is but a letter, and the letter occupies the object's place. This takes me back to the example I gave at the beginning of this essay: love of the unconscious as opposed to love of the poem.

In his speech entitled "The Meridian", on the occasion of receiving the Büchner Prize, Paul Celan maintains that: "The Poem holds its ground on its own margin. In order to endure, it constantly calls and pulls itself back from an *'already-no-more'* into a *'still here'*" (Celan, 1986, pp. 48–49).

One may say that the poem occupies a similar place to that of the letter: an intermediate zone that corresponds with the unconscious.

* * *

In an exhibition catalogue of Michal Rovner's photographs, I found an essay regarding her works as a confrontation with Leibnitz's question, "Why is there not nothing?":

> In Rovner's pictures, the answer is uncertain. It struggles. The pictures say: there is not nothing for a moment really. Nothing calls out to being, asking it to come back . . . it is as though in breaking down the photograph Rovner attempts to re-discover the building blocks. She presents matter as deconstructed, vague, weightless and experimental. [Madoff, 1993, p. 4]

When she photographs a house, she sees it as a sign of matter that uncovers itself. She exposes it as a letter, searches for signs in the matter, signs of a subject in the most elementary place—in the tension between nothing and something.

"The photograph has no referent," says Madoff. It requires an act of decoding, which will already expropriate the form's status as a sign, turning it into a signifier. The decoding will compose words of the letters, words that will be interdependent in a link that will render meaning. Rovner entitles the series of photographs *One Person's Game Against Nature*, in the sense of computer games. Man writes the program of the world in letters. But letters originate elsewhere—not from his symbolic set. Again, the letter appears simultaneously as an effect of discourse and as a pre-discursive place. Madoff quotes the seventeenth-century English writer Thomas Brown: "There is something in us that can be without us, but cannot tell how it entered into us" (Madoff, 1993, p. 6). This immediately brought to mind Lacan's definition of the object of love—something within us that is more than ourselves, and can be mutilated. That something is the letter. From the *already no more* to the *still here* . . .

CHAPTER NINE

The Act in psychoanalysis and art

When discussing Lacan, the focus is usually on language, the symbolic dimension, the chain of signifiers and the like, since French thought in the last decades—structuralist as well as post-structuralist—has often dealt with language and its importance.

It is also conventional to relate to psychoanalysis in terms of language, to use Lacan's words. That seems to be the obvious way to relate to it since language is the tool that psychoanalysts use, and also because speech is the principal activity in psychoanalysis. In psychoanalysis, people express their suffering verbally. In speaking, they ask for something, they want something from the analyst, and thus the opportunity for change opens up.

Through speech we try to bring about change in the structure of the subject. This is possible because the subject is also an effect of language. Thus, in analysis we try to cause a change in the patient's symptoms, to grant them meaning.

Lacan talked a lot about the signifier and the signified, metaphor and metonymy, the way patients relate to the material and to dreams, and unintentional declarations as texts to be deciphered—hence his famous saying, "The unconscious is structured like language".

Placing so much emphasis on the dimension of language, however, is liable to distort or be misleading—even for people interested in Lacan. This applies especially in the case of intellectuals who do not engage in clinical work; those who perceive psychoanalysis as merely another theory and who ignore the aspect of psychoanalysis that eludes language—the realm of the Real.

Since at this point I want to touch on the practice of art or artistic creation, I shall discuss Lacan from the aspect of the Act in relation to the Real, which deviates from the realm of language.

* * *

Lacan was neither a theoretician nor a philosopher, but a psychiatrist who, like Freud, evolved through clinical work. His clinical observations provide the basis of his theory and substantiate it. Psychoanalysis was born as a practice—not in a university.

It developed from the accounts of the hysterical women who told Freud of their desires. Through their complaints of their pains and anxieties and through the symptoms they exhibited, they showed him the difference between biological instinct and drive—the difference between bodily anatomy and the erogenous structure of the body.

* * *

Post-structuralists and post-modernists say that there is no meta-language—that the truth is in the text itself. The interpretation of a literary work is an inseparable part of the work itself. All statements are metonymic—interchangeable with other words of similar meaning. There is no object.

Lacan, however, insisted that metaphor is more important than metonym—metaphor cuts, which means in effect that a new dimension is added when something is expressed in different words. Sense arises from nonsense, and that which remains beyond sense peers out from metaphor as an object—hence the Act is a kind of cut.

I should add that meta-language exists in the Real rather than the imaginary realm—remaining an impossibility, even though it is unavoidable.

There is no language that does not have its external object. The motion of the chain of signifiers is not endless; rather, it orbits a particular void that embodies the lost object.

* * *

In reading Freud thus, Lacan found a philosophical context to anchor his psychoanalytic discoveries. Freud, on the other hand, hoped to have his discoveries anchored in biological or neurological findings. However, both points of view constitute different types of metaphor, each having developed from its own domain.

It has to be emphasized that psychoanalysis is not just another form of knowledge to be added to the universal body of knowledge. It is a form of ethics dealing with human desire—the desire that stems from something basic that is lacking. This lack is therefore vital to structure—it can only be filled fleetingly by substitute objects. Such objects cannot make the lack go away, but they certainly can make it hurt less.

Psychoanalysis deals, then, with that which is particular to each person—with the subject as a subject of desire. Hence, despite science's aspiration towards the universality of knowledge, psychoanalysis can be termed "The Science of the Particular".

* * *

So, psychoanalysis deals with what is lacking in human beings, a lack that cannot be formulated in words because it falls between the words.

Between the words lies concealed the desire for something else—always for something else. Any need can be fulfilled. Any object that is wanted is obtainable—except for love. The gap that lies between need and demand generates desire. Desire is persistent and cannot be eliminated. As far as desire is concerned, any object is only partial.

* * *

Lacan speaks of the alienation that develops in humans right from the start—at the stage termed the "mirror stage", when babies encounter their own reflection in the mirror and a figure of significance to the baby points to the mirror and says: "That is you!" The first alienation is connected with this primal phenomenon, which is also the basis for the construction of self-identity (the ego).

Lacan says that the role of the "mirror stage" is that of "imago"—the formation of the imaginary link between external reality and one's inner world. Here, of course, we encounter a fundamental disparity between the immaturity of the human child and the imagined completeness of the image in the mirror. Through that mirror image of another, the baby gains an initial notion of its own physical completeness and the control it has over its movements. While the baby can actually see these things, the inner sense of itself that it continues to have is referred to by Lacan as *corps morcelé* [dismembered body].

The illusion of unity is what fundamentally separates man from nature and what determines what is lacking in relation to nature. This primal image of the body constitutes the primal I and is that which gives form to the libido—meaning that it reorganizes the drive. The imaginary creation of the I alienates because it is based on the Other that is beyond the subject and also because imaginary identification divides the subject itself.

The I does not contain desire in its entirety: a certain amount remains surplus, on the exterior, continuing to impede us even as we remain unaware of it.

* * *

In Seminar II, Lacan contends that right from source there is something fundamentally wounded in the way humans relate to the world. Human desire, Lacan says (in the wake of Hegel's dialectic concept of master and slave), forms under the sign of mediation. First and foremost, man's desire is for his desire to be recognized, which is what determines the structure of desire as desire of the Other. The object of desire is essentially the object that is desired by the Other (Lacan, 1978).

The dream of the butcher's wife

An example of the aforesaid is the case of the butcher's wife's dream in Freud's *The Interpretation of Dreams*.

Desiring to prove to Freud that he was mistaken in interpreting every dream as the fulfilment of a wish, the shrewd wife of a butcher told him that she would relate the contents of her dream, specifically because it did not seem to be a response to a wish.

In her dream, *the butcher's wife had to prepare a meal but she only had a small piece of salmon. She wanted to go shopping for more but remembered that it was Sunday. She wanted to order by phone but the phone did not work.*

The manifest content of the dream contains the frustration of a pre-conscious wish—to give a dinner. Actually the butcher's wife does not like salmon, but her slim female friend, who wanted to come for dinner, does.

The butcher is fond of her slim friend, despite the fact that his usual taste is for plump women. His wife prefers caviar herself, but she asks her husband not to give her caviar—that is, not to give her what she likes.

What does the butcher's wife actually want of him? Not to give her what she wants—to leave the matter of desire an open question. What Freud discovered was that what the hysterical woman desired was the desire of the Other (Freud, 1908e [1907]).

* * *

Lacan continues his analysis of Freud and shows that the hysterical woman wants either to maintain the lack or give rise to it in the Other (Lacan, 1966a).

In the desire itself there is *jouissance*. What is the butcher's wife asking? What every woman would ask due to her being hysteric: How can another woman be loved by a man? In this case it is the patient's husband, who in fact could not be satisfied by her slim friend because he likes plump women.

Behind the desire for caviar is a kind of desire for unrequited desire. This question turns the hysterical women into a unique subject (which could be seen as a query in regard to the woman's essence). The woman thinks that the answer lies with the man or with another woman, but in the end the object does not have an answer because it, too, is lacking, it, too, lacks the word. Structure is built around this lack.

The Act in psychoanalysis

Now we can turn to examining the nature of the Act in psychoanalysis. The legend goes:

> When God appeared in order to give the law unto Israel, he did not appear only before Israel, he was revealed unto all nations and tongues. First he appeared before the sons of Esau and said unto them "Do *you* want to receive the law?" and they said unto him "What is written in it?" and he said "Thou shall not kill". They said unto his blessed visage "But Lord of the universe, killing is all Esau has" as it is said "And the hands were Esau's, and Isaac blessed him and said unto him thou shalt live by thy sword."
>
> And he took comfort and went unto the children of Amon and Moab. They asked what is written in the law ... in the end he reached the Children of Israel who replied in one voice "We will do and we will hear". [Bialik & Ravizky, 1936, p. 104; translated for this issue]

All the other nations first wanted to know what was written. They wanted to base their decision on knowledge, but the Children of Israel put everything on the line. Such is the Act, which is, according to Lacan's definition, a deed that has not been determined by any kind of previous knowledge, something that goes against the flow of knowledge.

Jacques Alain-Miller said of this that the manifold significance of thought, speech, and language are abandoned in favour of the Act.

* * *

The Act takes place when one detaches oneself from the guarantee of that Other with which, so it is believed, lies knowledge—the parent, the state, university. When it is realized that the Other is also lacking, inconsistent, and that it also desires, then a total gamble is embarked upon that may or may not fail, following which the subject changes, or, as Lacan put it: a new subject is born.

We will only know in retrospect that the Act took place, due to its effects. For example, a youth deciding on a particular profession, despite what he has been told: in such an Act there is a form of rejection of authority and knowledge, or what can be described as *initiation*—not something that can be interpreted: further discussion of it would be superfluous.

However, not all rebellions are Acts. In 1968 Lacan infuriated French students when he told them that the only aim of their revolt was to topple one master in order to identify with another, meaning that their case did not constitute an Act.

* * *

I emphasize that the Act transforms the subject. It occupies the place of enunciation (declaration, announcement, certainty), in the wake of which one should keep quiet.

Lacan said that the Act turns the chatter of the *phantasme* into the silence of the drive (Lacan, 1973).

Hamlet, for example, was not able to perform what had been demanded of him. His tragedy was actually the tragedy of rejection, procrastination, and inaction and of complaining rather than acting:

> Sir, in my heart there was a kind of fighting,
> That would not let me sleep: methought I lay
> Worse than the mutines in the bilboes. Rashly,
> And prais'd be rashness for it, let us know,
> Our indiscretion sometimes serves us well,
> When our deep plots to pall: and that should
> Learn us.
>
> [*Hamlet*, V:ii]

But Hamlet's Act could actually have been the refusal to commit what had been asked of him. I would add that in the context of the Act, Kierkegaard differentiates between the poet and the hero, saying thus:

> The poet or orator can do nothing that the hero does; he can only admire, love, and delight in him.... he takes nothing of his own but is zealous for what has been entrusted.... it is the sin of poeticizing instead of being, of standing in relation to the Good and the True through imagination instead of being that, or rather existentially striving to be it.... when the spirit cannot reach realization in its eternal world, it stands aside, rejoicing in the images reflected in the clouds and crying as they vanish. Then it is a poet.... [Kierkegaard, 1954, p. 34; translated for this issue]

In Kierkegaard's metaphor, a neurotic is a person who wants to be a hero so very much but cannot be because he is divided. He also does not allow himself to be a poet *because* of the fact that he wants to be a hero. In this state he turns to the therapist, who asks him to start talking: "Start composing so that you will be able to reach the point of being a hero, if you still want that. Look for the words that will enable you in the end either to reach the point of enunciating—or find your silence."

This differentiation between poet and hero could be described as being of an entirely imaginary nature, and Kierkegaard's lack is in his failure to recognize that an artistic creation can be an Act.

* * *

As mentioned, the Act functions against the flow of knowledge, as if cutting into language—interrupting. Assuming that language is dominated by phallic law, which says that there are those that "have it" and there are those who "do not" (or, there are those who have a phallus and there are those who are castrated), we perceive that the Act does not stem from phallic law, which determines that all scientific knowledge is connected to phallic law and every meaning leads in the end to phallic significance. The phallic signifier guarantees all meanings.

In the Act there is a kind of rejection of the phallus and creation of another kind. Women are not entirely subject to this law, which is why the Act takes place when that same veiled desire becomes apparent, shattering existing phallic frameworks. This secret desire is feminine desire—like that in the butcher's wife's dream: the desire for desire to be recognized, to open up lack. If this is so, perhaps it may be said that artistic creation tries to open up lack in the world.

Sublimation

The term that Freud instigated in regard to what motivates us is *Trieb* [drive].

The concept of drive is emphasized here because it is neither physical nor spiritual. It is not an entity—it is a dynamic that has an objective: to satisfy itself.

It can be satisfied by obtaining the same object that satisfied it in the beginning: the missing or lost object. Such an object could be in form of the mother's breast or her gaze—the gaze in which he saw himself loved, saw himself as an ideal. Since such objects have been lost, the subject finds all kinds of substitute objects for itself. Culture in its entirety is built on such substitute objects.

Sublimation is the process that deals with the challenge of satisfying drives not by affecting the drive (by repression or subjugation, for instance) but by transforming the object. Sublimation means displacement of the libido: drives cannot be subjugated but objectives can be shifted in ways that can grant them legitimacy from the social point of view.

* * *

Subjugation also involves resistance—the resistance of culture to the original satisfaction of the drive. Freud found similarity between the ways cultures develop and the way in which the libido of the individual develops. Drives, such as anal eroticism, for example, have to displace the conditions for their gratification, leading them to alternative paths. Sublimation of the drive enables the higher faculties (scientific, artistic, or ideological) to become active, to play such an important role in cultural life.

In this, there is an attempt to grasp the rope at both ends: on the one hand, the chance of authentic gratification; on the other, objects endowed with collective social value that have undergone development of the imaginary and phantasmic dimension. Sublimation is usually compared with desexualization, with the libidinal investment displaced from being a crude object (which is supposed to gratify basic drives) to a higher and more cultured form of gratification—for example, writing poetry instead of engaging in sexual intercourse.

Actually, though sublimation and desexualization are not at all connected, in Lacan's view (which relates to the object not as a specific object but as the presence of the absence of an object) this is the basic lack around which the entire structure is organized, the essential lack around which the drive is formed. The lack that is granted positive existence through the formless form of the Thing, *das Ding*.

The sublimated object, Lacan said, is an ordinary day-to-day object of no importance, elevated to the glorious level of the Thing—the embodiment of nothing-at-all.

Therefore, sublimated objects represent the paradox of the object that can only exist in the shadows, mediated, veiled, hidden away. In the XIth seminar, Lacan called it "the beauty behind the veil". The moment one tries to reveal the essence by driving away the shadows, all that is left is a simple and insignificant object.

* * *

Now for an example taken from Lacan's VIIth seminar, *The Ethics of Psychoanalysis*: Lacan relates that during the Nazi occupation of France he visited his friend the poet Jacques Prévert, at whose place he found a collection of matchboxes. That was the only sort of collection that was permitted at that time. It had been aesthetically arranged to form an arch. The surprising thing, which was also gratifying for the collector, was that those empty boxes revealed something that was not generally noticed: they revealed that they were not just an object, they were impressive due to their quantity and the manner in which they had been set out. The matchboxes were elevated to a glory that was not previously theirs (Lacan, 1986).

To return to Lacan's sentence, contending that sublimation elevates the object to the level of the Thing—this is, in essence, a veiled and hidden object that inevitably must be exposed by the movement that goes on around it. Approaching it when it is too close creates a sense of dread or of the uncanny. As Freud put it, complete sublimation is not possible: something wild is always left out, impossible to sublimate, and attempts to completely sublimate a drive are always likely to fail. They could even lead one to suicide attempts, either physical or spiritual, as in the case of many artists.

The drive that represents itself as the death drive erupts and detaches from the libido since, according to Freud, sublimation is paid for in living flesh (a statement that I shall refer to further on).

* * *

The object only appears when it is covered—that is, it is represented by something else, language. Picasso used to say: "I do not seek, I find." Obviously what is found is what has been sought after, but it is found via the paths of the signifier—of language. The question is, how does the connection between the person and the signifier—language—lead to a connection with the object that is beyond language? Perhaps this is the place of the Act. In reference to this, Lacan said that the signifier engraves furrows in the Real (thus, we could say that it is connected to the death drive that lies at the heart of the sublimated object).

So, there is language and there is beyond language; there is sublimation and there is that which cannot be sublimated; there is the "Law of the Father", which veils, and there is that which is not entirely subject to the "Law of the Father". Lacan called this leftover, this excess, *jouissance*. The Act therefore is likely to be connected to this leftover, this surplus, which can neither be enclosed nor defined but which lives and breathes and informs of its presence through the discontent that is in culture. From time to time it erupts like boiling lava, bringing about not inconsiderable changes in the structure of the culture.

The Act in art

According to Lacan, the Act on the part of the painter is in directing his gaze—an Act that transfers to something material, "If a bird were to paint would it not be by letting fall its feathers, a snake by casting off its skin, and a tree by letting fall its leaves?" (Lacan, 1973, p. 114).

Lacan likens painting to rain falling from the brush. The Act is the gaze. This is a special type of gaze followed by the appearance of a gesture, a movement of the brush that reaches the canvas and is trapped there.

* * *

Towards the end of his life, Picasso became captivated by the rhythm of repetitious motions, by the pulsation of variation. He would paint the same motif over and over again with slight variations. He said that he was particularly interested in the motion of painting, the dramatic transition from view to view in which the transition is not realized: "the movement of my thought interests me more than my thought itself" (Krauss, 1988, p. 74).

This leads to the question of whether modern art is interested less in objects than in the movement that occurs around such objects, in the hope that through such repetitious motion it will be possible to touch, through art itself, that which is beyond sublimation, to touch that unbearable remnant that continues to pulsate.

Following Plato, Lacan called this remnant *lamella,* a kind of living flesh beyond the symbolic envelope, a yolk continuing in motion, the kind of thing that finds good description in science-fiction movies.

* * *

Does the artistic Act create lack in the world? Perhaps this is what Lacan meant when he said that all art is organization around emptiness. In *The Ethics of Psychoanalysis* he illustrated this by referring to pottery—the oldest form of art in the world (Lacan, 1986). According to Lacan, the world was created by the potter, not by God. They both created the world out of nothing. How can something be created out of nothing, asks Lacan. By attaching a number to it. By counting the nothing as one and turning it into one nothing. This could be called an Act of creation: is nothingness created or does creation take place from within nothingness? Is nothingness located somewhere or is it nowhere?

* * *

Many are familiar with either the book *The Neverending Story* or its movie version. It begins with nothingness swallowing up the land of Fantasia. The will-o'-the-wisp, one of the emissaries hurrying to the ivory tower of the childish empress in an effort to save Fantasia, relates that Lake Foamingbroth disappeared one day:

> "'You mean it dried up?' Gluckuk inquired.
> "No," said the will-o'-the-wisp. "Then there'd be a dried-up lake. But there isn't. where the lake used to be there's nothing—absolutely nothing. Now do you see?"
> "A hole?" the rock chewer grunted.
> "No, not a hole," said the will-o'-the-wisp despairingly. "A hole, after all, is something. This is nothing at all."

The three other messengers exchanged glances.

"What—hoo—does this nothing look like?" asked the night-hob.

"That's just what's so hard to describe," said the will-o'-the-wisp unhappily. "It doesn't look like anything. It's—it's like—oh, there's no word for it." [Ende, 1979, p. 21]

There is no word for *that*: it is not represented, but it is clear that it has motion, which can only be stopped by linkage with a word or, to be more precise, by naming. That's the task of Bastian (a young boy, the central character in the story)—to give the childish empress a new name. This description adeptly clarifies the dimension that Lacan termed the "Real". The Real, then, is not empty; it is a dense mass of nothing at all. In order for something to be created, it has to be penetrated by lack, which is represented by the signifiers.

* * *

In pottery, emptiness is created from a mass of clay. The clay pot contains emptiness—which facilitates filling. The pitcher is the object produced in order to represent the existence of emptiness at the centre of the Real that is termed the Thing.

This emptiness is represented nihilistically—of nothing. Thus the potter creates the pot with his hands encircling that emptiness, forming it, like the mythical creator, *ex nihilo*—meaning the potter commences by making a hole, that is the entrance of the signifier, which is the pot. Within it the signifier contains the concept of *ex nihilo* creativity.

Lacan said that producing the pitcher does not represent a vessel but, rather, something more akin to a ring. There is emptiness both within and without—like Henry Moore's sculptures, in which void has positive form and the sculpture is penetrable.

The void is a part of it. If emptiness is the Real and the pitcher is the signifier, then the creator—the artist or artisan—is the mediator between them.

What man creates is itself of the realm of sublimation. In this sense sublimation is always determined by emptiness, which constitutes the realm of the death drive. In the end the created thing will always indicate emptiness because it can only be represented by another thing.

This concept of everything touching everything (when "everything" is bound by the formless whole) is an echo of what in the ancient world was called primeval, raw matter. Marlo Ponti termed this principle "the flesh of the world" (Lacan, 1973, p. 82) and contended that the visual field is an incision in that flesh.

In this context, one should bear in mind that Freud said that sublimation is paid for in living flesh. If that is so, we can say that sublimation is a kind of cut. If all things are connected and touching and if we want to define a field in which there are various discernable positions such as those of the observer and the observed, we have to insert an incision, a rift. If not, touching or being touched are liable to be indistinguishable from one another, like clasped hands. The reply to the Zen koan "What does one hand clapping sound like?" could be "Clapping thus is touching emptiness", meaning that art has produced this division, this lack—particularly modern art.

The hole in the flesh of the world

Modern art, particularly, indicates the formation of lack in our world in that it takes day-to-day objects from shops, rubbish dumps, and even theoretical texts and turns them into works of art. However, the sculptor taking a piece of marble from an Italian quarry is also expropriating for himself a concrete object from the world.

In any event, it is clear that the artist creates a rift in the flesh of the world—void in place of what previously was. What leads us to state that some form of object had previously been there is the fact that there is now nothing-at-all. That is absence—the lack that indicates the object.

Once the artist has "acted within" the piece of marble, it looks less like it originally did than do modern materials such as Andy Warhol's Cornflakes cartons.

What leads the beholder to suppose that what he is seeing is something other than a lump of marble or a load of Cornflakes cartons? Why should he not open a carton and eat from it? If this happens, it means that the artist has failed to achieve his objective. What, then, holds the artistic materials in place? What prevents them from returning to the place from whence they came? One reason is that the created object is empty—empty also of its daily usage.

* * *

Even if the carton is actually full, the fact of its being a work of art points against opening it or eating the contents. The difference, then, between a tin of food in a supermarket and that tin in a gallery is that in the gallery it is empty. The fact of its emptiness and its marked similarity to any other tin creates the effect of an optical illusion (*trompe-l'œil*), which is also its aim.

Another reason for the difference is, of course, context and syntax, like Jacques Prévert's matchbox collection: the manner in which the object is arranged in relation to its surroundings has to differ from that of, for example, a supermarket.

For Cornflakes cartons to become a work of art they have to be seen as something other than just cartons. The results of artistry must exceed the mere promise of gratification through devouring the contents. The beholder is supposed to be made aware that he is seeing more than just Cornflakes cartons by the fact that they are arranged in a manner indicating a factor beyond their own form or contents. If the observer knows what is *not* before him (as opposed to what he is seeing), the cartons will appear differently to him from how they would if they were on a supermarket shelf. In the same way, when we look at Michelangelo's *David*, we don't see it merely as a lump of marble.

As Freud notes in his dissertation "Negation", through negation we know something of the gap, the rift, about the lack in the subject (Freud, 1925h). The process is similar to the machinations of the unconscious: we can know more about something through negation or error than we would through being actually told about it. For example, when a person says of a character in one of his dreams "It wasn't my mother in the dream", it is even more obvious that the character he saw was, in fact, his mother than if he had stated outright, "It was my mother in the dream!"—we become aware of the unconscious through the resistance to it.

* * *

Lacan gave another example of visual deception with the old story of two artists—Zeuxis and Parrhasios—who compete to see who can paint a bunch of grapes so realistically that the birds will try to eat from the painting (Lacan, 1973). Zeuxis unveils his painting, and the birds indeed approach in order to eat from it. Beamingly confident of victory, he turns to Parrhasios and asks him to unveil his painting to see whether the birds will come to eat from it. Zeuxis loses the competition when it turns out that Parrhasios has only painted a curtain—to deceive not only the eyes of the birds but the eyes of the artist as well.

* * *

Returning to my contention: sublimation occurs in the face of resistance to the direct gratification of a drive. Sublimation displaces the objective of a drive from the object itself to whatever cloaks it. Lacan does point out that it lies beyond the symbolic realm, because it creates a fissure through which the object can peep out. Art is a mask that is intentionally left incomplete. Art does not belong to what other psychoanalysts call "the preverbal stage"; rather, it is verbal in the second degree, meaning that it causes us to express truth through the *structure* of language, without, in most cases, using language itself.

This enables art to pass on knowledge through non-academic channels and discover new knowledge, like the Act. The Act moves against the flow of existing knowledge, but in taking this different direction it invents new knowledge or metaphors.

* * *

In the illusion of sublimation, there is something through which the illusion destroys itself. Illusion shows that it is there only as signifier cloaking the void.

Art imitates the objects that it represents, but its purpose is not to represent them. In imitating the object it actually transforms, so it only appears to be imitating. The more the object is represented by imitation, the more and more it opens the realm in which illusion is destroyed and alludes to something else.

In other words, in that well-ploughed phallic meadow there still peeks a rock that has not been removed, or weeds still grow there—this is the feminine Act, which the phallus cannot cover. Perhaps this is the real objective of art.

I return to Lacan's fine saying about painting: "If a bird were to paint would it not be by letting fall its feathers, a snake by casting off its skin, and a tree by letting fall its leaves?" (Lacan, 1973, p. 114).

This, then, is the Act, committed through gazing—reorganizing that dripping or shedding in a new way.

I am concluding with one of Lorca's poems:

> I come to you with three wounds,
> The wound of life
> The wound of love
> The wound of death.

According to Lacan, a man relates to the world in a fundamentally wounded way. The point of the poem is what it does not mention. Perhaps the missing line should read: the poem itself has been written, the artistic creation masks those wounds while simultaneously revealing them.

CHAPTER TEN

The return of Orpheus—
a psychoanalytic view
on realism in contemporary art

The psychoanalytic viewpoint referred to in this chapter takes in two seemingly unrelated exhibitions. One is a retrospective exhibition, at the Metropolitan Museum in New York, of Lucien Freud's work. (Lucien Freud is Sigmund Freud's grandson and is considered to be one of the greatest realist painters of our time.) The other is Tsibi Geva's exhibition called *Blinds*, held at a venue in Tel-Aviv. Geva—one of Israel's best-known contemporary artists—used realist objects: ordinary aluminium or plastic venetian blinds, with a thin layer of black or white paint having been laid on the closed slats. Both exhibitions, each shown on a different continent, aroused mixed feelings.

Despite the critics' definition of the Lucien Freud exhibition as "THE exhibition of the 90s", The Museum of Modern Art in New York refused to exhibit it, claiming that his work does not fit in with the discourse of modernist art.

Regarding the Geva exhibition, it was said among other things that

> Geva has executed a conceptual turnaround here, moving from "pretty, bourgeois" paintings of tiles and Arab head-dresses—which form a kind of peep-hole into a neighbouring reality

150

that is in the process of disappearing—to avant-garde paintings that explore blindness in a direct manner. If to some critics it has seemed that Tsibi Geva represents the kind of painting that rejects contemporary intellectual discussion, then here he has tried to execute a complete turnaround with an exhibition that is wholly environmental and conceptual. . . . The question is whether this successful shift can indeed "save" him from the rapid changes so characteristic of our time, which have to be acknowledged. . . . [Lusky, 1994, p. 14; translated for this edition]

Another critic wrote:

Geva challenges the disciplined and tedious act of painting. . . . In doing that he is belittling not only the artistic act but also the standing of the artist in the community, an artist who today seems more like a passive seismograph than an avant-gardist shaping the taste of the community in which he lives. . . . [Blich, 1994, p. 20; translated for this edition]

I chose to discuss these two exhibitions because I believe that they question, and even turn the tide on, the concept of realist representation in art, and the difference between it and abstract representation. This approach stands in contrast to that of the critics, who attempt to assign paintings to existing categories such as contemporary vs. non-contemporary, descriptive vs. conceptual, avant-garde vs. familiar, and so on.

In both of these exhibitions there is an attempt to cross boundaries, such as the boundary between the realistic and the abstract, the representative and the Real, and so forth.

* * *

In this article I try to link the work of painting with traversing (or failure to traverse) boundaries, as well as the traversing and repetition that lies at the foundation of contemporary art (the psychoanalytic term "repetition" refers to movement—namely, an Act rather than an object). I must admit that because of the attempt to traverse boundaries and to pose the aforesaid question in a way that is simultaneously manifest and latent, both exhibitions gave me a sense of unease.

It felt as if the familiar had suddenly turned strange, like the feeling that Freud referred to as "the uncanny" [*das Unheimliche*].

The familiar, the realistic, arouses distress by emerging suddenly from the depths of another world, which is non-realistic but definitely Real.

This "other world" can be described through the myth of Orpheus, which can be viewed as Freud viewed it—as a representative metaphor—or as something that "deals with paradox or contradiction, not by dissolving the paradox or resolving the contradiction, but by covering them over so that they seem (but only seem) to go away" (Krauss, 1986, p. 12). The myth of Orpheus alludes to art, hence its relevance to this discussion of the two exhibitions.

Orpheus, son of Apollo and Calliope, leader of the Muses, inherited his musical talent from his father. It is said that when he played, wild beasts and other forces of nature would gather around him, enchanted. He loved Eurydice, and lost her twice. The first time a snake bit her and she descended into Tartarus. Orpheus then boldly descended into Tartarus to search for her and fetch her back. The second time he lost her was when he turned his head back to gaze at her, even though Hades, king of the Underworld, had made the sole condition for her to return to life that Orpheus would not turn back to look at her until they come out of Tartarus. At that moment of gazing, Orpheus lost his love, but rescued art. It is said of him that he devoted the rest of his life to playing the lyre, until the Sabines became so jealous that they tore him to pieces.

In descending into the underworld, Orpheus crossed the border that separates life from death. Thus the failure of his deed became inevitable.

* * *

The French philosopher Maurice Blanchot analysed in depth the myth of Orpheus as a model for the dilemma that lies at the foundation of modern literary work—work that deals with the search of its own origin, while the origin is unattainable. According to Blanchot (1982), gazing at Eurydice regardless of the poem, with impatience and recklessness that caused the law to be forgotten—that is inspiration.

When Samuel Beckett speaks about modern art, he contends that we must endure the creative panic of the plunge into the unknown even though no other option exists but failure. He says that to be an artist means to fail as no one else dares fail. An artist is a person for whom failure is his entire world (Miller & Nelson, 1984). As in the myth of Orpheus, Beckett regards failure as a condition for the existence of art, or at least of modern art. Orpheus' failure stands as a representative metaphor for this claim. In the catalogue of Lucien Freud's exhibition, he describes a process whereby each completed picture reveals to its maker a "great insufficiency that drives him on" (in Lampert, 1993, p. 11).

* * *

Yves Alain Bois, in his article "Painting: The Task of Mourning" (1993), claims that modern painting deals solely with the death of painting, and with the discussion and representation of its end. According to this discourse, abstract painting should have stated the final truth and thereby run its course. At that time, the discourse revolved only around death, in all kinds of art, as well as in history (the death of the subject, the death of the novel, the end of history, the death of interpretation). Art was thus perceived as representing that which it refers to, and, in this sense, the time of realistic representation in art is long gone.

Bois refers to the trap of originality: he identifies the shock of the new in the perception of Baudelaire, who saw modernism and the value of innovation as being a source of trouble, because of the inevitable process wherein the new becomes old. The search after the totally new in art turns into a moment that cannot stop. It was Baudelaire who saw the connection between fashion and death. But Baudelaire never admitted that the new, which he sought after all his life, was made of the same materials as fashionable merchandise and was governed by the same market laws in terms of everything repeating itself. The drive for innovation is a double myth, because of its immanent extinction. Today's new is tomorrow's old. Innovation is thus like a guise adopted by the commodity.

In his discussion on Baudelaire, Bois talks about repetition in the new—namely, about the repeated drive to find a new object. Failure, of course, lies in the search itself.

* * *

In spite of the abysmal difference between the two exhibitions discussed in this article, they both deal with repetition from a different point of view: as a repetition of the attempt to cross boundaries and touch death, perhaps to pass through it and reach the lost object once again.

The source of repetition—and especially of the compulsion to repeat in psychoanalysis—is the death drive. As an example of repetition, one can consider the repetition of a nightmare that originates from shell-shock, or the repetition of a behavioural pattern suffered by an individual. In psychoanalytic repetition there is a crossing of boundaries and a feeling of the uncanny, and it always ends in a failure to capture or recapture the object, like Orpheus' failure to bring Eurydice back to the land of the living.

The compulsion to repeat is the attempt to recollect through movement, through an Act. Therefore, it is not related to the realistic realm; rather, it touches the Real, that same dimension that is present, yet cannot be described, in words. The Real is defined as that which repeatedly returns to the same place, though not precisely the same spot. The rendezvous with it is always lacking. This gap causes the repetition to fail, but perhaps, as in the myth of Orpheus, it also allows for the existence of art. Rosalind Krauss calls it "the pulse of art" (Krauss, 1988)—that is, the rhythmic on/off pulse that is a basic law of the unconscious and appears and disappears where the flow of discourse breaks ("now you see it, now you don't"). Krauss claims that this pulse is the source of many modern works of art, which have tried to base the autonomy of seeing as depending not only on space but on time as well.

Freud described this pulse when he spoke of his grandson, who, in reaction to his mother's absence, played with a cotton-reel, tossing it away from him and pulling it back, saying: *"fort/da"*—gone/here. This pulse is composed of presence and absence, of charge and discharge of erotic *jouissance* and anxiety—it is the death drive that operates beyond the pleasure principle, by means of repetition.

* * *

In other words, the purpose of the drive is not the same as that of the hunter trying to capture a bird, just as the aim of art is not to innovate more and more. The purpose of the drive is that the hunter will actually succeed in shooting, in releasing the arrow from the bow, in the creation of movement, whereas the purpose of art is to point towards that movement or its representation. The object is only that which is surrounded by the drive.

When Lacan refers to the work of art, he claims that the object is structured in a process that empties it of meaning, a process made possible by the drive surrounding it. When Picasso says, "The movement of my mind interests me more than the thought itself" (Krauss, 1988, p. 74), he is perhaps alluding to the same thing.

* * *

As I see it, Tsibi Geva indicates it by emptying the object—the venetian blind (*see next page*)—of all meaning and blocking the movement of the gaze. Lucien Freud, on the other hand, speaks of the insufficiency of the painting that drives him forward, when in each painting it seems as if he tries to re-penetrate through the protective layers and screens and get to that pure thought, emptied of meaning. Many of his sitters are also painted asleep or with their eyes closed: "Not having the look of the sitter, being them" (in Lampert, 1993, p. 12).

To return to the myth of Orpheus, we can learn that which structures it and makes it potentially eternal. There are two components: Orpheus' very attempt to cross the border between life and death by entering the Underworld, and the forbidden gaze that is the expression of that crossing—not necessarily the object itself (Eurydice).

* * *

Here we have to ask what is meant when we speak of realistic representation in art. The representation of the object or of movement? Realism of the world outside or an internal reality? Both exhibitions touched upon this question. It is as though the blinds that belong outdoors are placed here inside, and they represent the inside outside, or the outside inside, as with Möbius strips—the skin of Lucien Freud's sitters is a kind of topographical map.

In the next round, after the death of painting, nothing is left but the desire for painting, and then the backwards glance returns— not to the old and not even to more of the new, as Baudelaire says, but a return to another attempt to cross the border. As in the works

Untitled, 1993, by Tsibi Geva

of Lucien Freud, who crosses the figurative border, the realistic representation, thus Geva crosses the conceptual border. Both, in my view, attempt to traverse the borders and touch the Real.

* * *

In order to explain the Real and the place of the object in psychoanalysis, one should return to philosophy and to the beginning of the formulation of the modern subject. The one to begin this was Descartes, with the notion of *cogito ergo sum*—I think, therefore I am. Descartes listened to himself thinking, and instead of saying, "I believe in all the knowledge that I learned from my teachers", he cast doubt on that knowledge, emptied himself of it all, and observed doubt itself—thought itself. The thought is real because Descartes doubts knowledge and suspends the correspondence between the thought and things as they exist—namely, he delays the question of truth. Sigmund Freud, Lucien's grandfather, claimed that it is particularly the mistake, the dream, the slip of tongue that strengthen the certainty regarding the existence of thought. The certitude of existence for Freud is based, therefore, on error. He does not say: "I think therefore I am." On the contrary, he says: "I exist just where thought stops—the place where I get confused."

Kant distinguished between the "I think" model of thinking and the thinking matter itself: self-awareness makes present and transparent "the Thing" [*das Ding*] inside me that thinks (Žižek, 1993).

There is the person, and there is the I (the subject), whose status, according to Kant, is of logical construction that is both necessary and impossible—impossible in the sense that its concept can never be filled with the material of experiential reality. For Lacan, this is the concept of the Real, which he defines as being impossible: "I think" only insofar as I am inaccessible to myself as a being that thinks. The Thing is a primary object, it is lost (in our myth, it is Eurydice), and the phantasmic object is the material of the I, which fills its void, and is the realism (Orpheus' wish to bring his lover back to life). The act of "I think" is not an object of inner experience or intuition, it is empty. This lack of intuitive content is what structures the I, and the inaccessibility of the I to the core of its being is what transforms it into the I (Žižek, 1993).

* * *

Gazing at Tsibi Geva's blinds and the bodies in Lucien Freud's painting, it seems as if they are both trying to touch the presence of something that is absent, the void that is portrayed by *objet á*, that which has no representation—namely, the representation of the void. It is similar to Kant's distinction between the I and its material: it is a distinction far more radical than the one between subject and object. It could be said that an attempt is being made here to cross the boundary between subject and object, between external and internal, or even an attempt to say something about that which is unspeakable—that I whose existence can be deduced but no experiential reality can describe. This can be accurately felt in Lucien Freud's paintings of Leigh Bowers, especially in the large painting of the sitter's wounded back, as well as in the painted border on some of Geva's blinds, between black and white.

Sigmund Freud claimed that one can never know anything about that which is not connected to some sort of representation with some sort of language, not even on the unconscious level. By definition, the perceived I lacks intuitive content—it is an empty representation of a hole in the field of representation. For this reason, Meir Agassi wrote thus about Lucien Freud's power: " His power is based on the creation of an expanse—empty and naked, laconic and Spartan—between the viewer and the painting" (Agassi, 1994, p. 26, translated for this edition). He refers to the void between the painting and the viewer, but, in my opinion, the void and its representation can be seen in the painting itself.

Since there is a hole, a lack, room is created for the movement of desire, but the lost object becomes not the goal of desire, but the reason for it. Therefore, the desire is presented in the Lacanian psychoanalytic discourse as inextinguishable, because it is set into motion through a lost primary object, and each and every one of its courses is a search for that same lost object. There is no new object, original as it may be, that can satisfy desire; its fate is to continue its movement. No object is "it", "the Thing". The loss occurs due to the necessary mediation in our contacts with the Real—the mediation of language, representations called "the symbolic dimension". This mediation cuts off the "natural" cycle of our needs: the symbolic order introduces the concept of death. Lacan pointed out that Freud studied the meaning of life not in order to say that life has no meaning, but to say that life has only one meaning, that in which desire is borne by death. The function of desire should remain profound contact with death (Lacan, 1986).

* * *

This explanation brings us back to the myth of Orpheus, to his bungled return to the Underworld and his failed attempt to bring back his lover, and his stubborn attempt to cross the border between life and death: the attempt to cut a furrow in the Real by means of the symbolic—namely, to arrive not at the secret of death, but at the secret of life. That is also the nature of art—to cut a furrow in the Real through the symbolic, thereby revealing something of the Real.

Orpheus' gaze killed the object of desire, in this case Eurydice; he lost the object and saved the movement of art. Bois (1993), therefore, at the end of his intriguing article, states that the game of modernistic art may be over, but this does not mean that painting is dead. After the discussion on the death of art, we are left with the desire for painting. And this desire is not entirely programmed or subsumed by the market. The desire is the sole factor of a future possibility of painting (Bois, 1993).

Assuming that the death drive makes desire possible, then if Orpheus had brought Eurydice back to life, he would have closed up the lack of the object, and then art would no longer be possible or needed. The death drive is therefore what makes art possible and what enabled Orpheus to dedicate his life to playing the lyre.

* * *

In analysing the story of Antigone, Lacan speaks of two kinds of death—biological and symbolic. Antigone could not forego the symbolic order in the burial of her brother and was therefore doomed to be buried alive. This is a death that is lived by awaiting it, a death that crosses the border into the sphere of life, and life that crosses over into the reality of death. When this border is traversed—the way that the living Orpheus descended into the Underworld—"the beam of desire", as Lacan calls it, is both reflected and refracted until it produces the strangest and most profound effects. This, according to Lacan, is the effect of beauty on desire. Along its way, beauty only cleaves desire, because desire is not annihilated when it captures beauty; the desire continues to move, though the feeling that it has fallen captive is generated (Lacan, 1986). This is revealed by the splendour and the glory of the area that captivated it. (It is not by chance that the word *zohar*, meaning "splendour", which is the name of the mystical book of Jewish thought, is also used in that book to denote "creation".) Beauty captivates the desire, but destroys the object.

* * *

That was what I sensed when I witnessed the exhibitions of Tsibi Geva and Lucien Freud. I felt the power of the death drive behind the painted object, the emptying of the object of meaning. With Geva, it is a realistic object that has lost its realism, and perhaps it represents death. Lacan says that "the function of the beautiful [is] to reveal to us the site of man's relationship to his own death, and to reveal it to us only in a blinding flash" (Lacan, 1986, p. 295). By this he means symbolic death, man's connection to the lack in his being.

The plastic blind, the material on which Tsibi Geva paints, is a typical part of the Israeli symbolic field and is therefore completely realistic. After all, everybody is born into a particular symbolic field, and in this sense the aesthetic environment is part of our symbolic field and part of our culture. From the moment they open their eyes, the Italians and the French see surroundings designed in the grand tradition of art and architecture, not only exhibited in a museum, but part of everyday life, in the street and in the market. When they raise their eyes, they see marble walls decorated with stone engravings, wooden doors with carved reliefs of saints, or powerful church structures, while the aesthetic world that Israelis are born into is the world of plastic blinds and housing projects. The plastic blind is a piece of the world, a part of the urban nature upon which our gaze falls everyday, and it is therefore part of our symbolic field. The object itself, the awareness of its ugliness and practicality, are part and parcel of the cultural dialogue around us.

***

Modern artists often take pieces of their world and transform them into works of art—for example, Andy Warhol's soup or soda cans, Duchamp's urinal—and other useful objects are perceived as works of art in a certain context. This is analogous to the work of art that Lacan refers to—that is, taking a piece of the world's flesh. Art cuts a hole in the flesh of the world, thereby creating a lack that makes room for the movement of desire.

Lucien Freud says:

> "I want paint to work as flesh, I know my idea of portraiture came from dissatisfaction with portraits that resembled people. I would wish my portraits to be of the people, not like them. Not having the look of the sitter, being them. As far as I am concerned the paint is the person. I want it to work for me just as flesh does." [in Lampert, 1993, p. 12]

Tsibi Geva takes such a piece of the world's flesh and goes even one step further. He paints this object, the blind, with black and white paint, thus emptying it of all meaning. Baudelaire wrote about windows:

> Looking from outside into an open window one never sees as much as when one looks through a closed window. There is nothing more profound, more mysterious, more pregnant, more insidious, more dazzling than a window lighted by a single candle. What one can see out in the sunlight is always less interesting than what goes on behind a window pane. In that black or luminous square of life, life lives, life dreams, life suffers. [Baudelaire, 1947, p. 77]

Tsibi Geva does not paint romantic windows lit by candles that conceal a mysterious beauty. His painting is blind painting, which exposes the Real in the gaze, even creating a feeling of the uncanny. It tries to draw out the real act from the symbolic language in a way that reminds one of the dragon in M. C. Escher's painting. The two-dimensional dragon stubbornly tries to become three-dimensional, tries and fails again and again; it inevitably fails, yet still does not give up. Attempt and failure are in the nature of Escher's dragon, and they are also in the nature of the work of Lucien Freud and Tsibi Geva, in the same way that Beckett formulated failure as the foundation of the artist's work. Out of the attempt and failure arises the movement of the inextinguishable desire, like Orpheus who stubbornly goes down to the Underworld to bring back to life that which had died.

* * *

Cocteau, in his film *Orphée*, locates the Underworld behind a mirror, through which Orpheus enters it. It is as though he were trying to enter through the body image that creates the alienated and the phantasmic ego, to touch the bubbling, real essence of life, of flesh. In order to touch them, he must pass through the mirror, representing the world of the ego, the phantasy, the image. The Real is in there, inside the imaginary screen. In this sense, the realistic representation is a screen that conceals but also reveals through its torn cracks—the pulsating Real. Since failure is inevitable, because the object is empty, and what exists is nothing but a screen or disintegration, then the moment of loss, Eurydice's second death, is also the moment of Orpheus' return to life. It is an impossible instant in which death touches life, passes through love, and gives birth to art.

In Tsibi Geva's *Blinds* there is an attempt to cross boundaries. The object (the blind), which is also a signifier in our culture, becomes the material on which one paints, whereas the painting denies the blind of all meaning, rendering it a meaningless Real. But unlike the myth, what the painting on the blind lacks is that same movement through love.

* * *

In this sense, the plastic blind is like the human skin, as Lucien Freud paints it. When Freud paints the human body, it seems as though he were trying to break through the defences and pass through the skin to touch the flesh and veins. It is an attempt to touch the living, moving, breathing flesh—an attempt destined, of course, to fail (because it is impossible to represent the Real), but thanks to this attempt, movement continues. The skin in his paintings is stretched over the Real like the mirror in Cocteau's film, a mirror through which the Underworld peers out. The mirror is where narcissism develops—namely, our imaginary self-love—which is why we can imagine that we were seeing in the works of these two painters the inside layer of the ego, narcissism in its ugly yet vital nakedness.

The blind is dead, perforated material that the gaze is supposed to pass through. Tsibi Geva empties it of its functional use by shutting it and sealing it with paint. Out of a dead object, a painting is created—the minimum of a painting, yet still the desire shows through. This painting is not a trap for the gaze, as Lacan says of painting; the gaze does not pass through it, but just slides along its surface, creating a feeling of discomfort and perplexity, because it diminishes the possibility of becoming caught up in the painting, being hypnotized by it. The impenetrability and the asceticism of the black and white paint create the feeling of discomfort and peeping at the Real.

As Geva said:

"It is a work of art which at times one does not want to look at. It is a work of art that does not belong to any seductive formation, it lacks the fundamental vitality that holds attraction, or that creates some sort of seduction operating on the viewer's gaze. The work of art must relinquish this place of seduction if it wishes mortality to be present within the object in a real, experiential manner. The moment death is present within the object, the object is almost no longer viewed, it vanishes." [in Shapira, 1997; translated for this edition]

* * *

Orpheus' crossing of the border, which is perhaps the main goal of art, is a movement between presence and absence, a pulse of saying and failure. The paint as bare flesh in Lucien Freud's work and the ascetic painting on the sealed blind both indicate the same movement or lack of movement. For this reason, I believe that precisely through this dialectic the two artists point to a recurring process of a new breakthrough to the desire, a desire that is, according to Bois (1993), "the only means for the future existence of art" (p. 243).

Octavio Paz summarizes it beautifully in his poem "Touch":

My hands
Open the curtains of your being
Clothe you in a further nudity
Uncover the bodies of your body.
My hands
Invent another body for your body.

[Paz, 1962, p. 114]

Through this poem he transmits to the reader his view on crossing the border between the symbolic and the Real and raises the notion of creating an additional body within the body, asking—what then is the "real" body?

PART V

DEATH, ENTROPY

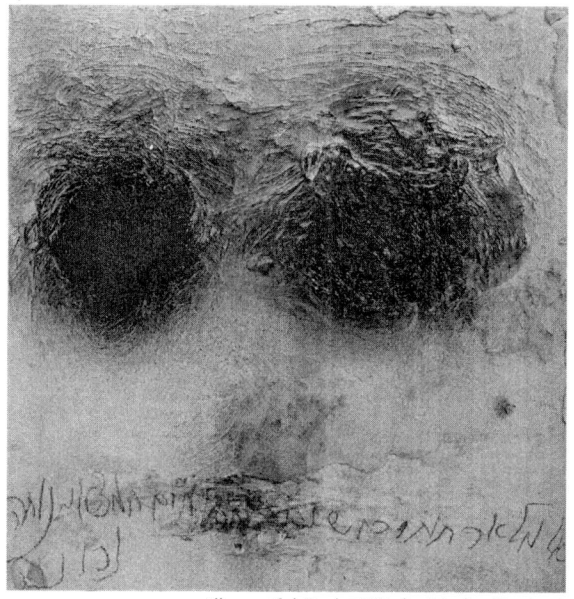

All-merciful God, 1995, by Moshe Gershuni

CHAPTER ELEVEN

True grace—the blood is the soul

> "Anxiety" describes a particular state of expecting the danger or preparing for it, even though it may be an unknown one. "Fear" requires a definite object of which to be afraid. "Fright", however, is the name we give to the state a person gets into when he has run into danger without being prepared for it; it emphasizes the factor of surprise.
>
> Sigmund Freud (1920g, p. 12)

This essay was born out of great fright. In 1995 we were surprised by four suicide bombings that occurred within the course of two weeks. The frightened eye that followed the horrifying sights on television came across the linguistic expression *Hesed Shel Emet* [True Grace] again and again, written on the back of the people who were busy collecting pieces of flesh into bags, in a desperate attempt to restore the parts into a whole; to turn the dismembered organism into a body, if only a dead one.

In his XXth seminar, Lacan says: "what is important is that all that hang together well enough for the body to subsist, barring any accident, as they say, whether external or internal. Which means that the body is taken for what it presents itself to be, an enclosed body" (Lacan, 1975a, p. 110).

* * *

At times I feel it is precisely language that provides an element of consolation in the face of fright, as though language is the last obstacle before the total disintegration.

"True Grace" makes you wonder. To what extent is the name linked to the task of collecting and burying human remains? As usual, Hebrew conceals two possible facets in one expression:

1. True Grace, as opposed, perhaps, to false grace (unequivocal, unambiguous grace).
2. Gracious Truth. Truth being kind to us (in an attempt to conceal the unbearable Real).

Grace

What is grace? An affect, an act; pertaining to love; perhaps a type of ethics; a function untouched by psychoanalysis although it does relate to love, to truth, to the body, and to the death drive. In a Biblical lexicon I found the following definition: "Originally, the word denotes God's love for human beings. Grace is one of the attributes of the Lord, who is 'compassionate and gracious'. His grace fills the earth, embracing even undeserving criminals. Thereafter, its denotation evolved to imply a relation of liking in general—a relation of mutuality" (Solieli & Barkoz, 1965, p. 297, translated for this edition). The later meaning is, in fact, lack of envy—that is, "perhaps he does not deserve it—but we will make an exception". According to Moses Maimonides, grace as a qualifier of God is embodied in the fact that the world exists.

* * *

That is to say, grace is exerted first and foremost by the Other—it is divine love, which is not associated with desire or lack. It can also be understood as Spinoza's *Amor Intellectualis Dei*—namely, Love that is linked to knowledge.

Upon waking, the first Jewish prayer is giving thanks to the Lord for returning our soul after the night's sleep, for, as the prayer goes: "great is thy faithfulness". God has faith in me, therefore I exist. I am the mirror reflection of the Other's faith. If he tells me "it is you!" I know this reflection is me, although at a later stage I will know that it is also not me but, rather, an image of myself, a *semblant*. I will know the "truth". But truth without grace, naked truth, it seems, is a psychotic, deconstructed truth.

The analytic notion of truth is linked to a lie. Lacan often discusses the truth and its relation to knowledge (Lacan, 1966b). He claims that there is no truth that, when passing through consciousness, does not lie (Lacan, 1973); that is what he means when asserting that truth has a fictive structure.

Following Lacan, Miller connects the reality of the unconscious with obscuring and misleading, while associating the concept of "repetition" (obsessive repetition of actions and thoughts that triggers anxiety and whose motives are unconscious) with the non-deceiving Real (Miller, 1991). In other words, the unconscious is not real, without being simultaneously false.

* * *

The first sentence of *Mesilat Yesharim* [The Oath of the Upright], one of the greatest Jewish ethics books, reads as follows: "It is fundamentally necessary both for saintliness and for the perfect worship of God *to realize* clearly what constitutes man's *true* duty in this world, and what goal is worthy of his endeavours throughout all the days of his life" (Lucato, 1969, p. 3, translated for this edition, emphases added). Saintliness [*hasidim*] and grace [*hesed*] share the same grammatical Hebrew root. The subject here is the uncovering of the ethical of the truth as a condition for grace.

* * *

Hasidim (as a concept rather than a movement) is, then, ethics that provide instructions on how to behave in a world where God is the first and last cause. It is suggested to the religious person to search for and verify his intentions; to adjust his own truth to that of the Lord's. Analysis, on the other hand, suggests to examine this truth in a world where, at best, God is unconscious; to question reality by encountering the Real. A religious person is confident that the cause is in the hands of God. This conviction, however, blocks his access to the truth. He compromises his own demand for the estimated desire of a God whom one must tempt and appease. In fact, Lacan believes that God is something that is encountered in the Real. He is inaccessible. He is characterized by that which does not deceive—anxiety (or, in religious terms, awe). In a seminar on the "Names-of-the-Father", which was comprised of a single lesson (given in the year of his excommunication), Lacan (1963b) refers to God and His name as revealed to Moses in the burning bush: "I am what I am". Yet, if one of God's qualities or names is grace, then this is a love story that differs from the story of temptation (see chapter two herein, "What Can We Know of Love?").

Love and truth in psychoanalysis

Regarding the connection between love and truth in analysis, Freud asserted that despite everything, the patient wants to proceed along the route of deceit when searching for the truth on account of love. Therefore, the patient moves towards recovery, abandoning the *jouissance* he derives from the symptom. Lacan believes that the deepest desire of human beings is not for knowledge but, rather, for ignorance. The desire for ignorance in the clinic assumes the form of love in the transference. Lacan sees love the way he sees truth: as a type of lie, a deceit. Transference love occurs as an inescapable obstacle. Truth can only be partially uttered, and love as embodied in the transference is deceiving, allowing us to get at the truth—that is to say, the deceit of love belongs to the dimension of truth. The subject is torn between truth and knowledge. He does not want to know, therefore he clings to the transference; yet this transference confronts him with his own subjective truth, enabling him to arrive at his unconscious knowledge. Hence, love can be regarded as a meeting point that introduces the dimension of truth into the analytic practice itself: analysis sees truth and love as similar in terms of their role in uncovering and covering repressed knowledge.

* * *

As opposed to religious truth, analytic truth is mobile, disappointing, evasive. Since there is no guarantee on the part of God, or some other Other, the praxis of analysis is bound to advance towards the conquest of the truth through the paths of deceit, and transference is precisely that—a transference to the nameless one who occupies the place of the Other. The truth in the analysis is not an expression of content. The truth is what happens in the encounter of the signifier with that which it does not signify, and the effect of this encounter is surprise. The truth is what surrounds the signifier, that which is in the margins. Freud says that the truth is the limit of what the psychic apparatus can bear. By the same token, transference is the effect of meaning, which lurks in the margins of what the patient does not say. Transference and truth are located in the encounter between the possible and the impossible.

* * *

At the end of analysis, says Leguil (1992) in a seminar on transference, the subject is that which can no longer be betrayed. He recognizes the fact that he has an unsubduable desire. He knows that his very being is not dependent on the ideal he finds in the Other but, rather, on something that is lacking there. When the movement is stopped, when the hole appears, the void must be filled by deceit (Leguil, 1992). Lacan says that at this moment the deceit is in some sense a fraud, but it liberates the "engine", the process. In a similar manner one can perhaps see the "fraud" of the *Hesed Shel Emet* people.

The body and the drive

In her essay "The Body in the Teaching of Jacques Lacan", Colette Soler (1995) quotes Lacan: the true, primary body is the language. It is the body of the symbolic. The symbolic is a body to the extent that it is a system of internal relations. Language is not a superstructure, it is a body—a body that gives body. "The first body makes the second by embodying itself." The body is, thus, not primary; rather, it is a reality structured through language, since the link that defines the signifying structure is already registered in it.

* * *

Lacan thought at first that the fragmentation is primary with regard to the image—that is, perceiving the body as a living organism that is defined as a whole by an image. During his investigation he shifted from the image—which is created through the gaze in the mirror that turns the organism into a body, a unity—to the understanding that the organism is, from the outset, a whole, and it is the signifier that creates a gap, that deconstructs. The body loses its unity because of the signifier. More than a rhetorical turnaround, I think this is a dual move. If we refer to wholeness and deconstruction on the imaginary level, it is the mirror that enables the representation of wholeness; from the point of view of the symbolic dimension, however, the signifier is that which disintegrates this perfection. The "truth" changes its appearance. This can be described as a three-dimensional hologram, fluctuating between the disintegrated or torn and the perfect, the whole. In any case, an Other—that something that is outside the organism—is required in order to define it. Lacan speaks of "ex-sistence", a persistent internal existence from without: it is the interior 8—two circles delineating three dimensions.

The shape of the interior 8 defines two areas of the body as a symbolic relationship that is related to sexuality, to the drive, and to the body as a living organism. When the unifying mirror is shattered or cracked, the invisible, intricate life of the flesh emerges. Maire Jaanus (1995) distinguishes between the body of the instincts, which is a body of need, and the body of the drives, which is a body of lack or demand. Both are equally Real insofar as they originate from the body. Yet, while a need involves the inside of the body, the inner organs, the drive involves the surface of the body and the erogenous orifices—those meeting points between inside and outside, which are interlinked in the form of ex-sistence, which is the form of the interior 8. Therefore, a transition between them, which can evoke fright or even horror, is possible.

The two levels of our being—instinct and drive—move fundamentally along two different routes. The instinctual level moves in organic rhythms of sleep and wakefulness, hunger and satiety, at times attaining rest. The drive, on the other hand, is like restlessness itself, seemingly irregular and non-characterized; within the drive, the constituent elements of the instinct are meaningless. The re-construction of both levels is discontinued and disjoined,

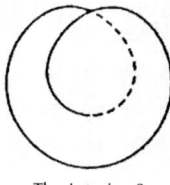

The Interior 8

mixing the natural with the unnatural, the mechanical with the sexual.

* * *

An infinite chain is thus rendered, which can only be limited, stopped, by the Real, the ostensibly small and worthless object, when it is charged with libido—that thing that is inextinguishable beyond all signifiers and bodies. That *objet á* is the nameless part of being—that which is neither phallic nor dependent on others. It is a primary *objet á*, different from the object as it is seen in the mirror. The object refers to a primary castration, before the constitution of language and the imaginary. It is the non-represented object ("abject"), unseen, unheard, odourless (Bataille, 1991). That part of *jouissance* that cannot be expressed but only experienced must happen. All forms of *objet á* are merely representatives or images of the immortal lost libido that is beyond the biological life. The *objets á* are "residues of the archaic forms of the libido". Lacan calls this libido *lamella*, defining it as "the libido, qua pure life instinct, that is to say, immortal life, or irrepressible life, life that has need of no organ, simplified, indestructible life. It is precisely what is subtracted from the living being by virtue of the fact that it is subject to the cycle of sexed reproduction" (Lacan, 1973, p. 197). Hence, the loss of various *objets á* is not a self-mutation, but a repetition of our original fall from immortality to mortality.

Freud had already noted that the object of the drive can be a part of the subject's body itself—that is, lost fragments of our very own body. Hence, according to narcissism, the first loss is the loss of physical substance. Castration first occurs in the body, in the loss of the primary object, and only then in language. In this sense, being is broken down into pieces. Physical castration that occurs within the body of the drive is as necessary as castration by language. This is not about trauma of meaning and meaninglessness as in language, but of being and non-being, immortality and mortality.

* * *

The "subject" of the drive, according to Jaanus (1995), is an object that is anchored in the Real by lost pieces of its own flesh. The subject is initially a partial object. It first plays with the pieces of its own body like the cotton reel with which Freud's grandson plays. It is a headless, languageless subject. In this sense, one may say that language is born out of the Real.

The drive is a movement around the fallen object; it is freedom from any visible object. According to Lacan, the essence of the drive is the inhibition of the act. Once it had encircled our body, sealing our empty erogenous orifices, as the breast filled the mouth and the voice filled the ears. These partial organs are part of a totality that is the *lamella*—the desexual libido, the immortal, indestructible life. Sexuality is what introduces death.

What happens to the drive when it transgresses in the direction of the instinct? It becomes excluded and enters a desexualized zone. "[T]he neutral real is the desexualized real . . . the subject has a constructive relation with this real only within the narrow confines of the pleasure principle, of the pleasure principle unforced by the drive . . ."(Lacan, 1973, p. 198). Only when the drive collides with the world of instincts can the sexual object once again become a mere parcel of meat, which is here to be consumed. In such instances, the sexual partner is reduced to a function of the Real and the reaction may be one of disgust, hysterical vomiting, or cannibalistic desire.

* * *

All this refers to the body, but there is also the subject. Soler (1995) describes the subject as an entity that is separate from the body. The subject exists before and after it has a body, before he is born—when talked about—and after he dies—in memory. Hence, it is language, says Soler, that ascribes the body to the subject, giving it to him thereafter. Thus, the subject's place is, first of all, in the other.

When focusing on the signifier, says Soler, it is not that important whether it is alive or dead, and this is the symbolic meaning of the body's burial. Essentially, burial is a way of refusing to recognize that the body, which was born through the signifier, becomes a cadaver, to guarantee its survival after the signifier gives it life—hence the great importance attributed by many cultures to burial ceremonies. Burial of an as-much-as-possible whole body is the grace, the kindness truth shows us, by hiding the Real under ground. The verse: "For dust thou art, and unto dust shalt thou return" (Gen. 3:19) refers to hiding and, at the same time, serves as an expression of the everlastingness of vitality, that which Freud entitled libido and Lacan called by this strange and vital name—*lamella*. Burial limits the flowing of *jouissance*, allowing the continuity of the insatiable desire, the inextinguishable power. According to Lacan, *jouissance* ranges between tickling and grilling. Soler translates this range to current language (before the terrorist attacks), locating *jouissance* between tickling and the suicidal bombers; from masochistic preening to the horrors of war.

Gathering pieces of flesh into a bag in order to bury the body as a whole is the last means for keeping the Real within some kind of a symbolic framework. The burial of the One is the return of bodily organs, instincts and objects, to their status as missing; only then can the drive move around them, and it is this movement that makes room for the Other of language.

The-name-of-the-father

At the beginning of the analysis, the analyst takes the place of the Other, the one who knows. Lacan warns the analyst repeatedly of identification with that place. The analyst need not be the knight of truth, says Lacan: neither a knight nor a dwelling place for the truth. The analyst need not interpret the transference—the patient will do it. The patient will develop the various ways in which he tries to seize the Other—namely, the analyst—in order to reduce the analyst to the complementary object, that which this Other lacks. Transference enables the subject to enter the path of deceit, for at the beginning of treatment the analysand thinks that there is a subject who is supposed to know, who knows the truth about truth. Lacan does not appreciate this knowledge, even if it is unconscious. The termination of transference is embodied in a glimpse into the Real, but this is not enough. The encounter with the drive raises a question: how can the unutterable be uttered? One cannot identify with the object, only situate it through signifiers around the hole. This is the only way to cross the plane of identification. There is a point in the operation where the subject who recognizes the castration is not represented by a signifier but is, rather, empty. The analyst, too, is but empty, since the subject finds out that he, too, occupies space. The truth uncovered by the subject is not within himself, not within the analyst; rather, it is in the latent object. The effect of this discovery is distress, and here lies, I believe, the place of grace, the place of "allowance to fellow men".

* * *

A non-crazy analyst, says Leguil (1992), must occupy the imaginary place (the *semblant*) within transference, while relying on the symbolic. It is the continuation of the lie that sets the machine in motion, implying that we believe what the patients say. The more they lie, the better we can discern their truth. The imaginary allows the psychoanalyst to wait for the required length of time until the Real stabilizes, for this is the point where one can no longer put oneself in the place of the *semblant*.

* * *

Returning to analysis, one must ask: what does the subject seek in the transference? What kind of love is this? The subject wishes to restore the father's status, the same father who cannot name the non-phallic *jouissance*, who cannot provide a guarantee. If God is unconscious, if He does not know what He is doing, then the world does not know where it is headed. The subject finds within the Other a word that he entitles God, which is the "Name-of-the-Father". The lack of being is filled, as it were, with the ideal signifier that is inscribed in the other as "Name-of-the-Father". If this is the truth, then the volunteers of "True Grace" cannot restore the father's status after the arbitrary disintegration, but they can adhere to the symbolic rules despite everything (as Antigone did when she insisted on burying her brother in spite of the king's prohibition) and, with these rules, create some kind of a screen that will cover up the father's absence.

"True Grace" is, thus, the ethics of truth which is related to the disintegrated body and to the drive that "complements" it—the movement away from the I, from the closed body, as reflected in the mirror, to the split I, in the sense of: "I am what I am". This is another way of reading Freud's *"wo es war soll ich werden"* ["where it was, I must come to be"].

* * *

When the patient discovers that the father does not know, and that God is no guarantee, he shifts to an identification with the symptom. Such identification enables him to cross the basic *phantasme*—"to settle an account" with the parents, to force them to recognize something: their sin, or the sin inherent in the primal scene. False grace is to turn from an accused to an accuser, or vice versa. True grace is to recognize their castration. Going beyond the castration complex implies an expropriation of the subject—that the subject himself move to the other side, the side that is beyond the pleasure principle. Once the subject crosses over to the other side, he realizes that the other is lacking. Beyond the castration complex there is the fact that the other is also castrated.

If first the *phantasme* says: "I know what the Other wants and I can get it", crossing the *phantasme* means putting *objet á* in the place of the unfulfilled desire. It means to recognize that the Other does not exist, and that he too desires. The *jouissance* this Other demands is not a pound of flesh or sacrifice of life but, rather, "plenty of nothing", to quote Porgy from *Porgy and Bess*. The invention of love is, then, love for the unknown—the desire for otherness. Or, as beautifully put by Lévinas (1982): "The pathos of love consists, on the contrary, in an insurmountable duality of beings; it is a relationship with what forever slips away. The relationship does not *ipso facto* neutralize alterity, but conserves it" (p. 67). Love is for that which is still not part of knowledge but, rather, part of the drive that evolves around any object. Or, as Freud puts it—they can be melted together. According to Freud, the material from which the drive is made is a melting-together of the object and the drive.

* * *

Thus, love—love that is also grace—no longer links the truth to the other. It does not link the truth to the Other, does not link the truth to the signifier, but, rather, to the subject's relation to that which triggers his love, to the cause of love—the object. Crossing the *phantasme* occurs when the subject notices that beyond, on the other side, there is a void. And the grace is to say: despite everything.

Grace is the ethics of the truth: death's grace to the living, truth's link to the physical. The element of the psyche is truth—"for the blood is the soul". Truth is gracious when it is revealed before us—the truth of castration, in body and language. Thus it also introduces the symbolic possibility of the One.

In conclusion, I am reminded of a verse from a prayer that praises the woman, the virtuous woman. It reads: "in her tongue is the law of kindness [grace]" (Prov. 31:26). Is it possible to accept the sphere of heroism as a phallic sphere, and the sphere of grace as a feminine sphere? If one can say that the other *jouissance* that is beyond the phallus is the *jouissance* of the female function, perhaps it is possible to say that grace as ethics of the truth is linked to putting oneself in the woman's place: recognizing castration as a female castration—Real in one sense, imaginary in another.

CHAPTER TWELVE

There is no such form—
Arbeit macht frei

"... affirming that the universe resembles nothing and is only *formless* amounts to saying that the universe is something like a spider or spit."

Georges Bataille (1985, p. 31)

"I can speak of the world of forms which I make as a liquid world. If I had to characterize this world I would say that it is a world of forms which are on the verge of disintegration, as if they are the last chance to hold to form in something that is falling apart, becoming threadbare, liquidizing.... And the last attempt to hold to any form is the challenge, because otherwise the painting is either ripped or liquified, and we talk of this big liquid thing from all points of view."

The artist Moshe Gershuni, speaking about his work
(in Golan & Lieber, 1996, p. 71; translated for this edition)

Anamnesis

In 1994, the organizers of The Freudian Place in Jaffa, Israel, held a public discussion with Moshe Gershuni, who spoke of the way he works and the connection between his work and his life. Among other questions, Gershuni was asked about the meaning of the expression "There is no such form (shape)" which he had used when analysing the work of a student. Gershuni was also asked about a basic form that is a recurring feature in many of his drawings—a crude line rising up, rounding off and falling.

In responding, Gershuni said, among other things:

> "Of course you could think, especially from the male viewpoint, of the phallic business, the business of erection or the wish for erection, and then this turning round . . . you can see here again the problematics of shapes. The problem of the shape of the breast for example, the mother's breast . . . the problem with the shape is that it is a boneless organ. You could say: 'there is no form (shape).'" [in Golan & Lieber, 1996, p. 72; translated for this edition]

* * *

Can there really be such a thing as an impossible form? Form can be related to as the equivalent of the symbolic register, because it puts limits on the Real. How, then, should we relate to topological forms—soft forms?

Shortly after the discussion with Gershuni, Yitzchak Rabin—the prime minister of Israel—was assassinated. "Nobody had even thought of" this intolerable, impossible act—but like the Real, it didn't stop it from not being registered.

Afterwards I visited an exhibition at a leading Israeli art gallery featuring works, in response to the murder, by Raffi Lavie and Gershuni. It was there that I beheld the *informe* in Gershuni's work—two apertures, with borders, that look as if they are in motion. Could these be the two holes pierced in Rabin's body? Or could they be the place where the breasts should be?

For me it was a moving embodiment of the death drive.

Definitions

Entropy: The expression is taken from a Greek word denoting "transformation". The concept of entropy is a mathematical measure of the disorganization of a system. It first arose as a name for the second law of thermodynamics—the theory of heat. The first law is the law of conservation of energy, which relates to the fact that the total quantity of energy in a closed system is invariant. The second law is concerned with the quality of this energy—that is, the amount of energy available in the system for doing useful work. Rudolf Clausius, who defined this law in the year 1854 and restated it in terms of entropy, meant the content of the transformation of a body or a system. Every irreversible change in the system will increase its entropy. That is to say, entropy is the result of the progressive fluctuation of every system—defined by form or content—towards an unpredictable state, as a process of unavoidable disintegration (Edwards, 1967).

* * *

Nowadays entropy is defined in terms of information theory. Entropy is that which measures lack of information about the structure of a system. Lack of information corresponds with actual disorder, and increase in entropy corresponds with progressive loss of information.

* * *

Negative Entropy: Any living organism delays its decay into thermal equilibrium (death) by its capacity to maintain itself at a fairly high level of orderliness (and hence fairly low level of entropy) by continually absorbing negative entropy from its environment (Edwards, 1967).

* * *

L'informe [Formless]: The opposite of form. Not its negation or absence, but a dialectic of constant movement, which is used for de-classification, in the double meaning of de-positioning and lowering on one the hand, and mixing confusion and disruption on the other.

The concept of *informe* is a structural concept. It enables us to cancel the dichotomy between form and content and to oppose the academic wish for the universe to "assume a form" and the need to divide the world into pairs of opposites—form versus matter, male versus female, life versus death, interior versus exterior, and so on. Bataille referred to such opposites as "mathematical fur coats" (Rozen, 1996).

* * *

Topology: The study of those properties of figures in space that persist under all continuous deformations. A topological space includes the notion of closeness. Topology is concerned with properties of "figures", and it studies, among other things, the concepts of limit and connectedness. Recently it has been used in the theory of catastrophes in order to classify the different ways in which a dynamic system can pass through a point of instability (Bullock & Stallybrass, 1992).

* * *

Death drive: Essentially, the death drive represents for Freud the basic inclination of every living being to return to an inorganic state. "Everything living dies for *internal* reasons" (Freud, 1920g, p. 38).

Freud established the essential conflict that exists between the drives in life: the libido, which includes the inclination towards unity and pleasure, and the death drives, which work towards disintegration and destruction. Nevertheless, these two types of drives are always encountered in combination with one another. On its own, the death drive would elude our perception because in itself it is silent. In the end, Lacan demonstrated how "The distinction between the life drive and the death drive is genuine in as much as it manifests two aspects of drive" (Lacan, 1973, p. 257). That amounts to every drive actually being a death drive, because in trying to go beyond the pleasure principle, it works towards its own extinction. While the pleasure principle drives towards homeostasis, creating balance and minimal stimulation, the aspect of the death drive brings the subject back towards excess—*jouissance* (and just as Freud claims the primacy of the death drive, so the Chinese sage Chuang-Tzu claims that the birth of each human being is accompanied by the birth of that human being's sorrow).

Lacan shifted the death drive to the realm of the symbolic order. He stated that the death drive is the action of culture, of language, upon the living being (see chapter eleven herein, "True Grace").

Initial thoughts—knowledge and truth

If "being" is a verb (a dynamic principle characterized by constant movement); if form and *informe* are a course of action created out of that possible movement from one to another, when *informe* is an entropic principle (a principle of loss of information, of shattering erosion that ultimately makes the creation of new forms possible); and if such labour is actually liberating (from fixation, from infinite repetition), then we have to examine this new place—something that is neither an object nor a subject but the dynamic between the two. We could, perhaps, use Bataille's term in referring to it as "abjection". Should we proceed along this way, perhaps we will be able to say more about the place of knowledge in relation to truth. We may also make some progress in regard to knowledge of non-phallic feminine sexuality—the other sexuality, which has no definitive form—the sexuality that lacks a signifier in culture.

* * *

The pleasure principle strives for balance, invariance, inertia and strives to ensure that the level of tension will be constant—namely, leaving entropy and negative entropy at a constant level. If we cancel the dichotomy between form and content, life and death, and relate to that element of the libido that cannot be annihilated, then entropy is indeed an element of erosion, an element of extinction that works within existing form—an element that, although it opposes change, ultimately leads to disintegration of the existing order and to the possibility of creating a new order.

This libidinal element could be described as a sort of skin, as the border of an elastic topological body inside which operate both the first principle of conserving energy and the second law of extinction. Each of these principles constitutes a mode of being, and the two operate simultaneously. Thus, through silent work—which is the way the death drive functions in the humdrum of life—arises the possibility of new bodies being created (beyond sexual reproduction).

* * *

What, then, is the minimum that guards the border and connectedness of the topological body? What is the minimal opposition to the death drive? The minimal information?

According to Gershuni:

> "The painter's job is a thousand times harder than God's. For God it is no big deal, he made real bone and stretched muscles and sinews over it. Now I have come from the outside without the help of a bone and through a depiction of two lines of drawing to give the feeling of a form that has inner resistance." [in Golan & Lieber, 1996, p. 71; translated for this edition]

Those two drawn lines of which Gershuni speaks are the way culture operates on the object, on the body. As Lacan says in his essay on the symptom (1975b): "It is always with the help of words that man thinks. And it is in the encounter between these words and his body that something takes shape. . . . This is where he places meaning" (p. 13). But as meaning is generated, movement in the body is stimulated that eventually leads to *informe*, taking the body to the point where it eludes the exact place of fixation by meaning. The body will be just a few micro-millimetres away. Rosalind Krauss (1993) considers *informe* as a conceptual matter that shatters the limits of signification and disintegrates the known categories in order to dislodge the meaning from its position, to lower it.

* * *

Entropy, then, is the work that is going on inside the existing form, the work of *informe* inside the form, of extinction in the navel of the "is". We could say: the silent movement; movement rather than flow. When Heraclitus says, "everything is in a state of flux", he means continual movement, which, as shown in the paradox of Achilles and the Tortoise, brings us to the paradox of the impossibility of movement.

I am referring more to a kind of movement that is created when one begins to throw stones into the ever-flowing river. In the beginning, the stones create a disruptive movement that slowly fades away, but they also have a silent result—they pile up one on top of the other unnoticed, and then, one day, the river is suddenly shifted from its course. If the imperative in the scientific discourse is, as Lacan says, to "continue knowing"—namely, information is put in the place of the master—then *informe* is that which overthrows the master. In psychoanalysis, knowledge is supposed to move from the known to the unknown—namely, within knowledge itself. This is the symbolic parallel to form, and there is an expectation of chaos, disorder, and no-knowledge. This type of movement does not move in a developmental direction but in the direction of death. As Lacan (1978) put it in Seminar II: "The libido is drawn towards death along the paths of life" (p. 80). From the point of view of the libido, this is an infinite journey: the movement towards death can enable a reawakening of life. It could be said that the conjunction of knowledge-form with the element of *informe* is the *point de capitone* of truth with knowledge and the point of freedom from the discourse of the master.

Freud and Beyond the Pleasure Principle

Freud, in fact, uses entropy as a metaphor for fixation. In referring to the Wolf Man, he draws attention to a characteristic feature that caused the Wolf Man to reject anything new. The Wolf Man stubbornly defended any position of the libido that he had assumed in the past, for fear of what he would lose if he gave that up and due to lack of belief in any possibility of finding a complete substitute in the new expected position. "So that in considering the conversion of psychical energy no less than of physical, we must make use of the concept of entropy, which opposes the undoing of what has already occurred" (Freud, 1918b [1914], p. 116). In "A Case of Paranoia . . ." (1915f), he defines entropy using the Jungian term of "psychic inertia", as a phenomenon that fights against inclinations for progress and recovery, that remains active even after the formation of neurotic symptoms. This inertia is not general, intimates Freud, but specific:

> If we search for the starting-point of this special inertia, we discover that it is the manifestation of very early linkages— linkages which it is hard to resolve—between instincts and impressions and the objects involved in those impressions. These linkages have the effect of bringing the development of the instincts concerned to a standstill. [Freud, 1915f, p. 272]

* * *

There is a seeming contradiction here. Entropy according to Freud is connected more to fixation, to a fixated restriction, meaning non-movement. Freud did not continue his research as Lacan did. Lacan distinguished between the principle of inertia and the principle of entropy. According to him, we are concerned here not with non-movement but with an island around which there is movement. Like in the allegory of the flowing river, this is an island that was created gradually, around which a new kind of movement is created; a shifting rather than a flowing movement. Figuratively one can say that what is formed is the death of the former track and the creation of a new track. This track can proceed in the direction of degeneration or development, corresponding with the respective dosages of the death drive and the libido, but motion goes on forever.

* * *

The pleasure principle operates according to the law of energy conservation, which is the law of inertia (which could even be described as mechanical). The pleasure principle is the emissary of homeostasis, and, thanks to it, the living creature survives. But if we go with homeostasis to the end—that is, reducing tension to its minimal quantity, to its annihilation—then we may become confused and reach the death drive. Therefore, the pleasure principle is nothing but the principle of minimal tension required to maintain life. Contrary to that, *jouissance* is something that overflows. *Jouissance* is not exactly interested in survival—death can definitively be a part of it. That is why Lacan suggested that the pleasure principle puts a limit to *jouissance*.

Repetition

Fixation, which is situated in the heart of the symptom, indeed fixates the early relations but is also a focus of *jouissance*. Therefore, we must begin with the symptom, we must give the symptom a form through words. When work is done, part of the energy is used and heat is produced; development is created, but part of the energy is lost. According to Lacan, into this part that is lost, entropy may insert new information, new knowledge, and the negative entropy can generate miracles. In his XVIIth seminar, Lacan intimates that repetition in this sense is not just a cycle of need and satisfaction; rather, it is a cycle that includes and brings with it the disappearance of life as such—returning to the non-living, a point outside the flow chart (Lacan, 1991a). This repetition belongs to the domain of *jouissance*; it is based on repetition of *jouissance*. Repetition denotes loss of vitality. Conservation of energy is the power of the master, although, in the binding force of repetition as such, there is also loss of *jouissance*, something that is unwilling to return to the starting point. This repetition is the principle of entropy, and this is the principle that in my opinion may be able to liberate us from the cycle of infinite knowledge—from this imperative to "continue knowing"—and lead us to truth.

Déjouer

When Bataille considers the birth of art, he sees art not only as creation, but also as defacement, self-mutilation (Krauss, 1993). The little child who smears excrement on the walls of his room is not necessarily "creative" but may be trying to cancel the difference. This difference that generates forms cancels the boundary between his body and the outside world; it is a kind of anti-narcissism. The intention is not to produce the forms of language—male or female—but to produce the absence of difference: *informe*. According to Bataille, the drive to cancel the difference traces back to the paintings of primitive man on the walls of caves. On the same wall on which the noble bison and mighty mammoth were painted, humans are depicted merely as grotesques. Even then, the desire of the artist was not for representation, but for alteration—in state and in time. This is the place of the *informe*: not an opposition to form as matter versus form, male versus female, life versus death, inside versus outside, vertical versus horizontal—but chaos that exists in the heart of every form. The *informe* is something that form, as such, produces—this is the possibility of activity in the heart of form through the principle of extinction. Bataille names this act *déjouer*: a structure that disputes the rules of the game while at the same time follows these same rules. Is it not that which Lacan did to psychoanalysis by returning to Freud? Is it not a fundamental principle that guides psychoanalysis? Disputing the rules of the game that were determined by the Other as a place of the ideal, through following and examining these very same rules?

The object

I return to the pulse of the unconscious, to the rhythm of disruption of motion that in the end produces a shifting in motion—that element that is the minimal limit necessary in order for topological form to be created. It is the object, the primal lost object, that in essence is a soft form. This object operates as a point of passage to the subject: the breast. This is a kind of object that, at a certain stage in the life of the baby, holds the origin of satisfaction of the need, the desire, and the drive altogether. This is the mythological mother (remember the gigantic milk-squirting breast that pursues Woody Allen in *Everything You Wanted To Know About Sex, but Were Afraid to Ask*).

To repeat Gershuni: "The problem with the shape of the breast is that it is an organ without bones inside it. One can say: 'There is no such form'" (in Golan & Lieber, 1996, p. 71, translated for this edition).

And, indeed, there is no such form, and there is no such an object, and there is no such mother (a mythological one). As the object is lost in advance, and the loss is a prerequisite to the obstacle course of desire, that ultimately also includes the artistic creation.

* * *

In the wake of Lacan we could say: something is forming in this encounter between body and matter. The breast is supposedly the object that words cannot give form to. Therefore, we can say: "there is no such form." But if there were no words, to what could a man give testimony? In Gershuni's art, there are painted words that take on the dimension of a body (as is the case in Peter Greeneway's last film, *The Pillow Book*, where he tries to make a connection in the Real between language as calligraphic writing and sexuality). "If I didn't paint a soldier," says Gershuni, "I wrote 'soldier' and then it exists in there, in the painting" (in Golan & Lieber, 1996, p. 67, translated for this edition).

And he paints with his fingers: "I had a visual image of the finger as a seismograph, as I said before this is calligraphy, and it is not for nothing that letters or sentences come out of the seismographic finger . . . it binds me to occupation with death" (in Golan & Lieber, 1996, p. 68, translated for this edition).

* * *

And how do you paint the *informe*? The breast in this case is the object of this *informe*. The formlessness of the breast is probably connected to libido and life, as opposed to the word "soldier", which is associated with death. The seismograph registers occurrences in real time. It testifies. It gives information. And I return to the expression that the functionaries of the Nazi regime confiscated from the fund of signifiers and that therefore received horrific connotations—"work liberates". Horror is produced when trying to disintegrate the forms not with entropy, with loss of information, but, on the contrary, by putting information above all value and turning human beings into so many "numbers" in such information.

Work liberates

The work of the *informe* liberates from testimony associated with death and facilitates organization towards new meanings and new bodies.

Information management has become a more and more common vocation. The job of information managers is to collect information. They operate in the direction of negative entropy, trying to organize the overflow of information that is dispersed in the computer into meaningful bodies, producing form out of this chaos of information. It is a kind of an instrument for helping researchers and scientists find their way in our information-bombarded world.

* * *

There is a lot of anxiety about the future of knowledge in our information-rich world but I don't think that there is real cause for worry. We may bless the law of entropy, because it shows us that truth will always elude us. There will always be loss of information, a place for the possibility of chaos. The hysteric will peep through each fissure that the obsessive gatherer of information leaves open and will create desire anew. The psychotic will always astonish us by revealing entropy in the heart of accumulating knowledge.

Is truth situated in the place of the principle of entropic movement? And will we be able to know more about the function of feminine sexuality when we continue our research in this direction?

CHAPTER THIRTEEN

Myth and Act on the crater's edge

If one stands on the cliff edge of the Ramon crater, near the town of Mitzpe Ramon, one sees, on the one hand, an astonishing landscape, reminiscent of the moon, that cannot fail to arouse within one a sense of awe and loftiness. On the other hand, the town appears miserable, graceless, and half-deserted, almost a ghost town. Between the Ramon crater ("nature") and the town of Mitzpe Ramon ("culture") lies an abyss almost as deep as the crater itself.

The rest of the town used to be "separated" from the cliff edge by the structure of the deserted municipal cinema, an ugly, prefabricated, asbestos-roofed building. This was the place of "culture"—an intermediate place, a space for phantasy. This was where the working people who lived their lives in this isolated place could go in order to forget, if only for a short while, their hardships. Here flickered images of characters and tales from another world, images far removed from the world of the inhabitants, yet

---

This essay was written several months before the murder of Yitzchak Rabin, the prime minister of Israel. It was written following the Co-Existence project run by the Artists' Museum group in Mitzpe Ramon, during Passover 1995.

familiar—Clark Gable, Gary Cooper, Marilyn Monroe, all occupying the unachievable realms of the imagination, like a utopian promise of a better world.

* * *

In the last years of its existence, the cinema—without a screen, without seats, the screening-hall in ruins—embodied perhaps more than anything the harsh reality of a merciless, promise-less land. Where the screen used to be there was now graffiti sprayed in black: "We shall not withdraw from the Golan [Heights]. Rabin [the then prime minister who was later assassinated] is an asshole—he betrayed his wife" and also "Motherfuckers". The Hebrew for "from the Golan" is *min haGolan*. The Hebrew word for "from", *min*, when spelt with a slight difference, also means "sex". In this case, the militant political context of the graffiti would require *min* to be spelt as in "from", but it was actually spelt as in "sex"—an intoxicating combination of Eros and violence carved into the wall by graffiti, the signature of the masses.

* * *

In *Group Psychology and the Analysis of the Ego*, Freud (1921c) claims that what binds people together to make them a crowd or the masses are mutual libidinal ties that have been diverted from their original goals. Among the features of the individual in the masses, Freud enumerates weakness of intellectual ability, lack of emotional restraint, being incapable of moderation, inability to control one's emotions, and the urge to exceed every limit in expressing them and giving vent to them through action. Freud felt that the picture that this assortment of features reveals is a regression of mental activity to that of an earlier stage of development.

Man is not a herd animal, says Freud, but a horde animal; a horde governed by a leader. All individuals in the group must be equal to one another, but they all wish to be ruled by the one. The leader can be either a figure or an ideal. In this context, Freud uses the myth of the primal horde: the primal father who prevented his sons from directly satisfying their sexual desires, forcing them into abstinence. As a result of the sexual repression, the sons developed libidinal ties aimed at a goal other than that of sexual conquest.

The father's sexual fanaticism and intolerance eventually causes the psychological phenomenon of the group. Having been driven out of the group and separated from their father, the sons advance from mutual identification to homosexual object-love, thereby achieving the freedom to kill the father (Freud, 1921c).

* * *

The writing on the wall at the cinema characterizes such a horde, the ties between the members of which are strengthened by the attempt to kill the father. Rabin, in this context, was the father that had to be killed because he held the secret of taking *jouissance* in women. In opposition to Rabin, who becomes a negative leader, the horde gathers around a national ideal that has been charged with libidinal values: the Golan assumes the shape of a tempting seductive woman, the same woman who Rabin "betrayed", and who is, according to Freud, the source of temptation for the mythical act of murder. She is the reward that will go to whoever wins the battle.

* * *

Again and again psychoanalysis shows us the very same phenomenon that Humanism tries to deny: that the intensity of the drive makes "culture" possible (because it allows sublimation) on the one hand, while, on the other, it operates as a destructive factor in the midst of "culture" (the death drive).

Speaking the language of the masses, the language of sex and violence combined with identification with the national ideal, is that remnant that democracy can neither overcome nor do without—a remnant that does not succumb to symbolic law.

According to Slavoj Žižek (1991)—who tries to deal with the structural failure of the democratic nation-state with psychoanalytic–Lacanian methods—the subject of democracy is tainted with a "pathological" stain (the term "pathological" is taken from Kant's discussion of the love-object, which makes the universality of the categorical imperative fail; the object is pathological in that it makes one ready to "break the law" for the sake of desire). Žižek identifies this stain as the ethnic mixture that is perceived as a "nation". Democracy is always connected to the pathological non-democratic fact of a nation-state. Any attempt to establish a "global" democracy, based on a community of all people as equal "citizens of the world", inevitably fails in the end. The subject of democracy can be created only through an alliance with some national goal, which is never in itself democratic or egalitarian (for example, "The State of the Jews", "A Palestinian State", etc.). The goal, or cause, is what Freud calls *das Ding*—the Thing—which embodies *jouissance*. The national goal is the way in which the subjects of a certain nation contrive their collective *jouissance* with the aid of national myths. Or, to use Freud's terms, it is that ideal that channels towards itself identification between the subjects and creates the masses.

* * *

Associating the Golan Heights with sex turns it into such a myth, and the association of the leader who wishes to shatter that myth with sexual betrayal turns him into the father whom, in order to maintain the unity of the horde, it is permitted to kill. Rabin becomes the Other, who has gained access to *jouissance*, thereby threatening the *jouissance* of the horde, the masses.

Žižek's main point is that democracy is made possible only if it incorporates its own impossibility, limitation, irreducible "pathological" remnant. This remnant demonstrates the Lacanian logic of *pas tout* [not everything]. According to the *pas tout* logic, we may say that the symbolic law can be applied to everything save *phantasme*. *Phantasme* resists universalization, because it is the particular way in which each of us structures the impossible connection to the traumatic Thing.

The factor that binds a particular community together cannot be reduced to symbolic identification. The connection between the members of the community always conceals a common attachment to the Thing, to the embodied *jouissance*. National identification, by definition, is maintained by the connection to the nation as the Thing. This connection to the Thing, which is structured through collective phantasies and is called "our way of life", is that which is endangered by that Other that holds the secret of the Other *jouissance*.

* * *

The law of the masses attempts to apply symbolic order to everything, even to sexuality—"The people are with the Golan" (a common Israeli political slogan of those opposed to waiving such territory in the framework of a peace agreement).

Freud claims that, within the masses, there is no place for the woman as a love object and that ties of love between men and women are consummated outside the realm of the masses. However, it can be said that the invocation of sexuality for the sake of uniting the masses is precisely what gives it a threatening strength. The Golan, indirectly presented as a tempting woman whom must not be dismounted, becomes that pathological remnant. This woman belongs to everybody. Loyalty is owed to her, and, in the name of such loyalty, anything is allowed. Any sacrifice is conceivable.

* * *

To this place came the artist, and this is what he found—a deserted cinema in a wretched town, on the edge of the most beautiful cliff in the world. He also found the strength that remained in the hands of the masses—shadows of phantasy and a dripping black spray of political pornography or pornographic politics.

In this possibly delusive-hypnotized, possibly horrifying setting (precisely in it, and not in a neutral place outside it), the artist defined a single frame and turned it into a *kaffiyeh* [the traditional Arab headscarf]. It is a provocative act, since the *kaffiyeh* is the symbol of the enemy (on whose account Rabin betrayed his wife, the Golan?), of the threatening Other, and, as far as the masses are concerned, a symbol of betrayal. Yet, in Hebrew *kaffiyeh* is also an anagram of "compulsion" [*k'fiyah*] and "reverse" [*hipukh*]. The painted *kaffiyeh* has a lacy quality to it, almost bird-like, fluttering, touching-yet-not-touching. A *kaffiyeh* whose borders are sharply and accurately defined as if frozen in time, and in its margins there is an empty space—for translation subtitles, translation of such a delusive reality, such a divided and monstrous reality. Out of the violent pornographic image itself, the artist draws the fluttering, shivering Eros, Eros who blows little birds over precise distances and by doing so confiscates the setting from the masses and turns it into a work of the individual.

In this context, the artistic act—a *kaffiyeh* painted above the inscription—constitutes more than just an aesthetic act or a political

Untitled, 1993, by Tsibi Geva

statement. It is an action on the ethical plane, an act that indicates the existence of a particular *phantasme*, that evades the attempt of the masses to enforce the same law on "everything". The deserted cinema in Mitzpe Ramon had been home to the voice of the masses until the moment when the artistic act was set. From then on, it became the voice of the individual.

* * *

At the end of *Group Psychology and the Analysis of the Ego* (1921c), Freud lists different phases of the libido. He begins with being in love, which is based on the existence of sexual desires as well as aim-inhibited desires. In this phase, says Freud, there is no room except for the ego and the object. The second phase is hypnosis, in which, as in being in love, there is room for two only, yet it is entirely based on aim-inhibited desires, and the object replaces the Ego ideal. This process occurs in much greater force in the masses, but in the masses there is also identification with other individuals.

Neurosis, according to Freud, deviates from this line. It appears wherever sexual repression towards aim-inhibited desires has not been entirely successful. The neurotic has been forsaken, says Freud, and therefore he has no choice but to replace the large mass assemblies from which he was alienated with symptoms. He creates for himself an imaginary world of his own, a religion of his own, a set of lunacies of his own (Freud, 1921c). In other words, the neurotic is a captive of his own *phantasme*.

* * *

In this sense, the act of the artist is closer to that of the neurotic, in that he creates for himself a unique world of his own, a world that evades the logic of the masses. Yet, unlike the world of the neurotic, it is based not on regression but, rather, on a creative act; it is not expressed in symptoms and not asking to be cured but, rather, is closer to the psychoanalytic interpretation.

The artist takes the phantasmatic material and structures it in a different dimension.

If such is the case, could it be said that his action is more like the action of the psychoanalyst?

PART VI

EVOLUTION

CHAPTER 14

Is interpretation possible?

"Millions of people alone, and if already alone then let it be in motion."

Line from a song of a famous Israeli pop group

Two essential discoveries emerged from Irma's injection dream that Freud analyses in *The Interpretation of Dreams*: the formula, or the power of the word, and the Real. The Real was revealed through Irma's open, frightful throat into which Freud looked, yet did not awake from the nightmare but, rather, kept on dreaming and found the solution, the formula. He found the meaning, the language—and founded the theory of the interpretation of dreams. One may say that Lacan's motion is the reverse: from the formula—the meaning, the language—to the unbearable, the Real; from the signifier to the sign; from the subject in his relation to the object to the *ex-time* object. Lacan refers

---

Lecture given at the symposium "Psychoanalysis in the Year 2000: Centennial of Freud's Dream about Irma's Injection", January 1996.

to the subject as a lack in being. The Jewish French philosopher Emmanuel Lévinas (1982) reminds us of Heidegger's reference to being: Heidegger stresses that being is not a noun but, rather, a verb. It is not an entity but, rather, an act. And if being is occurrence, then the lack must also be some kind of a flexible topological place, a place in movement. Lacan's *manque á être* is not a lack in being but, rather, a lack in the actions, the occurrences of being; some kind of a black hole within the movement, yet a moving hole. Lévinas (1982) distinguishes between "said" and "say", which is much more important (similar to Lacan's *énoncé* and *énonciation*: the uttered words and the very act of uttering). The "say" (as in "Say to the Israelites") is important not so much on account of its informative content, as because it addresses the interlocutor; it is related to discourse. Lévinas, like Lacan, gives precedence to the very act of utterance, which is always bound up with transference. Like "being", "transference" too is a verb, referring to movement rather than to a fixed state.

One may say that the interpretation does not point to the object; rather, it produces it.

* * *

In a fascinating lecture given by Lyotard at the Van Leer Jerusalem Institute, he discussed art, using psychoanalysis as an analogy.

Lyotard referred to the stable object, rendered by interpretation, as motion itself. The stable object is the motion, motion that is also its own time. It is not just any movement; it is the movement of *fort/da*, of presence and absence. Lyotard calls it a "spasm". The spasm is a repetition of presence and absence alternately. Not a +/− that creates a chain of signifiers; rather, a 0/1 that evokes anxiety. Will another 1 come after the 0? This, of course, is linked to the temporal realm.

To use an example from the field of painting, it can be said that the pictorial movement is registered in the artwork and is arrested there, just as the interruption of the analytic session stops the flow of speech.

The work of art is, thus, an object, like Freud's grandson's cotton reel, through the motion of appearance and disappearance. The artwork is an object within culture. The motion of interpretation in speech renders the object and is therein arrested. A tension is built between motion and arrest, between appearance and disappearance, when it is precisely the subject's disappearance that attests to his presence, precisely the interruption of speech that attests to the unconscious. These are not two separate movements but, rather, one. It is absence within presence.

* * *

If interpretation is supposed to lead to the construction and crossing of the *phantasme*, then they both must have a similar structure that is two-directional, Möbian, as in the *phantasme* described by Freud in his essay "'A Child Is Being Beaten'" (1919e). In this *phantasme*, the beating is simultaneously both a punishment and a source of pleasure. The structure of the *phantasme* is one of "but also". It holds simultaneously two contrary positions: active and passive, genital and anal, sadism and masochism. It goes beyond contradiction as in the structure of the unconscious. Freud discusses this in *Beyond the Pleasure Principle* (1920g), where he writes of the same two movements discussed above.

Behind the contradictory contents of the *phantasme* lies a form, a beat of loading and relief of tension. According to the pleasure principle it is the beat of + and −, or presence and absence, as opposed to Lyotard's spasm, which is not structured upon a principle of recurrence guaranteeing that an "on" will always follow the "off". Rather, it is a principle of interruption, cessation; 0–1, 0–1; existence and extinction; a repetition per se, repetition of nothing.

Anxiety arises precisely from this force of rupture that is not experienced as the onset of yet another contact, but as an absolute break, a discontinuity that touches death. It is the death drive, which operates together with the pleasure principle, alternating between pleasure and extinction. As Lyotard said, the passion of love concentrates around the turmoil towards separation. The painting is a desire for colour.

The spasm interrupts the transformation of the object into a real object; thus there is threat.

Even Lacan's *objets á* are all soft, topological objects—the breast, the faeces, the gaze, and the voice. The gaze seems to be the sharpest of them; this is perhaps why Lacan says it can best escape castration. Perhaps that is why Lacan also refers to it as the "evil eye".

In his lecture, Lyotard asserted that the painter must give up blindness in order to paint. This is like the psychoanalyst who must forget his knowledge and yield his understanding in order to listen.

The analysand sketches an associative anamnestic web, within which the analyst attempts to find structure. This associative verbal mesh is boundless; it flows. The act of interpretation is an arrest of movement, but only a temporary one. The act of interpretation is always a move in time. In fact, the arrest of movement by interpretation aims at resuming the movement of desire.

* * *

The associative web can be compared to the phenomenon of the grid in art. The grid in modern art is one of the most popular and stable structures employed during the twentieth century. Many modern artists, such as Mondrian and Jasper Johns in painting, or Frank Lloyd Wright in architecture, create grids. In her essay "Grids", Rosalind Krauss (1986) asserts that the grid in modern art declares, *inter alia,* art's desire for silence; it declares its hostility to literature, to narrative, to words. Grids were not painted in the nineteenth century, though they were present in the form of perspective sketches. Yet perspective is not a grid; it is projected upon the world as some organizing structure. It attests to the way in which reality and its representation can be mapped one into the other, to the way in which the painted image and the referent in the real world refer to each other. Perspective is a form of knowledge about the world. The grid, however, does not map the space of the room, or the landscape, or the group of images on the pictorial surface. It maps only the pictorial surface itself.

One may say that interpretation in Freud's time is comparable to perspective—a form of knowledge that refers to the representation of reality—whereas interpretation according to Lacan is closer to the grid. It refuses speech; it bars it. It deals with the structure in and of itself.

The grid can be read in two ways. The first, a centrifugal reading, according to which the work of art is like a fragment, a tiny piece torn arbitrarily from a much larger fabric; thus, the grid operates from within the work of art outwards, coercing our recognition of a world beyond the frame. The second reading is a centripetal one, working from the external borders inwards. According to such a reading, the grid is a representation of anything that separates the work of art from the surrounding world.

The grid is an internalization of the boundaries of the world into the work. It is a form of repetition whose content is the conventional nature of art itself. In analogy to analysis, it can be read as a laboratory, as part of the totality of life, where the interpretation strives to the general, the universal, as opposed to a reading that separates the world and the subject, striving for the particular. Again we come to an *ex-time* object that is defined by the interpretation as grid.

* * *

Manipulated by the laws of the market, the contemporary world tries to force objects to be objects by subjecting them to the law of rating—how many viewers came to the exhibition, how many read the book, how many go to analysis as opposed to other therapeutic methods. In this manner, we attempt to eliminate the threat of absence, to freeze the movement.

Another common method is putting objects in the museum. We live in a museum-oriented era, says Lyotard; an era that places the entire history and the surface of the Earth in museums, a culture that sanctifies memory.

It is an era that threatens, I fear, to put Freud, too, in the museum—pay him his due respect while, in fact, sentencing him to death.

Perhaps we should consider how to avoid putting Lacan, too, in the museum. It would, indeed, allow the arrest of motion and the relief of the spasm of being, but a motionless object is a dead object, and the object in psychoanalysis is located in the movement of absence and presence.

CHAPTER FIFTEEN

About narrow-mindedness and the Real

For my teacher, Andrew Cohen

Spinoza

"... it is made finite through its cause, which is necessarily God. Further, if it is finite through its cause, this must be so either because its cause could not give more, or because it would not give more. That he should not have been able to give more would contradict his omnipotence; that he should not have been willing to give more, when he could well do so, savours of ill-will [narrow-mindedness], which is nowise in God, who is all goodness and perfection." [Spinoza, 1660, pp. 51–52]

I interpret this statement by Spinoza as meaning that the literal meaning of narrow-mindedness is vision of limited perspective. While man is afflicted by narrow vision, the vision of the Divine is absolute, and therefore the divine abundance is of an absolute nature.

Freud

In his essay "Remembering, Repeating and Working-Through" (1914g), Freud referred to treatment by analysis as broadening one's view: "and now we can see that in drawing attention to the compulsion to repeat we have acquired no new fact but only a more comprehensive view" (p. 151). Through analysis Freud sought to broaden one's point of view and reduce the limitations of one's perspective.

Holarchy

From an evolutionary perspective, there is direction in the way life on earth is developing and there is natural hierarchy in the world, which Arthur Koestler referred to as "holarchy".

Reality is comprised of a whole/fragments or "holons". Holons are simultaneously complete in themselves and components of a greater whole. Every thing is a holon of something else. Reality is comprised of neither things nor processes, but of holons, and is infinite.

* * *

Holons appear in holarchy, or natural hierarchy—an order of ever-increasing perfection: from particles to atoms to cells to organisms; from letters to words to sentences to paragraphs. What constitutes a whole on one plane becomes a fragment in relation to a higher plane. The lower does not include the higher, but the higher does include the lower.

Evolution tends towards increasing complexity, further differentiation/integration, further organization/construction, increasing relative autonomy, and more and more *telos* [purpose].

Each evolutionary level transcends, yet includes, its subordinate level. Each new level is innovative, as metaphor is to language (Wilber, 2000).

* * *

In his book *The Fragile Absolute* (2000), Slavoj Žižek shows us that psychoanalysis functions in the intermediate zone of the contrast between factual "objective" knowledge and "subjective" truth. Psychoanalysis exposes deceit uttered under the guise of truth (such as by obsessive personalities whose statements, while precise, actually deny their desire). It also exposes the speakers of truth under the guise of deceit (the hysterical process, or slips of the tongue that reveal the subject's desire) (Žižek, 2000).

The value of such truth is not what is important in psychoanalysis. What is important is the manner in which the transition between truth and deceit reveals the desires of the patient.

* * *

When a female patient contends that her father sexually abused her, the important factor is not the abuse as such; rather, it is its role in her symbolic economy and the manner in which the event was subjectified. It is not the event itself that is important but the way in which it is related to and the ability to register it in the make-up of the psyche, conscious or unconscious. Lacan interpreted thus what Freud called "the reality of the psyche".

If the evolutionary holarchic model is applied, we will be able to state that what is deceit on one plane becomes truth on another plane, while the transition between the planes reveals the desire. Desire for what?—for further expansion of consciousness or broadening of perspective. When there is no transition, if things get stuck, desire gets jammed—a symptom into which *jouissance* is drained.

The experience

After many long years of psychoanalysis, that female patient has reached the point of certainty—she circumnavigates and surrounds the rock of the Real, that which cannot be described, which cannot be healed. She will have to bear that wound all her life; all that is left to do is "identify with the symptom", adjust oneself more comfortably to the symptom, and accept it.

She considers the *passe* as an option, instead of which she opts for a spiritual workshop in India. After a week of meditation, contemplation, silence, and detachment from all that is known, the teacher speaks of the Real—in his own terms. "Get real!" he says, using "American" terminology. What comes to her mind is "Coca Cola—The Real Thing", and she chuckles derisively.

Then, seemingly from nowhere, the barrier—the Real—pops up from the very depths of her being. Doubt assails her—could this really be the Real? At that very moment of the question arising, the Real melts away and it is as if it had never been present. The world turns upside down. There is a sense of wonder and blissful dizziness, and an almost unbearable ease. That same dark god that had controlled her, to whom she had sacrificed so much, around which her whole life had revolved, has crumbled away in front of her like a cheap illusion. For her it was a leap in consciousness that made the Real imaginary. So where is the "real" Real hiding? If we see the evolution of consciousness in spiral form, the only Real that there is is the Absolute, or full, perspective—unlimited all-encompassing vision. Every other Real can only be relative.

* * *

Two years later, the effects of the experience have taken root, stabilized, and her perspective continues to broaden.

The flower

Hegel

Hegel distinguished between dialectics as a science (knowledge)—the "synchronous" motion within the world of complete knowledge—and dialectics as a journey (truth), which is the movement towards it. The analogy is taken from the realm of flora—the journey of the tree from bud to fruit:

> In the same way when the fruit comes, the blossom may be explained to be a false form of the plant's existence, for the fruit appears as its true nature in place of the blossom. But the ceaseless activity of their own inherent nature makes them at the same time moments of an organic unity, where they not merely do not contradict one another, but where one is as necessary as the other; and this equal necessity of all moments constitutes alone and thereby the life of the whole. [Hegel, 1807, p. 68]

* * *

210   EVOLUTION

Hegel speaks of evolutionary leaps while comparing them to the birth of a child or to building a new world:

> It [the spirit] is indeed never at rest, but carried along the stream of progress ever onward. But it is here as in the case of the birth of a child; after a long period of nutrition in silence, the continuity of the gradual growth in size, of quantitative change, is suddenly cut short by the first breath drawn—there is a break in the process, a qualitative change—and the child is born. In like manner the spirit of the time, growing slowly and quietly ripe for the new form it is to assume, disintegrates one fragment after another of the structure of its previous world. That it is tottering to its fall is indicated only by symptoms here and there. Frivolity and again ennui, which are spreading in the established order of things, the undefined foreboding of something unknown—all these betoken that there is something else approaching. This gradual crumbling to pieces, which did not alter the general look and aspect of the whole, is interrupted by the sunrise, which, in a flash and at a single stroke, brings to view the form and structure of the new world. [Hegel, 1807, p. 75]

Thus dialectics stem from the fact that there is tension (contradictions) within the system of concepts. This tension cannot be relieved at the level of our current conceptual system. In order to solve it, new ideas have to be generated, but these also have to preserve some of the logic of the preceding stage that generated the tension.

Lévinas

In the aforesaid context, it is interesting to note the apparently opposite position that Lévinas took. To Lévinas, evolution occurs in retrospect—from absolute to relative. Opposite the analogy of the blossom that develops into fruit, we can bring Lévinas's reference to a Talmudic problem in the Shabbat tractate (page 88, 71–72), as it explains the verse from the Song of Songs: "As the apple tree among the trees of the wood, so is my beloved among the sons . . " (Song of Songs, 2:3). This passage from the tractate tells of Rabbi Hama, son of Rabbi Hanina, asking why in this verse the

Israelites are compared to an apple. Rabbi Hanina answers that, as is the case with the apple whose fruit precedes its leaves, so the Israelites preceded doing to hearing (Lévinas, 1968).

The fruit precedes the leaves and the flowers. The Torah is received prior to any inquiry, outside of gradual development. The epilogue precedes the story—"We will do and we will hear". The Torah in this sense is the Real.

The "yes" in "we will do" does not mean volunteering for doing per se, it does not envelop a wonderful "praxis" that precedes thought, while the blindness, even if it is the blindness of a trusting individual, is bound to bring about disaster. On the contrary: this "yes" is about sobriety without hesitation, without a guiding hypothesis, without a clue, without cognitive examination. It is about an evolutionary leap.

Lacan

In the XXth seminar, Lacan said: "the ego [*moi*] can also be a flower of rhetoric, which grows in the pot of the pleasure principle that Freud calls '*Lustprinzip*,' and that I define as that which is satisfied by blah-blah" (Lacan, 1975a, p. 56). We know that the ego mediates between the subject and reality. We know that the reality that the ego mediates is actually made of the pleasure principle, which it represents. In this seminar, Lacan focused on symbolic language as a parasite of primal *lalangue*, the language of *jouissance*. However, it seems that when he spoke of the ego's "blah-blah", he meant a third form of speech—speech as self-importance and empty "authoritative" knowledge, as a false mask that covers the living knowledge that pulsates within the Real—that stems from the unknown and is exposed more and more in the course of evolution.

Trauma and opportunity

Žižek

In *The Fragile Absolute* (2000), Žižek referred to the connection between the structure and its own event. On the one hand, the event is the impossible Real of a structure, of its synchronous symbolic order, the violent gesture that generated it. Synchronous structural order is a kind of defensive formation against the event that establishes it. On the other hand, one could contend the opposite: the status of the event itself (the mythic narrative of the primordial, violent establishing gesture) is phantasmic. This is phantasmic construction that is intended to relate to what cannot be related to (the sources of order), through concealing the Real of the structural antagonism (lack of possibility) that prevents synchronous structural order from achieving balance.

* * *

The Act as Real is an authentic Act, located between time and eternity. Žižek quoted Kant and Schelling regarding the Act. They see it as the point at which eternity intervenes in the process of time, the point at which the temporal causal chain is disturbed. Something appears, generated from emptiness (the revelation). Something that cannot be explained occurs as a result of the preceding chain. On the other hand, the Act is simultaneously the moment at which time rises from eternity. This voids the balance—this is the paradox of the eternal gesture that simultaneously realizes eternity while opening up the realm of the temporal/historic.

Eternity is not above time, in the simple sense of existing beyond time. Eternity is the name given to the event or the cut that supports and operates the temporal dimension as a sequence of failed attempts to capture it.

* * *

Psychoanalysis refers to this Act as "trauma". Trauma is eternal and cannot find form either in time or in history. It is the point of eternity around which time revolves. This is an event that is only accessible in time through the multiplication of its traces. Eternity and time are not mutually exclusive, in the simple sense of the word. There is no time without eternity. Temporality is maintained by our failure to grasp/symbolize/historicize the eternal trauma. If trauma enters the temporal/historic, the dimension of time itself will collapse into the eternal now, devoid of time. Eternity is that which is excluded—the exception that enables historical reality to preserve its consistency.

* * *

Psychoanalysis includes within it acceptance and admission that all of our verbal exchange formations are eternally haunted by "a leftover that cannot be divided". It is a ghost of traumatic remnant that resists confession—that is, integration with a symbolic world: it cannot be liberated, completed, or allowed to rest. This relates implicitly to the traumatic core that continues as an obscene remnant of a living-dead that keeps the world of verbal exchange "alive". Without the addition of this ghost, there is no life. Therefore, the ultimate objective of psychoanalysis is not the attainment of peace through confessing trauma but, rather, acceptance that our life also has an irreparable core of trauma. There is something in us that cannot find release—ever.

Evolutionary opportunity

Like Freud, Žižek (2000) halts in the face of trauma. By his description, it appears that the trauma does not enable an evolutionary releasing process. However, later in the book he wrote:

> Judaism stands for the paradox of Universalism which maintains its universal dimension precisely by its "passionate attachment" to the stain of particularity that serves as its unacknowledged foundation. Judaism thus not only belies the common-sense notion that the price to be paid for access to universality is to renounce one's particularity; it also demonstrates how the stain of unacknowledged particularity of the gesture that generates the Universal is the ultimate resource of the Universal's vitality. . . . [Žižek, 2000, p. 99]

What did he mean when he spoke of Judaism? Was he unwittingly speaking of the same Act that Lévinas was also referring to, whose significance becomes apparent only in retrospect, an Act connected with revelation and that leads to redemption—because trauma is simultaneously a threatening fixation that leads to anxiety while also offering the opportunity to awaken—*tuché*—the opportunity to take an evolutionary leap?

Something has occurred—an event that can be neither suppressed nor forgotten. Something has to be done—before and in place of recognition.

* * *

From a holarchic and evolutionary perspective, trauma is the opportunity to approach that place of broader perspective. When truth rises to a higher plane, what might be experienced by us as real in the context of the psyche can become imaginary.

GET REAL!

CHAPTER SIXTEEN

Eppur si muove!—
nevertheless, it does move

This short essay gives an initial outline of a broader research project. The project was conducted in order to re-examine some of the conclusions reached from viewing psychoanalysis not as a form of scientific, philosophical, or even psychological research, but as research that includes the researching subject—meaning that psychoanalytic research is inseparable from clinical work.

The purpose of such research is not merely to gather information or knowledge, but to reveal elements relating to truth and cause, in a way that will influence and bring about change, transformation. This concept is valid in relation to both praxis and, in a different way, learning. Transformation is movement of the psyche—in a specific direction.

* * *

With the opening of the Clinical Section in Paris in 1977, Lacan established the couch as the clinic. He said that we have to "clinicize"—to lay the patient down. He meant that the term "clinic" should lead us to reconsider our own clinical work: the treatment we give, our transition from the position of analysand to that of analyst, and the way we relate to transference. Lacan used the opportunity to assert that "Clinical psychoanalysis must consist not only of analytic examination but also examination of the analysts" (Lacan, 1977b).

I feel that it is too easy for us to forget what Lacan really meant by allowing ourselves to be satisfied merely by the more interesting intellectual and theoretical elements of psychoanalysis.

Sometimes even testimonies regarding the *passe* process seem to be no more than a creative way of expressing analytic insights, devoid of real effects. This is both stimulating and worrying. A glance at working relationships within the analytic institution, for example, can leave one wondering in regard to the effect that psychoanalysis has on the analysts themselves.

At this point, I tend to believe that we fail to apply our professional ethics in our personal lives. As soon as we get up off the analyst's armchair, we stop being ready to listen freely and openly, to cast off our tendency towards narcissism and to contemplate in a way that is free of ego.

* * *

There is a difference between curiosity about psychoanalytic knowledge and studying it, because we have a sense that our fate depends on there being new breakthroughs in the field. When questions do start to be asked, genuine answers are generally found, but the real answers can seem too big for us to deal with, because they require transition from the known to the unknown and a change in our ethical position. That is why we tend to bury the answers in a sheath of knowledge—"Interesting, I'd like to look into that." That is how we make sure that we will always be students. This course of action involves a lot of *jouissance*, identification with psychoanalysis as an ideal, and identification with the ideals of psychoanalysis.

The critical question relates to the motive behind the research— or the desire that empowers the research. The individual that approaches psychoanalysis in order to know also wants to know about himself and his place in the world. I call such knowledge "living" or "erotic" knowledge—the opposite of the knowledge of universities. Whether or not a person admits it, there is a sense of dissatisfaction with what already exists, a hunger for deeper experience of being.

* * *

So psychoanalysis is really a kind of psychic motion. Or, more precisely, psychoanalysis deals with the conflict between the dynamics of progress, regression, going round in circles, or being stuck in one place—a dynamic of internal and external events, of drives and representations, occurring within the framework of time.

The libido

Such dynamics are based on Freud's concept of libido. Lacan's initial definition of libido aided him in constructing the "mirror stage", the stage at which the ego becomes fixated. Miller used Lacan's scheme to illustrate the imaginary connection that runs between a and a', with the libido in a circular motion, representing complete connection at the level of *jouissance*—the level of libidinal drive. His definition is based on Freud's essay "On Narcissism" (Freud, 1914c). The connection at the imaginary level interferes most foully with the intersubjective connection, blocking it, making it fixed and repetitive (Miller, 1995–96).

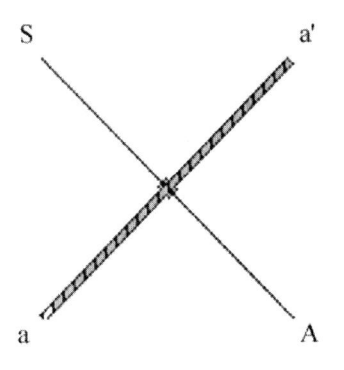

The axis upon which the libido registers obstructs the subject's symbolic connection with the Other, even to the point of disconnecting it. *Jouissance* cuts off the genuine connection with the Other. As Miller put it, in psychoanalysis one has to overcome the libidinal connection in order to facilitate a genuine connection with the Other. When treatment is steered in the right way, *jouissance* ultimately gives way, allowing for the motion itself to be transformed.

* * *

Lacan distinguished between two opposing types of libido:
1. Libido in a repetitive cycle from the ego to the world outside, in narcissistic terms—libido that can be transferred.
2. That which he termed "The libido of phallic auto-eroticism"—fixated, stagnant libido.

"The imaginary function is what Freud formulated. It governs the object's investment as a narcissistic object" (Miller, 1995–96).

The permanent element of this circulation is phallic. In distinguishing between the two opposing forms—transitory and fixated—Lacan established the basis of what he later called the model of *jouissance*.

In *The Four Fundamental Concepts of Psycho-Analysis*, Lacan wrote:

> Everything that Freud spells out about the partial drives shows us the movement that I outlined for you on the blackboard last time, that circular movement of the thrust that emerges through the erogenous rim only to return to it as its target, after having encircled something I call the *objet a*. I suggest—and punctilious examination of this whole text is a test of the truth of what I propose—that it is in this way that the subject attains what is, strictly speaking, the dimension of the capital Other.
>   I suggest that there is a radical distinction between *loving oneself through the other*—which, in the narcissistic field of the object, allows no transcendence to the object included—and the circularity of the drive, in which the heterogeneity of the movement out and back shows a gap in its interval. [Lacan, 1973, p. 194]

Lacan located the libido of Freud in that gap created by the periodicity of the drive. In Lacan's XIth seminar (1986), he saw libido not as energy but as an organ, the substance of the Real: biological life, unlimited by life or death. The libido represents life as something that cannot be annihilated, the pure drive of life—beyond the genealogical chain of sexual procreation. The libido, therefore, is a result of the separation between biological sexuality and human sexuality—as dictated by the symbolic order.

* * *

When Lacan began to teach, he thought that it would suffice to contend that it is not the signifier that attracts the libido but the image, the reflection. In time, he discarded this explanation because he discovered that the signifier itself is saturated with libido. He noted the material dimension of language and then distinguished the split subject as a non-libidinal effect of the signifier—a dead subject, an effect of signifiers—from *objet á* as a loaded effect of the signifier. The signifier therefore has both a fatal effect in regard to the subject and a life-giving effect—*jouissance*.

In this context, *objet á* is the symptom.

Fixation—the ego

The remarkable similarity between Buddhist teachings and the way Freud and Lacan establish the ego as an object was, for me, a novel and exciting revelation. According to both views, the object is formed out of the building blocks of identifications and is structured as a shield or screen to protect from unmediated encounters with the bodily or worldly Real.

The ego serves as a defence mechanism in the face of the dynamic uncertainty of the subject of the unconscious, its inherent otherness, and the sense of the uncanny that accompanies such encounters. Because of the imaginary fixation on the ego as our identity (Eastern wisdom refers to such fixation as "attachment"), the ego resists movement or change in desire. In analytic practice, the ego is considered to be a source of resistance and fixation. Reinforcing it merely serves to increase resistance. The attachment of the ego is the personal, imaginary perspective, which puts a stop to motion.

By undermining the attachment to the ego, psychoanalysis tries to restore the movement of desire, of its dialectic, to open up a free space in which the subject can dwell and move more freely through life's contingencies.

* * *

For Lacan as for Freud, the ego is not a subject but an object, constructed out of fixated identifications. It is but a structure formed by identification with the specular image of the "mirror stage". This is the place where the subject becomes alienated from itself, becoming its fellow men. In a structural sense, such alienation is similar to paranoia. Therefore, the ego is an imaginary product, the locus of resistance.

Thus, Lacan was very much against the idea that psychoanalysis should reinforce the ego. Since the ego is the seat of our illusions, reinforcing it only serves to facilitate further alienation and fixation of the subject.

The ego therefore constitutes the principal source of resistance to analysis. Since it is essentially fixed in the imaginary realm, it resists all subjective growth and change and also the dialectic motion of desire. By undermining the fixation of the ego, analysis attempts to restore the dialectic of desire and to usher in the subject's being.

Where does Lacan locate the ego in the make-up of the psyche? In the XXth seminar (1975a), Lacan distinguished between the two bodies that psychoanalysis relates to. One is the body defined by language—what is said about it and the way it is treated and touched. It is a sexual body in a process of birth and death. The other is the organism—that conglomeration of flesh imbued with inextinguishable life.

In this sense, language constitutes a kind of parasite on the organism, constructing as it does the symbolic body. We have two bodies—one mounted on the other, and two languages—one mounted on the other. Language is mounted on the *lalangue*. The process of recognition or the revelation of this is a reverse process: from the body to the organism. There is language and there is *lalangue*. However, I believe that the kind of speech that comes from the ego that Lacan refers to as "blah-blah" constitutes a third type of speech. This third form of speech is the talk of self-importance and knowledge that bestows authority—it acts as a screen that covers the living, pulsating knowledge in the Real, which is connected with the unknown (Lacan, 1975a).

Perhaps for Lacan the ego was a hybrid creature, connecting the organism—the body per se—with the symbolic body, or connecting the speaking being [parlêttre] with the subject when it is based on the pleasure principle.

I contend that in place of the non-existent sexual connection, we tend to construct an imaginary sexual link with our own ego, which becomes one of the principal obstacles to analysis. We are trapped in phallic *jouissance* in regard to our own self-image—our thoughts, moods, ideas, and so forth. They seem to us highly unique and important, whereas they are, in effect, the cause of our suffering. We find such suffering so very hard to give up because it constructs our "identity".

Time after time we come across clear examples of this phenomenon in our clinical work. However, apart from it being critical to psychoanalytic training, how will the analyst, when captivated by his own ego, be able to apply, for example, free-floating attention? (free of self-image, identifications, the known).

Horizontal and vertical movement

Relating to the psyche and the world in the fundamental context of motion is not unique to psychoanalysis. Thousands of years ago the Buddhist philosopher Chuang Tzu said that the primal elements of the universe are dynamic systems, transitional stages in the constant flow of variability and transformation.

According to Heisenberg:

"[In modern Physics], one has now divided the world not into different groups of objects but into different groups of connections.... What can be distinguished is the kind of connection which is primarily important in a certain phenomenon.... The world thus appears as a complicated issue of events, in which connections of different kinds alternate or overlap or combine and thereby determine the texture of the whole." [in Fritjof, 1975, p. 291]

Thus, the concept of motion has come to occupy a central position in modern science. The world is experienced as a dynamic inseparable whole that also includes the observer. In this experience the traditional concepts of time and space, individual objects, and cause and effect lose their significance. Quantum theory, for example, recognizes the interconnecting relations that underlie the universe, showing that the world cannot be disassembled into independently existing units. Our world is formed of these links, which are in a constant state of motion and change.

* * *

In psychoanalytic terms there are two forms of motion: there is repetitive cyclic motion, the motion of drive around the object causing *jouissance*, and there is also the developing form of vertical motion.

Thus, the subject can go from fixation and compulsive repetitiveness to acting from free choice.

* * *

Ken Wilber (2001), an influential contemporary thinker and expert on Eastern and Western knowledge, distinguishes between the two functions offered by religion, but the distinction he makes can also apply to various fields in our culture—particularly psychoanalysis.

Wilber distinguishes between horizontal and vertical movement. He refers to horizontal movement as "translation"—motion that generates meanings, deepening understanding, stories, interest, and interpretation. Horizontal motion only serves to reaffirm and reinforce the I. It cannot bring about a change in our level of awareness. It cannot liberate us from the ego.

There is also vertical movement—the movement of radical transformation and liberation. This kind of movement is characteristic of a tiny fraction of the population. Instead of reinforcing the fixated ego, it has the potential to destroy it. It is about emptiness rather than fullness, as well as revolution. Wilber refers to it as "transformation". Vertical motion puts the very process of translation in doubt, shatters it. With translation, the I finds new ways of thinking about the world. Transformation means changing the world rather than translating it.

* * *

The process of translation gives legitimacy to the I and its beliefs. Without translation there will be social chaos. Individuals who cannot translate with a reasonable level of integrity and precision—who are unable to construct a world of significance—fall into psychosis. The world ceases to be understood, and the boundaries between the world and the I begin to disintegrate. This is not a breakthrough—this is a crisis, disaster rather than transcendence.

While translation has a vital function, there is a point at which it can no longer console and no new paradigms or myths can allay the sense of distress. The only way out is transformation—individually and collectively.

From the personal to the particular via the universal

Psychoanalytic treatment is a bit like starting out on a journey and having to visit various places on the way—starting from the personal, passing through the universal, and arriving at the unique, the particular.

At the initial session with a new patient, my first question is "What brings you here?" or "Why are you here?"

During the last session following nine years of treatment, one of my patients asked me, with tears in her eyes, "What have you brought me up for?" Her question came as a surprise for me, like a retrospective interpretation, shedding light on the entire nine-year process. It had a hair-raising effect, akin to her asking: "My God, My God, why hast thou forsaken me?" Was *that* what I had been doing in her analysis? Bringing her up?

In his essay "The Subversion of the Subject and the Dialectic of Desire in the Freudian Unconscious", Lacan said, referring to his investigation of the unconscious, "to the point at which it gives a reply that is not some sort of ravishment or takedown, but is rather a 'saying why'" (1966a, p. 283). He refers to the cause.

* * *

I believe that the route along which analysis flows runs between the three questions, "what?" "what for?" and "why?"

Patients respond to the first question in personal terms—their personal complaint, the story of their life, their own personal pain and anxiety. Treatment revolves around repetitive elements of their tale. From the repetition arise the symptom, the complex, and a structural diagnosis. The universal nature of his suffering—the structural character (i.e. neurotic, psychotic, perverse, etc.)—comes as an unpleasant surprise for the subject. The chaos of the signifiers is reduced to a kind of formula. The personal has to be taken through the universal prism, which changes the position of the subjects and their narcissistic investment in "being special". That is the first step. The next is the recognition of the *jouissance* that is bound up with the subjects' suffering and adhesion to their symptom. The subjects assume responsibility for their position regarding sexuation—their sexual preference—man or woman (beyond biology and sex) and that special combination of verbal *jouissance*. These are the particular aspects of their subjectivity.

* * *

Only through adopting the position of "I don't know but I want to know" can they "pass through" and grow from the personal to the particular.

In this respect, drive belongs to the realm of universality. Drive is the movement around the fallen object, freedom from any object that can be perceived. Lacan defined the essence of the drive as the trace of the Act. Once it used to encircle our bodies, sealing off our empty erogenous orifices, just as the breast blocked our mouths and voices blocked our ears. Such partial organs are part of the totality of the *lamella*, that part of the libido that is desexualized—immortal, inextinguishable life.

Sexualization introduces death—the trace of an Act rather than the Act itself. The movement of drive, the *jouissance* and satisfaction involved, are the movements of an automaton. They belong to the realm of cyclic, horizontal motion, and are not evolutionary. Not so desire, which can never be satisfied. It has a metonymic possibility—replacing one object with another. There is also a dialectic faculty in Hegelian terms: generating a new metaphor when it engages [*tuché*] with the Real.

* * *

The gist of philosophy, including Eastern philosophy, has dealt with horizontal movement rather than with evolution. Even in referring to movement—"Everything flows" or "All is one"—it is the whole, the absolute, that is being referred to. In psychoanalysis, the phallic dimension constitutes a part of this totality. Like the movement of a pendulum—creation and extinction—there is and then there is not. The libido, too, has been characterized by the movement of here/there, life/death, *fort/da*. Even in the Borromean context, which refers to four dimensions—symbolic, imaginary, Real, and the object that connects them—the connection is still cyclic: pincer grasped by pincer, dimension gripped by dimension; a chain of signifiers. In the past, vertical motion was the realm of the religions, but they, too, failed to refer to the evolution of consciousness, focusing instead on the development of morality.

Although in the realms of science—quantum physics—the border between matter and consciousness has been rent asunder, to the best of my knowledge the subject of research is not evolution—the new. There is a field, and there are things that affect that field. Psychoanalytic practice, however, deals with evolution—personal, universal, and particular. This occurs through praxis rather than theory. Analysis cannot be discussed without discussing evolution—recognition of repetition, the fall of the ideal, giving up *jouissance*, and so on.

The next step is to stop trying to become: to recognize the fact of partiality of the various passions and their limitations and to break free of them—that is, liberation.

* * *

The various scientific theories regarding the expansion and contraction of the universe also have an evolutionary element. This element exists in the anomalous, in the "not everything". Transition is the subject here—from the phallic to the feminine, giving up *jouissance*, inventing knowledge, identification with the *sinthome*. What does psychoanalysis exist for if not to prevent repetition? To liberate from fixation, to create a space for desire to move in, to improve the representation of drive with new metaphors? To fell the ideal? To leave identification behind?

Lacan also referred to the *passe* as a possibility for evolution of knowledge through transmission.

The movement and training of the analyst

In referring to the training of psychoanalysts, Miller (2002) talked about "formation"—training—and what lies beyond training— "transformation".

The question of training becomes more refined when the objective is not only to accumulate knowledge but that certain subjective conditions should emerge: transformation of the subject's being, or training for wisdom, like in Zen—that is, subjective transformation without transmitting any specialist knowledge.

Training requires that the psyche mutate. Genuine training transmits spirit and a path and is realized when the individual develops a new character. In real training we are always ready for surprises and the unknown—in the same way that interpretation works as an Act that leads to change in psychoanalysis. Study is not training. Miller's concept, in the wake of Lacan, says that proper training always starts after study. It includes within it ignoring what one already knows" (Miller, 2002). Its aim is perfection. In training—as in therapy—subjective transformation is what is sought after.

REFERENCES

Adorno, T. (1962). Commitment. In: A. Arato & E. Gebhardt (Eds.), *The Essential Frankfurt School Reader* (pp. 312–318). New York: Continuum, 1982.

Agassi, M. (1994). Lucien Freud and Howard Hodgkin. *Studio, 50*: 24–31. [Hebrew]

Améry, J. (1977). *Jenseits von Schuld und Sühne. Bewältigungsversuche eines Überwältigten*. Stuttgart: Klett Cotta Verlag.

Arendt, H. (1996). *Love and St. Augustine*. Chicago: University of Chicago Press.

Atar, T. (1979). *The Lunar City*. Tel-Aviv: Hakibutz Hameuchad. [Hebrew]

Azaria, Rabbi M. (1884). *Kanfei Yona* [Vol. 4]. Lamberg.

Bataille, G. (1985). *Visions of Excess—Selected Writings 1929–1939*. Minnesota, MN: University of Minnesota Press.

Bataille, G. (1991). *Documents 1920–30*. Paris: Editions Jean Michel Place.

Baudelaire, C. (1947). *Paris Spleen*. New York: New Directions.

Bergmann, M. (1987). *The Anatomy of Loving: The Story of Man's Quest to Know What Love Is*. New York: Ballantine Books.

Berman, S. J. (1980). Kol isha. In: L. Landman (Ed.), *Rabbi Joseph H. Lookstein Memorial Volume* (pp. 45–66). New York: Ktav.

Bialik, H. N. & Ravizky, Y. H. (1936). *Sefer Ha'agada*. Tel-Aviv: Dvir. [Hebrew]

Blanchot, M. (1982). *The Gaze of Orpheus and Other Literary Essays*. New York: Barrytown.

Blich, B. (1994). The artistic functionality of the blind. *Ha'ir*, 21 January, p. 20. [Hebrew]

Bois, Y. A. (1993). Painting: The task of mourning. In: *Painting as Model*. Cambridge, MA: MIT Press.

Bullock, A., & Stallybrass, O. (1992). *The Fontana Dictionary of Modern Thought*. Tel-Aviv: Am Oved. [Hebrew]

Cameroon, E. (1988). Should Paul Celan have been accepted in Israel? *Al Hamishmar*, 29 January, p. 17. [Hebrew]

Celan, P. (1972). *Poems of Paul Celan*. New York: Persea Books.

Celan, P. (1976). Out of the shattered. In: *Selected Poems and Prose*. Tel-Aviv: Hakibutz Hameuchad Publishing, 1994. [Hebrew]

Celan, P. (1986). *Collected Prose*. New York: Sheep Meadow Press.

Celan, P. (1988). *The Rose of Nothingness. Selected Poems*. Tel-Aviv: Sifriat Poalim. [Hebrew]

Celan, P. (1994). *Selected Poems and Prose*. Tel-Aviv: Hakibutz Hameuchad Publishing. [Hebrew]

Chalfen, I. (1991). *Paul Celan: A Biography of His Youth*. New York: Persea Books.

Dolar, M. (1996a). At first sight. In: S. Žižek & R. Salcel (Eds.), *Gaze and Voice as Love Objects* (pp. 129–154). Durham, NC: Duke University Press.

Dolar, M. (1996b). The object voice. In: S. Žižek & R. Salecl (Eds.), *Gaze and Voice as Love Objects* (pp. 7–31). Durham, NC: Duke University Press.

Edwards, P. (Ed.) (1967). *Encyclopedia of Philosophy II*. New York: Macmillan.

Ende, M. (1979). *The Neverending Story*. London: Penguin Books, 1990. [First published Stuttgart: Thienemann Verlag.]

Felman, S., & Laub, D. (1992). *Testimony: Crises of Witnessing in Literature, Psychoanalysis and History*. New York: Routledge.

Freud, S. (1900a). *The Interpretation of Dreams*. *Standard Edition*, 4 & 5.

Freud, S. (1905d). *Three Essays on the Theory of Sexuality*. *Standard Edition*, 7: 125.

Freud, S. (1908e [1907]). Creative writers and day-dreaming. *Standard Edition*, 9: 143.

Freud, S. (1910a [1909]). Five lectures on psycho-analysis. *Standard Edition*, 11: 3.

Freud, S. (1910h). A special type of choice of object made by men. *Standard Edition*, 11: 165.
Freud, S. (1912d). On the universal tendency to debasement in the sphere of love. *Standard Edition*, 11: 179.
Freud, S. (1914c). On narcissism: An introduction. *Standard Edition*, 14: 69.
Freud, S. (1914g). Remembering, repeating and working-through. *Standard Edition*, 12: 147.
Freud, S. (1915c). Instincts and their vicissitudes. *Standard Edition*, 14: 111.
Freud, S. (1915e). The unconscious. *Standard Edition*, 14: 161.
Freud, S. (1915f). A case of paranoia running counter to the psychoanalytic theory of the disease. *Standard Edition*, 14: 261–272.
Freud, S. (1918b [1914]). From the history of an infantile neurosis. *Standard Edition*, 17: 3.
Freud, S. (1919e). "A child is being beaten": A contribution to the study of the origin of sexual perversions. *Standard Edition*, 17: 177.
Freud, S. (1920g). *Beyond the Pleasure Principle*. *Standard Edition*, 18: 3.
Freud, S. (1921c). *Group Psychology and the Analysis of the Ego*. *Standard Edition*, 18: 67.
Freud, S. (1925h). Negation. *Standard Edition*, 19: 235.
Freud, S. (1927e). Fetishism. *Standard Edition*, 21: 149.
Fritjof, C. (1975). *The Tao of Physics*. Berkely, CA: Shambala. [Reprinted London: Flamingo, 1982].
Galliano, C. (1998). The encounter with the real. *Machbarot Freudianiot—Journal of the Clinical Section*, 5: 2–21. [Hebrew]
Geva, T. (1994). Center: Itzhak Golombek. *Studio*, 55: 42. [Hebrew]
Golan, R., & Lieber, S. (1996). Two meetings with Moshe Gershuni. *Studio*, 76: 62–73. [Hebrew]
Hegel, G. W. F. (1807). *The Phenomenology of Mind*. New York: Harper Torchbooks, 1967.
Jaanus, M. (1995). The demontage of the drive. In: R. Feldstein, B. Fink, & M. Jaanus (Eds.), *Reading Seminar XI* (pp. 119–138). Albany, NY: State University of New York Press.
Kandinsky, W. (1982). Sounds. In: K. C. Lindsay & P. Vergo (Eds.), *Complete Writings on Art* (pp. 291–340). Boston, MA: G. K. Hall. [Reprinted Cambridge, MA: De Capo, 1994.]
Kirkegaard, S. (1954). *Selected Writings*. Tel-Aviv: Dvir. [Hebrew]
Kirkegaard, S. (1990). *The Diary of Soren Kirkegaard*. New York: Carol Publishing.

Krauss, R. (1986). *The Originality of the Avant-Garde and Other Modernist Myths*. Cambridge, MA: MIT Press.

Krauss, R. (1988). *The Impulse to See: Vision and Visuality*. Seattle, WA: Bay Press.

Krauss, R. (1993). *The Optical Unconscious*. New York: MIT Press.

Lacan, J. (1962). Kant with Sade. *October, 51*: 55–75.

Lacan, J. (1963a). *On Anxiety* [Seminar X, lesson 22/5/63]. Unpublished seminar.

Lacan, J. (1963b). Introduction to the names-of-the-father seminar. In: *Television* (pp. 81–97), trans. J. Mehlman, ed. J. Copjec. New York: Norton, 1990.

Lacan, J. (1966a). *Écrits*. New York: Norton, 2002. [First published Paris: Éditions du Seuil.]

Lacan, J. (1966b). Science and truth. *Newsletter of the Freudian Field , 3*: 3–40.

Lacan, J. (1973). *The Four Fundamental Concepts of Psycho-Analysis*. London: Peregrine Books, 1986. [First published Paris: Éditions du Seuil.]

Lacan, J. (1975a). *Encore: On Feminine Sexuality, the Limits of Love and Knowledge* [Seminar XX, 1972–73]. London: Norton, 1998. [First published Paris: Éditions du Seuil.]

Lacan, J. (1975b). Geneva lecture on the symptom. *Analysis, 1*: 7–27.

Lacan, J. (1977a). Desire and interpretation of desire in Hamlet. *Yale French Studies, 55/56*: 11–52.

Lacan, J. (1977b). At the opening of the clinical section, Paris [unpublished].

Lacan, J. (1978). *The Ego in Freud's Theory and in the Technique of Psychoanalysis* [Seminar II, 1954–5]. Cambridge: Cambridge University Press, 1988. [First published Paris: Éditions du Seuil.]

Lacan, J. (1986). *The Ethics of Psychoanalysis* [Seminar VII, 1959–1960]. London: Routledge, 1992. [First published Paris: Éditions du Seuil.]

Lacan, J. (1991a). *L'envers de la psychanalyse* [Le Séminaire XVII, 1969–1970]. Paris: Éditions du Seuil.

Lacan, J. (1991b). *Le transfert* [Le Séminaire VIII, 1960–61]. Paris: Éditions du Seuil.

Lampert, C. (1993). *Lucien Freud: Recent Work*. London: Whitechapel.

Laplanche, J., & Pontalis, J.-B. (1973). *The Language of Psychoanalysis*. London: Karnac, 1988.

Lauterbach, J. Z. (Trans.) (1933). *Mekhilta de-Rabbi Ishmael* [Vol. 2]. Philadelphia: Jewish Publication Society of America.

REFERENCES

Leguil, F. (1992). *Transference in the Lacanian Clinic.* Tel-Aviv: GIEP Israel. [Hebrew]

Lev, Rabbi A. (1971). *Baer Ha-Gola* [Drush Al ha-Torah]. Jerusalem.

Levi, P. (1988). *The Drowned and the Saved.* New York: Vintage Books.

Lévinas, E. (1968). *Nine Talmudic Readings.* Bloomington, IN: Indiana University Press, 1990. [First published Paris: Éditions de Minuit.]

Lévinas, E. (1982). *Ethics and Infinity.* Pittsburgh, PA: Doquesne University Press, 1985. [First published Paris: Librairie Artheme Fayard.]

Lucato, Rabbi M. H. (1969). *Mesilat Yesharim.* Jerusalem: Levin Epstein. [Hebrew]

Lusky, H. (1994). Successful turn. *Yediot Aharonot,* 21 January, p. 14. [Hebrew]

Madoff, S. H. (1993). *In the Zone of Transition.* Chicago: The Art Institute of Chicago.

Margaliot, Rabbi R. (Ed.) (1960). *Sefer Hasidim.* Jerusalem: Rabbi Cook Institute.

Medini, Rabbi H. H. (1963). *Sedei Khemed.* Tel-Aviv: Klalim. [Hebrew]

Miller, J.-A. (1987). The sinthome, a mixture of symptom and fantasy. *Psychoanalytic Notebooks of the London Circle, 5:* 9–31.

Miller, J.-A. (1988). Jacques Lacan and the voice. *Psychoanalytic Notebooks of the London Circle, 6:* 93–104

Miller, J.-A. (1991). Ethics in psychoanalysis. *Lacanian Ink, 5:* 13–27.

Miller, J.-A. (1992). Mazes of love. *Pulmus, 7:* 7–11. [Hebrew]

Miller, J.-A. (1995–96). Drive is Parole. *The Symptom, 1.* Retrieved 27 June 2004, from http://www.lacan.com/drivef.htm

Miller, J.-A. (1996). The Lacanian orientation: On die wege der sympombildung [Seminar of Barcelona]. *Psychoanalytic Notebooks of the London Circle, 1 :* 11–67.

Miller, J.-A. (2002). In exposition to the AMP conference on the formation of the analyst, Brussels.

Miller, W. J., & Nelson, B. (1984). *Samuel Beckett's Waiting for Godot and Other Literary Works.* New York: Monarch Press.

Paz, O. (1962). Touch. In: A. Weinberger (Ed.), *The Collected Poems of Octavio Paz, 1957–1987* (p. 114). New York: New Directions, 1991.

Raz, Y. (Trans.) (1995). *Crazy Talks: Zen Acts.* Tel-Aviv: Modan. [Hebrew]

Regnier-Bohler, D. (1992). Literary and mystical voices. In: C. Klapisch-Zuber (Ed.), *A History of Women: Silences of the Middle Ages* (pp. 427–482). Cambridge, MA: Harvard University Press.

Rozen, O. (1996). Re-dealing the cards of modernism: About the exhibi-

tion "l'informe" at the Pompidu Center in Paris. *Studio*, 73: 25–27. [Hebrew]
Salecl, J. (1988). *(Per)Versions of Love and Hate*. New York: Verso.
Sandbank, S. (1983). The sky as chasm: About "No-One's Rose". *Yediot Aharonot*, 27 May, pp. 14–16. [Hebrew]
Schmitt Pantel, P. (1992). The woman's voice. In: P. Schmitt Pantel (Ed.), *A History of Women: From Ancient Goddesses to Christian Saints*. (pp. 473–480). Cambridge, MA: Harvard University Press.
Semin, D., Garb, T., & Kuspit, D. (1997). *Christian Boltanski*. London: Phaidon.
Shapira, S. (1997). *Interview with Tsibi Geva*. Unpublished. [Hebrew]
Shatner, M. (1999). A completely normal Nazi. *Ha'aretz*, 13 August, p. 34. [Hebrew]
Schmitt Pantel, P. (1992). The woman's voice. In: P. Schmitt Pantel (Ed.), *A History of Women: From Ancient Goddesses to Christian Saints*. (pp. 473–480). Cambridge, MA: Harvard University Press.
Schocken, Z. (1970). Upon Celan's death. *Ha'Aretz*, 15 May, p. 20. [Hebrew]
Semprun, J. (1994). *L'écriture ou la vie*. Paris: Editions Gallimard.
Soler, C. (1995). The body in the teaching of Jacques Lacan. [Trans. L. Watson.] *JCFAR*, 6: 10–38.
Solieli, M., & Barkoz, M. (1965). *Lexicon Biblicum*. Tel-Aviv: Dvir. [Hebrew]
Spinoza, B. (1660). Short treatise on god, man, and his well-being. In: *Spinoza Selections* (pp. 45–93), ed. J. Wild . New York: Charles Scribner's Sons, 1930.
Weinberg, Rabbi Y. Y. (1999). *Sridei Esh* [Vol. 2]. Jerusalem: The Committee for Publishing Rabbi Weinberg's Writings. [Hebrew]
Wilber, K. (2000). *A Brief History of Everything*. Boston, MA: Shambala.
Wilber, K. (2001). A spirituality that transforms. *What Is Enlightenment?*, 20: 34–40, 172–173.
Winkler, M. (1970). Paul Celan. *Davar*, 11 September, p. 26. [Hebrew]
Wolowesky, J. B. (1986). Modern orthodoxy and women's self-perception. *Tradition*, 2: 65–81.
Žižek, S. (1991). *Looking Awry: An Introduction to Jacques Lacan through Popular Culture*. Cambridge, MA: MIT Press.
Žižek, S. (1993). *Tarrying with the Negative*. Durham, NC: Duke University Press.
Žižek, S. (2000). *The Fragile Absolute*. New York: Verso.

INDEX

Act:
    in art, 133–149
    feminine, 148
    in psychoanalysis, 133–149
Adorno, T., 112, 122
Agassi, M., 158
Allacoque, M., 89
Allen, W., 188
Alterman, N., 1
ambivalence, 39
    logic of, 38
Améry, J. (H. Meier), 105, 119–120
anaclitic love, 25–26
anal eroticism, 141
anamnesis, 179
Anna O, 3
annihilation, 105
anorexia (clinical examples), 73–77, 116–119
appetite, 22
"Arbeit macht frei", 179–190
    and entropy, 112
archetypal Other, mother as, 8
Arendt, H., 22
Aristophanes, 29, 32
Aristotle, 129
art:
    and psychological creations, xiii
    vehicle for testimony, 121–226
Atar, T., 1
Augustine, St, 22, 24, 87
Auschwitz, 105, 116–122
Azaria of Pano, Rabbi, 84

Bar-Hiya, Rabbi Y., 79
Barkoz, M., 168
Bataille, G., 112, 173, 179, 181, 183, 187
Baudelaire, C. P., 153, 155, 161
Beckett, S., 152, 153, 161
Ben David, Rabbi A., 81
Benigni, R., 123
Bergmann, M., 23
Berman, S. J., 82
Bettelheim, B., 106, 119
Bialik, H. N., 138
Bingen, H. von, 87

Blanchot, M., 152
Blich, B., 151
body:
    and drive, 171
    image, 36, 37, 162
Bois, Y. A., 153, 159, 163
Boltanski, C., 122
Borromean Knot, 128
Bowers, L., 158
Brown, T., 131
Buber, M., 9
Büchner, G., 67–69, 131
Bullock, A., 182

Cameroon, E., 66
Camus, A., 30, 113
castration, 5, 38, 60, 64, 90, 92, 118, 176, 178, 204
    anxiety, 28, 41, 177
    of mother, 58
    primary, 173
Catherine of Siena, St, 75
Celan, P., 31, 47–72, 114, 119, 124, 131
chain of signifiers, 6
Chalfen, I., 51, 54–58
Chelem, wise men of, 41, 45
Chuang Tzu, 221
Chun, Emperor, 86–226
Clausius, R., 181
Cocteau, J., 162
Cohen, A., 206
conscious intention, 5
conscious phantasy, 37
cotton-reel game (*fort/da*), 39, 154, 174, 202, 225

Dahan, G., xvi
daydream, 36, 37, 38, 42, 43
death:
    drive, xiii, 40, 50, 60, 62, 64, 71, 88, 89, 108, 142–145, 154, 159, 160, 168, 180–186, 193, 203
    definition, 182
    eroticization of, 64
    and love, 22
deceit in love, 28

de Folignio, A., 89
déjouer, 187
de Saussure, F., 3, 4, 92
Descartes, R., 42, 157
desexualization, 70, 141
desire, 2, 10, 11, 16–17, 22–26, 31–33
　feminine, 140
dialectics, 118, 209, 210
discourse, 3, 15, 16
　jouissance in, 12
Dolar, M., 30, 31, 86, 87, 94, 95
dream, 9, 14, 37, 40, 42, 137, 147, 157, 201
　of burning child, 36, 40, 110–111
　of butcher's wife, 136–137, 140
　function of, 36
　and reality, 36
　secondary processing of, 36
　about trauma/traumatic, 110–111
drive(s):
　and body, 171
　death, xiii, 40, 50, 60, 62, 64, 71, 88, 89, 108, 142–145, 154, 159, 160, 168, 180–186, 193, 203
　definition, 182
Duchamp, M., 160

Edwards, P., 181
ego, 14, 42, 91, 162, 211, 217–222
　fixated, 222
　formation of, 36, 136
　"his majesty the ego", 43
　ideal, 25, 197
　psychology, 14
　vs subject, 3
Eichmann, A., 107
Ende, M., 145
entropy, 122, 183, 185, 187, 190
　definition, 180–181
　formlessness, 112
　law of, 112
　negative, 181, 183, 186, 189
　　definition, 181
erotic investment in object, 26
Escher, M. C., 161
eternity, 212
European School of Psychoanalysis
　Israeli Group, xvi
evolutionary opportunity, 213–214

father:
　identification with, 25
　"Name of", 8, 58–59, 62–66

paternal metaphor, 59
primal, 94
Fellini, F., xv
Felman, S., 101–105, 113
feminine voice:
　in Jewish culture and psychoanalysis, 78–99
　and music, threat to male language and law, 85
fixation, 25, 183–185, 213, 219–222, 225
　incestuous, 25
　narcissistic, 25
fore-pleasure, 44
fort/da (cotton-reel game), 39, 154, 202, 225
free-floating attention, 221
Freud, L., 150, 153, 155, 157–163
Freud, S. (*passim*):
　Anna O., 3
　"castration", 5
　cotton-reel game, 39, 154, 174
　dream:
　　burning child, 36
　　butcher's wife, 136–137, 140
　on error as certitude of existence, 157
　on love, 22–34
　on negation, 147
　on phantasy, 35–48
　pleasure principle, 50
　seduction theory, 108
　symptoms as "hieroglyphs", 10
　"the uncanny", 15
　"The Unconscious", 9, 12
　Wolf Man, 24, 25, 41, 185
Freudian Place
　(Jaffa, Israel), xvi, 179
Fritjof, C., 221

Galliano, C., 109
Garb, T., 122, 123
Gary, R., 119
Gershuni, M., xvi, *19*, *165*, 179–180, 184, 188
Geva, T., xvi, 129, 150–151, 155, *156*, 157–163, *196*
Gleitmann, B., xvi
Goder, L., xvi
grace, 168
Greeneway, P., 188

Hama, Rabbi, 210

Hanina, Rabbi, 210, 211
Hegel, G. W. F., 2, 120, 136, 209, 210
Heidegger, M., 2, 5, 113, 202
Heiman, M., xvi
Heisenberg, W. K., 221
"hieroglyphs", symptoms as, 10
Hisda, Rabbi, 80, 97
holarchy, 207
Hölderlin, J. C. F., 55
Holocaust, 49, 54, 57, 61–65, 75, 101, 123
 see also Shoa
Holzweg, 113, 123
Huller, S., xvi
hypnosis, 197

idealized object, 11
identification(s), 3, 4, 14
 imaginary, 9
imaginary dimension, vs. symbolic dimension, 4
imaginary object, 9, 36
incentive bonus, 44
incestuous fixation, 25
infantile sexuality, 11
l'informe, 112, 180, 181, 183, 184, 185, 187, 189
 definition, 181
intention, unconscious, 5
interpretation, 2, 10, 15, 16, 201–205
 and meaning, 9
Isaac, Rabbi, 80

Jaanus, 172, 174
Jackobson, R., 92
Jewish culture and psychoanalytic theory, feminine voice in, 78–99
Johns, J., 204
jouissance (passim):
 in discourse, 12
 feminine, 49–72, 88, 90, 95–98
 indications of, 12
 and music, 87
 pathological, xv
 phallic, 50, 89, 176, 221
 ultimate, 62
 verbal, 224
Joyce, J., 130
Jung, C. G., 2, 23
juvenile sexuality, 2

Kandinsky, W., xi

Kant, I., 41–42, 62, 89, 115, 157–158, 193, 212
Kierkegaard, S., 30, 127, 139, 140
knowledge:
 and the Act in psychoanalysis, 138
 analyst's, 14, 29, 204
 and art, 148–168
 Descartes's doubt of, 157
 desire for, 2, 33, 76
  and psychoanalysis, 2
 disclosed, of the "one", 130
 erotic, 216
 and the ethical, 127
 future of, 189
 historical, 112
 infinite, cycle of, 187
 limitations of, 2
 living, 216
 and love, 21–34, 168
 objective
  vs. subjective truth, 208
 and the Real, 107, 109, 122, 211, 220
 repressed, 170
 scientific, 140
 and sexuality, 32
 subjective, 74, 109
 and truth, 169, 170, 183, 185
  "intolerable", 107
 unconscious, 14, 29, 32, 113, 170
Koestler, A., 207
Kosman, A., 78–99
Krauss, 38, 144, 152, 154, 155, 184, 187, 204
Kuspit, 122, 123

Lacan, J. *(passim)*:
 Freud, return to, 1–2
 I vs subject, 3
 jouissance, kinds of, 89
 on language, 3
  as tool of psychoanalysis, 3
 on love, 23, 21–34
 objet á, 32, 88, 92–98, 118, 158, 173, 177, 218–219
 "Other", the, 8
 on phantasy, 35–48
 "sign", 12
 study of, 2
 on symbolic dimension, 15
 therapy as social link, 6
Lackner, R., 56

lalangue, 12, 211, 220
lamella, libido as, 144, 173–175, 224
Lampert, C., 153, 155, 161
language (*passim*):
   and analysis, 13
   diagnostic and therapeutic value of, 6
   and object, 5
   primal, 12
   and psychoanalysis, 3
   and reality-testing, 4
   without meaning, 12
Lanzmann, C., 101
Laplanche, J., 37
Laub, D., 101, 103, 105, 113
Lauterbach, J. Z., 83
Lavie, R., 180
Law of the Father, 59, 89, 96, 143
Leguil, F., 171, 176
Leibnitz, G. W., 131
letter as place, 127–132
Lev, Rabbi A., 85
Levi, P., 103–107, 119–121
   suicide of, 119
Lévinas, E., 177, 202, 210–213
libidinal drive, 37, 217
libido, 24–26, 50, 88–89, 112–113, 136, 142, 182–186, 189, 197, 217–219, 225
   archaic forms of, 173
   displacement of, 141
   of I, 25
   as lamella, 144, 173–175, 224
   and love, 22
   of object, 25, 26
   as organ, 22
   and partial drives, 22
   types of, 218
Lieber, S., xvi, 179, 180, 184, 188, 189
life drive, 182
linguistic disorder and psychosis, 5
linguistic unit as signifier, 3
linguistics, 2
Lonshitz, Rabbi E. of, 84
Lorca, G., 149
love, 21–34
   anaclitic, 25–26
   /apathy antithesis, 27
   and death, 22
   deceit in, 28
   falling in, 26, 31
   as imaginary screen, 26
   love/hate antithesis, 27
   narcissistic, 25, 27, 29
   neurotic, 24
   and partial drives, 22
   and truth, in psychoanalysis, 170
   loved/beloved antithesis, 27, 28
Lucato, Rabbi M. H., 169
Lusky, H., 151
Lyotard, J.-F., 38–40, 202–205

Madoff, S. H., 131–132
Maharal (Rabbi Y. Lev ben Betzalel), 85
Margaliot, Rabbi R., 82
masochism, 39, 203
masturbation, 15, 42
material reality, 37
Medini, Rabbi H. H., 85
memory:
   limitations of, 104
   and trauma, 93
meta-language, 134
Michelangelo, 147
Miller, J.-A., xvi, 28, 30, 42, 91, 113, 138, 169, 217, 218, 226
Miller, W. J., 153
mirror stage, 37, 91, 135, 136, 217, 220
Mondrian, P., 204
Moore, H., 145
Moses Maimonides, 168
mother as archetypal Other, 8
myth and Act, 191–200

Na'aman, M., xvi, 47
Name of the Father, 8, 170, 175
narcissism, 25, 26, 29, 91, 162, 173, 187, 216
narcissistic fixation, 25
narrow-mindedness, 206–214
negation, 14, 30, 147, 181
Nelson, B., 153
normal love, 23, 24

object(s), 5, 8, 9, 11, 17, 188
   desexualization of, 70
   idealized, 11, 70
   imaginary, 9, 36
   and language, 5
   primal, 11, 17, 24, 92
   lost, 11
objet á, 32, 88, 92–98, 118, 158, 173, 177, 218–219
Oedipus complex, 8, 58, 59
Orpheus, myth of, 150–166

"Other", the, Lacanian meaning of, 8

paranoid psychosis, 13
parlêttre, 12
Parrhasios, 147, 148
paternal metaphor, 59
Paz, O., 163, 163
penis envy, 90
perversion, 41, 42
phallus, 28, 58, 60, 65, 67, 140, 148, 178
  symbolic law of, 118
phantasme, 7, 11, 17, 36–44, 65, 139, 177–178, 194, 197, 203
  primal, 37
  and the Real, 101–125
  testimony, 106
phantasy:
  beauty as, 71
  definition, 37
  unconscious, 36
Philo of Alexandria, 79, 80, 82, 83, 88
philosophy of science, 2
Picasso, P., 142–143, 155
Plato, 25, 28, 86, 144
pleasure principle, 26, 39–40, 50, 88–89, 154, 174, 177, 182–183, 186, 203, 211, 221
Pontalis, J. B., 37
Ponti, M., 146
post-modernism, 134
post-structuralism, 133, 134
pottery, 71, 144, 145
preverbal stage, 148
Prévert, J., 142, 147
primal horde, 192
primal object, 11, 17, 24
primal scene, 41, 42, 177
projection, 15
psychical reality, 37
psychoanalysis:
  as ethics, xii
    of the Real, xiv
  as "science of the particular", xii, 135
psychoanalytic theory and Jewish culture, feminine voice in, 78–99
psychosis, 11, 5, 13, 92, 223
  and linguistic disorder, 5
  paranoid, 13
psychotic, 12, 13

quantum theory, 221, 225

Rabin, Y., 180, 192, 193, 194, 195
Rashi (Rabbi Shlomo Itzchaki), 80
Ravizky, Y. H., 138
Raz, Y., 35
Real, the (*passim*)
  order of, 27, 90, 96, 97, 128
  to *phantasme*, 101–125
  testimony, 106
reality:
  material, 37
  psychical, 37
Regnier-Bohler, D., 86
repetition, 112
  compulsion, 40, 108, 109, 114, 154, 169, 207, 222
  and trauma, 108
repression, 14
resistance, 14, 15
Rilke, R. M., 63
Rovner, M., xvi, 125, 131
Rozen, O., 181
Rybnicki, A., xvi
S
Sade, Marquis de, 41, 62–63
sadism, 39, 203
Salecl, J., 93
Sandbank, S., 63, 64, 65, 66, 67, 68
Sartre, J.-P., 2
Schelling, F. W. J. von, 212
schizophrenia, 5
Schmitt Pantel, P., 85
Schocken, Z., 63, 65
secret bearers, 101–125
seduction theory, 37, 108
Semin, D., 122, 123
Semprun, J., 120
sexuality, 11, 23, 32–33, 64, 78, 88–90, 97, 172, 183, 188–190, 195, 219
  feminine, 88–90, 183, 190
  juvenile, 23
sexual trauma, primary, repressed, 37
sex drive, 83
  vs love, 27
Shakespeare, W., 33, 60, 61, 139
Shapira, S., 163
Shatner, M., 107
Shesheth, Rabbi, 80
Shoa, 101–103, 112, 115, 117, 121–123
  see also Holocaust
signification, 4, 5, 6
  etymological, 5
  truth of, 4

signifier(s) (*passim*):
    chain of, 6, 71, 92, 133, 135, 202, 225
    linguistic unit as, 3
    symbolic, 17
sinthome, 130, 225
slip(s) of the tongue, 9, 208
Socrates, 2
Soler, C., xvi, 171, 174, 175
Solieli, M., 168
Song of Songs, 21, 22, 29, 210
Sophocles, 79
Spinoza, B., 115, 168, 206
Stallybrass, O., 182
structuralism, 2
subject vs ego, 3
subjective truth, 6
sublimation, 70–71, 80–81, 84, 140–146, 193
    illusion of, 148
    spiritual, and music, 87
suicide, 33, 120, 121, 142
    Paul Celan's, 49, 56, 63, 103
    Primo Levi's, 119
superego, 13
symbolic dimension, 5, 9, 14–16, 40, 64, 133, 158, 172
    vs. imaginary dimension, 4
symbolic order, 7–8, 12–13, 16, 43, 76, 92, 96–97, 128, 158–159, 182, 195, 212, 219
    synchronous, 211
symbolic register, 108, 180
symbolic signifier, 17

talking cure, 3
testimony, 104
topology, definition, 182
transference, 13–14, 17, 28–29, 171, 176, 202, 216
    interpretation of, 175
    love in, 170
    love out of, 17
transformation, subjective, 226
trauma, 37, 63, 64, 93, 105, 108–110, 122, 173
    as absence, 109
    and opportunity, 211–214
    and repetition, 108
truth:
    analytic, 171
    intolerable, 107
    and knowledge, 183
    and love, in psychoanalysis, 170
    religious, 171
    subjective, 6, 103, 170

uncanny, the, 15, 67, 69, 92, 102, 108, 115, 123, 142, 151, 154, 161, 219
unconscious, the, 3
    meaning of, 9
unconscious intention, 5
unconscious phantasy, 36, 37
unconscious wish, 37, 118

Van Leer Jerusalem Institute, 202
voice:
    and drive, 174
    of the Father, and feminine voice, 94–99
    feminine, 78, 81, 83, 84, 86, 94, 96, 98
    as *objet á*, 88–99
    woman's:
        erga, 82, 95
        erva, 78–98

Warhol, A., 146, 160
Warshawsky, R., xvi
Weinberg, Rabbi Y. Y., 85
Wiesel, E., 103
Wiesenthal, S., 103
Wilber, K., 207, 222
Winkler, M., 66, 67
wish fulfilment, 38
    unconscious, 37, 118
Wolf Man, 24, 25, 41, 185
Wright, F. L., 204
writer, creative, 43, 44
writing:
    Hieroglyphic, 129
    phallic value of, 130
    Phoenician, 129

Yehuda, Rabbi, 85, 130

Zeuxis, 147, 148
Žižek, S., xvi, 42–43, 128, 157, 193–194, 207–208, 211–213
Zupnik, M., xvi